A Reader's Guide to *The Silmarillion*

A READER'S GUIDE TO

The Silmarillion

PAUL H. KOCHER

HOUGHTON MIFFLIN COMPANY BOSTON 1980

*Library of Congress Cataloging
in Publication Data*
Kocher, Paul Harold, date
A reader's guide to The Silmarillion.
Bibliography: p.
Includes index.
l. Tolkien, John Ronald Reuel, 1892-1973.
The Simarillion. I. Title.
PR6039.032S534   823'.9'12   79-25959
ISBN 0-395-28950-5

Printed in the United States of America

S 10 9 8 7 6 5 4 3 2 1

The author is grateful to George Allen &
Unwin Ltd. and Houghton Mifflin Co.
for their permission to use the Map of
Beleriand showing the realms Noldor and
Sindar, by Christopher Tolkien, which
originally appeared in *The Silmarillion*, by
J. R. R. Tolkien, © 1977 by George Allen
& Unwin (Publishers) Ltd.

Contents

May '80 publ. 6.63

I	A Mythology for England	I
II	The Providence of Ilúvatar	14
III	The Valar and the Elves	31
IV	Fëanor	50
V	The First Two Battles of Beleriand: Dagor-nuin-Giliath	74
VI	The Realms of the Noldor	86
VII	Of the Coming of Men	107
VIII	Beren and Lúthien	124
IX	The Battle of Unnumbered Tears: Nirnaeth Arnoediad	145
X	Túrin Turambar, Master of Doom	155
XI	The Ruin of Doriath	176
XII	Tuor and the Fall of Gondolin	183
XIII	Eärendil and the War of Wrath	191
XIV	*Akallabêth:* The Downfall of Númenor	204
XV	*Of the Rings of Power and the Third Age*	227
	Chronology of the First Age	253
	Notes	265
	Bibliography	273
	Index	277

A Reader's Guide to *The Silmarillion*

I

A Mythology for England

In a paper read at Exeter College, Oxford, in 1912 J. R. R. Tolkien praised the mythological ballads of *Kalevala*, Finland's national epic, as being "full of that very primitive undergrowth that the literature of Europe has on the whole been steadily cutting and reducing for many centuries with different and earlier completeness among different people." And he added, "I would that we had more of it left —something of the same sort that belonged to the English."[1]

In other words, Tolkien, looking about him at extant Anglo-Saxon literature, saw that it had lost much, or most, of its early mythology, as compared with the Norse-Icelandic *Eddas* and sagas and with the *Kalevala*. All that survived were *Beowulf*, the Christian legends of Cynewulf, some historical war poems, one or two minstrel reflections like *Deor's Lament*, letters between husband and wife, miscellaneous charms and riddles, and the like.[2] Not promising materials on which to build a mythology.

Tolkien therefore set out upon the heroic task of remedying this lack by creating "a mythology for England." He wrote in 1914 a poem, "The Voyage of Eärendil, the Evening Star," inspired by Cynewulf's *Crist*. By 1917 he had composed "The Fall of Gondolin" and also "The Children of Húrin," part of which he derived consciously from the story of Kullervo in *Kalevala*.[3]

Writing of this ambition many years later, Tolkien said,

"Do not laugh! But once upon a time . . . I had a mind to make a body of more or less connected legend, ranging from the large and cosmogonic to the level of romantic fairy-story—the larger founded on the lesser in contact with the earth, the lesser drawing splendour from the vast backcloths—which I could dedicate simply: to England, to my country. It should possess the tone and quality that I desired, somewhat cool and clear, be redolent of our 'air' (the clime and soil of the North West, meaning Britain and the hither parts of Europe; not Italy or the Aegean, still less the East) and while possessing . . . the fair elusive beauty that some call Celtic (though it is rarely found in genuine ancient Celtic things) it should be 'high,' purged of the gross, and fit for the more adult mind of a land long steeped in poetry. I would draw some of the great tales in fullness and leave many . . . only sketched. The cycles should be linked to a majestic whole, and yet leave scope for other minds and hands, wielding paint and music and drama. Absurd."[4]

In spite of the defensive modesty which led Tolkien to speak of his undertaking as absurd and laughable, he was utterly serious in his design to create a mythology for England. His lifelong labors on it show that. What is important for us to mark well at the outset, in order to understand his purpose, is to see clearly the qualities which Tolkien intended his myths to have and not to have. He wanted them to be "cool and clear . . . redolent of our 'air,' " possessed of "a fair elusive quality," and finally "high, purged of the gross."

He need not have been so critical of his own patriotic wish to provide England with a fitting mythology. The minstrel singing the opening Runo of *Kalevala*, for instance, had no such hesitations. He roundly declared to his Finnish audience that he would sing "the people's legends, / And the ballads of the nation" in order to instruct them, and especially the younger generation, in their heroic past.[5]

Noteworthy in Tolkien's prescription for his new mythology is the number of other mythologies it *excludes*. It
will not resemble Roman and Greek myth. Nor will it
borrow from "ancient Celtic things." Since it is to be "high,
purged of the gross," it cannot very well look too closely
to *Kalevala* either, because Tolkien himself, although enjoying its songs, characterized its heroes as "unhypocriti-
cal, low-brow, and scandalous."[6]

Tolkien's prescription for the subject matter of his
myths inevitably dictated also the prose style in which he
presented them. He was capable of writing in many different styles, of course, but the "cool, clear, high" theme of
The Silmarillion seemed to him to require a manner which
was lofty, and perhaps a little archaic. This style takes some
getting used to but, once accepted, its poise can be seen as
highly appropriate to its theme. It must be added that some
of Tolkien's critics have not accepted it yet, to their own
loss.

The mythologies of Rome, Greece, Finland, and the
Celtic past having been excluded as models for his new
mythology for England, what other mythologies were left
to inspire Tolkien and help guide his way? The one which
dominated "the hither parts of Europe"—Denmark, Ger-
many, Norway, and especially Iceland—before Christianity came to expunge it, dealt with the Norse pantheon of
gods headed by Odin. With this mythology Tolkien was
already acquainted as early as 1913, and the more he studied
the Icelandic *Elder Edda* (Poetic) and *Younger Edda* (Prose)
the more engrossed he became.[7] For them and for the great
individual Icelandic sagas, like those that told of Grettir
and Njal, he developed a lifelong affection. At the University of Leeds[8] he set up an informal reading club known as
the Viking Club, and later at Oxford the Kolbitar,[9] in order
to discuss them outside the classes he taught. Indeed *The
Silmarillion* resembles *The Elder Edda* in that both are collections of tales more or less loosely tied together, although

The Silmarillion's linkage is much tighter and more dramatic, as well as more weighty in meaning.

Account must also be taken of the fact that as a devout Catholic Tolkien rejected much of the world outlook assumed by Norse-Icelandic mythology, although this rejection did not prevent him from admiring the artistic power with which it was often stated, and even accepting into *The Silmarillion* those of its contents most closely akin to Christianity, or those which he could transform into Christian acceptability. No doubt Tolkien told himself, in effect, that the England for which he was inventing a new mythology was officially Christian in his day, that many of his readers would likewise be Christian, and that his proffered mythology ought to be one which could be conceived of as a precursor to that religion, or at least not inimical to it.

One portion of Norse-Icelandic mythology which he cut off cleanly and completely was its polytheistic assembly of some twelve gods (e.g., Odin, Thor, Tyr) and an equal number of goddesses (Frigg, Freya, Var), often their wives. Like the Christian Book of Genesis *The Silmarillion* has, of course, only one God, known as Eru the One or, in his creative aspect, Ilúvatar.[10] It likewise rejects the three Norns or Fates, Urd (Past), Verdandi (Present), and Skuld (Future). These three predetermined the fates not only of men but also of the Norse gods themselves, and nobody could say them nay. Such a doctrine was abhorrent to Tolkien, who believed passionately in free will, as all his writings demonstrate.[11]

As to the origins of the world, Norse-Icelandic mythology taught that it all began with a Void (Ginnunga, gap), "a grinning gap," as it has been strikingly translated.[12] This was likewise the view in the Book of Genesis; so Tolkien had no difficulty in transporting it into *The Silmarillion*. What he could not accept was the Norse belief that the first physical occupant of this emptiness was the frost giant Ymir, said to have been composed of poison drops from

some unknown somewhere, perhaps from Elivagur, meaning the Milky Way. The sweat of Ymir's body became
nodules which developed into other frost giants. According
to *The Elder Edda* there was also a cow (Audhimla), which
by licking salty ice blocks uncovered a manlike being
named Buri,[13] whose son Bor sired the first gods of the
Norse pantheon, Odin, Vili, and Ve. These three then
killed Ymir in order to use portions of his body to build
Midgard (Middle-earth). Out of his blood they made rivers,
lakes, and the sea encircling Midgard; from his flesh, the
earth; from his bones, the mountains. Man (Ask) and
Woman (Embla) were shaped by Odin and his brothers
from two trees they found along the seashore, bestowing on
them spirit, understanding, speech, and all the senses
proper to humankind. And the three gods used the sparks
and burning embers blown out of Muspell to make stars,
sun, and moon to light heaven and earth.

For obvious reasons this complex and all too physical
account of Creation did not attract Tolkien. And, like the
Book of Genesis, *The Silmarillion* puts into the Void only
pure Spirit, God the Father (Eru-Ilúvatar) and the angels
(Ainur) he has brought into being. For Men, as the second
Children of Ilúvatar, Tolkien had plans different from both
the Norse and the Biblical narratives, as will be seen.

Like the Norse myth of the world's beginning, the Norse
conception of its ending in the Twilight of the Gods (Ragnarök) was quite uncongenial to Tolkien and won no place
in *The Silmarillion*. For one thing, Ragnarök had all been
predestined by the Norns and could not be prevented even
by the gods on Asgard. Indeed all its events were well
known to them in advance. The Fenris wolf would devour
Odin. Thor and the Midgard Serpent would kill each other.
The hosts from fiery Muspellheim led by Surt would come
riding to burn the whole of Midgard and cause it to sink
under the sea. Wolves would swallow both the sun and the
moon. On the plain in Asgard called Vigrid, the Einherjar

(those bravest of warriors slain in battle and brought to Valhalla by the Valkyries) would fight in vain to the last man against the invading armies from Muspellheim. Universal anarchy would follow.

This grimmest of prospects threw a shadow over Norse temperament and its whole outlook on life. It had to be endured, however. As Tolkien remarked in his lecture "Beowulf: the Monsters and the Critics,"[14] the poem called upon man's heroic will to face the fact that human life is tragic. Norse mythology is full of tales showing Odin wandering about in disguise to gather from the Wise all the information he can get, not to avoid Ragnarök, which he knows cannot be done, but to find out, if he can, when it will come and what, if anything, will happen afterward. That, for example, is the object of Odin's questioning of the Sybil in *The Elder Edda*. In *The Silmarillion* this atmosphere likewise ruled the Noldor exiles in Beleriand, for they had heard the Doom of Mandos, telling them as they left Valinor that they would never win their war against Morgoth. And they knew that Mandos spoke for Ilúvatar. Yet they fought on, their leaders and their cities falling one by one.

There is a kind of happy ending after Ragnarök for the world, for gods, and for men, Sybil tells Odin. True, he and all the other gods must perish in Ragnarök, but their sons will survive to take over their powers. Odin's Vídar and Váli will dwell in Asgard in his stead. Thor's sons Modi and Magni will wield his great hammer Mjöllnir. Moreover, Baldr the beloved will return from the underworld to rule an earth newly risen from the sea. A man and a woman, Lif and Lifthrasir, hidden from Surt in a wood, will be alive to start the human race again. All will be Utopian.

There are hints here and there in *The Silmarillion* that Middle-earth will be destroyed in a Last Battle, but Tolkien prefers not to give even the vaguest details about it or about its aftermath, if any.[15] Specifically, he is too good a Christian himself to bring into his epic another Baldr, or to promote him as some kind of Christ figure. Baldr was a good and just god but he did not voluntarily die on the Cross, or anywhere else, to atone for the sins of the human race as Jesus did.

It is worth mentioning that Loki may have given Tolkien a hint or two for the character of Melkor, before he graduated into full evil as Morgoth. Both are spirits of malice, and both like to perpetrate their plots secretly through others who shield them from all blame. Melkor's method of spreading vile and harmful rumors so subtly that they cannot be traced back to him is well known to readers of *The Silmarillion*. Similarly Loki, having learned that Baldr the beloved is vulnerable only to arrows of mistletoe, does not shoot one at Baldr himself but covertly persuades blind Hödur to do so, killing Baldr. And when Hel, the ruler of the underworld, agrees to release Baldr if every living creature on Midgard will weep for him, Loki assumes a disguise and alone refuses to join in the universal weeping, feeling safe enough behind his change of shape. Finally, at Ragnarök he turns against his fellow gods and guides the fire giants from Muspell to the plain of Vigrid, where the Einherjar are all to be defeated and slain again. So Loki is no mere mischief-maker, as he is sometimes portrayed by some who write about him today, but a full-fledged evildoer, a murderer.

We have read so much about Elves and their mighty deeds in Tolkien's writings that we have come to accept them as possessing always the immortal bodies and splendid minds with which he endowed them. The fact is otherwise. Since at least as far back as Shakespeare's *Midsummer Night's Dream* and Drayton's *Nymphidia* in the sixteenth century, Elves had come to be regarded as tiny, pretty, and fairylike, mere playfellows for young children. Against this conception Tolkien waged incessant war. He did so in his Andrew Lang Lecture "On Fairy-Stories" delivered at the

Scottish University of St. Andrews in 1938.[16] And again at
the very end of Appendix E to *The Lord of the Rings* (1955).
And yet again in that nostalgic short story, "Smith of
Wootton Major" (1967).

Now it happens that Elves are quite prominent in the
two *Eddas*, although no detailed physical description of
them is given.[17] The Light Elves have a home region (Alfheim), as do the Dark Elves (Svartalfheim). The former
seems to lie in Utgard, the outer edge of Earth, the latter
underground. "The Light Elves," says *The Prose Edda*,[18]
"are fairer than the sun to look upon, but the Dark Elves
blacker than pitch."

The Light Elves are friendly with the gods of Asgard. In
"Loki's Flyting," when Aegir, god of the sea, gives a feast
he invites elves as well as gods and all sit at the same table
side by side.[19] In "Skirnir's Ride" the sun is called "Glory
of Elves."[20] In the same poem Frey, desiring to possess
Gerd, laments, "no elf, no god will grant my prayer," and
when Skirnir comes to her, Gerd asks him, "Are you one
of the elves, are you one of the gods . . . ?"[21] This close
juxtaposition of gods and elves is constant in *The Elder Edda*
and indicates that the elves have qualities which are god-
like. Examples of this nearness could be multiplied. Finally, we get in "Words of the All-Wise" a list of the names
given by Elves to a dozen natural phenomena. These help
to reveal the character of elves in Norse mythology.[22]

OBJECTS NAMED	NAMES GIVEN BY ELVES
Earth	Growing
Heaven	Fair-Roof
Moon	Tally-of-Years
Sun	Fair-Wheel
Clouds	Weather-Might
Wind	Traveling-Tumult
Calm	Day-Quiet
Sea	Water-Charm

Fire	All-Burner
Forest	Fair-Bough
Night	Sleep-Pleasure
Seed	Water-Charm

Why the elfin names for Sea and Seed should both be Water-Charm is hard to say, unless it is because Seed also needs water to charm it into growth. The names, on the whole, show imagination, close observation, and a feeling for language.

Consequently it seems more than a mere guess that Tolkien built upon the suggestions of the *Eddas* in reaching his conception of what an Elf truly was, and why he resisted centuries of tradition in formulating it.[23]

*   *   *

The Dwarves of Midgard raise for us the same sort of questions: Whence did they come? What were their true natures? And did they perhaps help Tolkien in conceiving the Dwarves who appear in *The Silmarillion, The Hobbit,* and *The Lord of the Rings?*

At the outset be it noted that he had no such long tradition of prettification to combat in the case of the Dwarves as he had in the case of the Elves. At least he nowhere inveighed against it when describing Dwarves. It would seem that in Western folklore and legend Dwarves had always been craftsmen of superlative skill who lived by preference underground or in caves.

According to "The Deluding of Gylfi" Dwarves began as maggots tunneling through the body of Ymir.[24] Hence their propensity for digging down under the surface of Midgard. But by decree of the Aesir gods "they acquired human understanding and the appearance of men, although they lived in the earth and in rocks. Módsognir was the most famous, and next to him, Durin."

At this point *The Elder Edda* tells in "Song of the Sybil"

(stanzas 13 ff.) how the gods took counsel as to which of the Dwarves should "mold man by mastercraft / From Ymir's blood and limbs," and chose Durin for the task. Under his direction the Dwarves made "many man-forms . . . from the earth." The names of several dozen Dwarf workmen are then listed. This account of the creation of mankind contradicts the account in *The Prose Edda* that the first man (Ask) and first woman (Embla) were created by the gods out of two trees they found on the seashore. Be that as it may, the tale in *The Elder Edda* establishes the ability of the Dwarf race to plan and execute works of the highest difficulty.

Like the Elves, the Dwarves have dwellings of their own on the outer edge of Midgard, in regions appropriately called Darkdale and Everfrost since the Dwarves prefer darkness and a far northern region where the sun is weak and cold.

Among the chief works forged by their skills are a sword which will never rust and will easily cut through iron ("The Wakening of Angantyr"); a ship, Skidbladnir, which will always have a favorable wind wherever it sails, can hold all the gods, and when not in use can be folded together like a cloth and be kept in a pocket ("The Deluding of Gylfi"); and a mead which makes anyone who drinks it "a poet or a scholar" ("Poetic Diction" in *The Prose Edda*).

Like the Elves, the Dwarves have given names to many natural objects and times ("The Words of the All-Wise"):[25]

Heaven	Dripping-Hall
Moon	The Bright One
Sun	Dvalin's Doll [Dvalin is a Dwarf king]
Calm	Day-Rest
Sea	Dark-Deep
Night	Spinner of Dreams

These namings reveal an imagination and a love of beauty not usually attributed to the dour Naugrim.

Tolkien, however, has always insisted upon their love of beauty. In *The Silmarillion* the Dwarves who build Menegroth of the Thousand Caves for Doriath take the pride of the artist in their work. And in *The Lord of the Rings* Gimli goes into rhapsodies as he examines the sculptures in the caves of Aglarond in Helm's Deep.

Taken all in all, Norse mythology ordains a grim life and a death by fire or by monsters for all the races and the gods of Midgard. In *The Silmarillion* Tolkien, too, has chosen to narrate a series of mistakes and mishaps which are almost uniformly dark, and in which the moments of happiness are few. Not that these errors are predestined, as are those in the *Eddas* and in other early Icelandic lays and sagas. There are no Norns in *The Silmarillion*, only free choices made by free wills. Yet these choices are used by Ilúvatar to help bring about the designs of his Providence. He foreknows them all and fits them into his plans for the future, whatever these may be.

So dismal is the trend of events in *The Silmarillion* "from the high and beautiful to darkness and ruin" that Tolkien appends to its conclusion what is almost an apology, and an extenuation. The woes just related, he declares, were due to the marring of Arda by Morgoth, that is, to the working of Evil in the hearts of Elves and Men, and even in some of the Ainur (p. 255).

The present chapter contains no mention of Hobbits, the sturdy, brave little Halflings whom many of Tolkien's admirers have taken to their hearts as the best of all his creations. But Hobbits were not to settle in the Shire until the Third Age, thousands of years after the events recounted in *The Silmarillion*. The First Age, of course, deals primarily with Elves, and for them at least as good a case can be made as Tolkien's masterpieces. These potent beings, about

whom Norse mythology offered many attractive general
hints but few details, became in Tolkien's mind and imagination a wholly new race, the Firstborn Children of Ilúvatar, immortal and wise, superbly worthy to be one of the
races for whose sake Eä, an entire world, came into existence. Considering the many ancient misrepresentations of
Elves which Tolkien had to overcome, his achievement is
amazing. Only less so are his Dwarves, unlike any other
race of Dwarves before or since.

But lest Tolkien's skill in creating new races as neighbors
for Men absorb all our attention, we should consider also
their place in the overall structure he planned for them.
How were all the different elements of *The Silmarillion* to
be bound together into a coherent whole? "I had a mind,"
wrote Tolkien to a friend, "to make a body of more or less
connected legend, ranging from the large and cosmogonic
to the level of romantic fairy-story." And he added that he
wanted to "draw some of the great tales in fullness, and
leave many only placed in the scheme, and sketched. The
cycles should be linked to a majestic whole . . ."[26]

This structure was, in fact, just about what Tolkien
achieved. The Music of the Ainur *(Ainulindalë)* and the
names and works of the Valar *(Valaquenta)* in the task of
creating and serving Eä provide the cosmogony he desired.
From it he proceeded to an account of the flight of the
Noldor from Valinor and the varying fortunes of their
battles against Morgoth (certainly "large," if not "cosmogonic"). And thence to short sketches like the rescue of
Maedhros by Fingon and the quest of Aredhel, the White
Lady of Noldor. From these to "great tales in fullness,"
such as the stories of Beren and Lúthien, of Túrin Turambar, and of Tuor's journey to Gondolin.

One can see why Tolkien might not have greatly cared,
especially in his old age, about the fact that some episodes
of *The Silmarillion* had been fully explored and others only
summarized. His design was flexible enough to accommo-

date every sort of incompleteness save that of a major story left unfinished. There is none such.

When comparing *The Silmarillion* with either *The Elder Edda* or the *Kalevala* we find that these latter two collections start with a Creation and then present a number of tales or lays, in no particular order, about the people created. These tales vary greatly in length and complexity. Tolkien is in the mainstream of mythological writing in all these respects except that as an artist he prefers to give a tighter, more pervasive order to his stories and a more developed theocracy, under Ilúvatar.

II

The Providence of Ilúvatar

To STUDY the Providence of Ilúvatar is to study Ilúvatar himself, for his nature reveals itself in whatever he does or fails to do. The design of the All-Father pervades the whole of Tolkien's great work, side by side with the freedom of choice which he has given to all intelligent beings on Eä. A close examination of *The Lord of the Rings*, however, is outside the scope of this book. For our purposes here it must suffice to concentrate on *The Silmarillion* in some detail, beginning with the Music of the Ainur and moving on through its subsequent parts, selecting those episodes which reveal most.

Several *caveats* must be kept in mind, however. As is well known, Tolkien himself was a dedicated Roman Catholic. But *The Silmarillion* tells of a time long ages before Christ came, and Tolkien never forgets that fact. Also, he never consciously imposes his own beliefs upon his narrative. Indeed, he much prefers to keep himself out as much as he can. Yet an author's ability to suppress his own views can never succeed entirely, and it will not do merely to rule out all Catholic influence *in toto*.

There is no doubt that Ilúvatar is far more merciful than Odin, for example. He is patient even with the great destroyer and tempter, Morgoth. Although he has no Church through which to speak, he does have Manwë and Mandos

as his spokesmen to the Valar. Manwë is notable for a
softening compassion, Mandos for strict justice.

* * *

Out of love for the Children (Elves and Men) whom he
would later create, Ilúvatar, the All-Father, designed in the
Void a world for them to inhabit. He might have made it
alone but, also out of love, he first made the holy, angelic
Ainur who, being the offspring of his thought, were his
children too, though of a different race. And these he
taught to sing together in harmony.

Then he gave them three themes which they were to sing
harmoniously, each adorning them with his own sub-
themes if he chose. In this he left them free. But Melkor,
on whom Ilúvatar had bestowed "the greatest gifts of
power and knowledge, and . . . a share in all the gifts of his
brethren" (p. 16),* abused this freedom by introducing not
sub-themes but counter-themes. For already this most potent of the Ainur had searched the Void for the Imperishable Flame with which to create living beings subject only
to himself, not to Ilúvatar. And this, too, Ilúvatar permitted, knowing that the Flame was his and could not belong
to any other.

So into the three themes Melkor introduced his own
destructive discords against the harmony commanded.
Others of the Ainur chose to sing with Melkor against
Ilúvatar. In this also they were left free to follow their own
wills. But in the third theme Ilúvatar's theme captured
Melkor's most triumphant passages and wove them into
the divine pattern. And Ilúvatar, angered, brought all the
music to an end in a single conquering chord which included all the discords and transcended them.

---

*All page references given in parentheses in the text are to *The Sil-
marillion* unless otherwise noted.

Then Ilúvatar warned all the Ainur, but especially Melkor and his adherents, that every sub-theme or counter-theme which they might think was theirs came ultimately from him, and would always be absorbed into his themes, making them more wonderful than before (p. 17). In short, Ilúvatar would permit selfish, rebellious Evil to exist but would always transmute it so as to serve the ends of his divine Providence. Not that there were no limits to what he would allow, as witness his wrath in bringing the third theme to an end. Nor that Ilúvatar would not punish Evil for its crimes, as Melkor when he became Morgoth was to discover.

Having issued this warning to the Ainur, Ilúvatar took them out into the Void. Adding the power of sight to the sense of hearing they already had, he showed them afar the fresh new world composed by their Music, already living and growing and beginning to develop a history. In it, Ilúvatar told the Ainur, each of them would recognize, besides the All-Father's own central design as expressed by the three themes, whatever thought each had added in the sub-themes. And to Melkor especially he repeated his warning that Melkor would see expressed there all his thoughts, however secret, and would perceive "that they are but a part of the whole and tributary to its glory." Let him not think that he could keep any thought of his hidden from Ilúvatar or prevent his Providence from turning it, evil though it might be, to his own divine uses.

At this point Ilúvatar revealed to the Ainur that his Providence contained an important element not previously described to them. In every age of the world would happen, he said, "things that are new and have no foretelling, for they do not proceed from the past" (p. 18). That is, there would always be events which had no prior natural cause. Such uncaused supernatural events were in effect miracles of Ilúvatar, new creations out of nothing. This necessary and liberating element freed Ilúvatar from his own world, from the chains of causation which ran through it by means of physical, psychological, and other natural laws. Consequently, in viewing *The Silmarillion* we should not expect to be able to explain every happening in the light of its predecessors. One prime example of this freedom of Ilúvatar is the coming of his Children, Elves and Men, in whose creation the Ainur had no part and who appeared at times not foreknown by them.

But being loyal servants of the All-Father and inheritors of his love, most of the Ainur, watching the history of Middle-earth unroll and the Children of Ilúvatar appear according to his pleasure, loved them as he did. For these Children were "beings other than themselves, strange and free." They were unlike the Ainur in being of a different race, but like them in having the same freedom to make their own moral choices, as did all the intelligent races of Middle-earth, including Elves, Dwarves, Hobbits, and Ents. To Elves and Men, accordingly, throughout *The Silmarillion* Ilúvatar offered an untrammeled liberty to make their own decisions between Good and Evil. And all too often they chose Evil, as will be seen.

When the Ainur realized that the world being shown them by Ilúvatar had been created by him as a dwelling place for his Children, and that they themselves also had been unwittingly preparing it for that purpose, many of the mightiest among them longed to descend into it in order to help with the task. Even Melkor half persuaded himself that he wanted to go there for the Children's good by gentling the extremes of heat and cold which he himself had generated during the Music. But his true motive was to subdue Elves and Men to his will and make them his slaves. Yet Ilúvatar did not forbid him to go.

Others of the Ainur, however, were genuinely attracted to the idea of doing helpful work on Middle-earth. And

Ilúvatar pointed out to each the labors for which he was best fitted by the gifts given him at the time of his creation: Ulmo for ruling the seas, rivers, and other waters; Manwë, "the noblest of the Ainur," for governing airs and winds; Aulë for taking charge of the fabric of the Earth; and so on also for the other Ainur.

Then suddenly came Darkness, which the Ainur had never experienced before, since the Void had in it neither Light nor Darkness. And it snatched away their vision of the changing Earth just before the time came for the Dominion of Men in the Fourth Age, as told in *The Lord of the Rings.* Then, as intended by Ilúvatar, the Ainur became restless, wanting they knew not what, except that the sight of Middle-earth should never again be taken from them.

Therefore Ilúvatar revealed to them what their longing was—that what they have seen as a world "should verily be, not only in your thought, but even as you yourselves are, and yet other" (p. 20). Until now the new world has had only the degree of reality that a dream has for a dreamer. Their wish was to have him give it full metaphysical Being (in the Thomistic sense). This status Ilúvatar proceeded to confer by divine *fiat,* as in Genesis: "*Eä!* Let these things Be!"

Then he sent forth to Earth across the Void the Flame Imperishable, which belongs to Ilúvatar alone and which is necessary to Being. So the Ainur saw the new globe like "a cloud with a living heart of flame" and knew that it had ceased to be a vision and had become a new thing, "Eä, the World that Is." Tolkien's capital letters here accentuate the importance of the full Being which Middle-earth has just attained.[1]

Now it became possible for the Ainur to go down to Eä. And, although some of them chose to remain in the halls of Ilúvatar, many of the greatest among them elected to descend, accepting the condition he imposed upon them that they would never leave Eä but would use their powers for its benefit so long as it should last. In this way the Ainur who descended became the Valar, the Powers of the World.

And indeed their powers were sorely needed from the first. Much to their surprise they found that the Earth was raw and unshaped and without any history whatever, quite unlike the ordered world they had seen in their Vision. So they had to begin all things from their first beginnings despite the meddling of Melkor who undid whatever was done, to the extent that Providence permitted. Moreover he claimed the whole world as his own, but Manwë denied his right, saying that many others had labored here as much as he.

Then, remembering that all their labors were for the Children of Ilúvatar, the Valar clothed themselves in the Children's shapes, some male, some female, as they had appeared in the Vision, in order that the Children, whenever they came, might the more readily approach and love them. But open war with Melkor soon broke out, and Manwë called to his aid not only the other Valar but also many Maiar, who were Ainur of lesser degree. And although in the end Middle-earth, being continually spoiled and corrupted by Melkor, never became as perfect as the Valar had planned, yet at last it was shaped and made firm as well as they could manage. As in the Music, Ilúvatar's Providence accepted the admixture of Evil with Good and of ugliness with beauty, to the degree which seemed sufficient to him.

*   *   *

Of all the Ainur who descended to Eä, Manwë was dearest to Ilúvatar and best understood his purposes, the aims of his divine Providence. Therefore the All-Father appointed him King, "lord of the realm of Arda and ruler of all that dwell therein," including the other Valar (p. 26). When difficulties arose King Manwë communed silently with Ilúvatar, in the manner of prayer, to discern his Will and publish it to all his subjects. Often enough, though not always, he was granted the knowledge he sought and became the spokesman of the divine Will.

Now Mandos, who kept the Houses of the Dead in Valinor, knew all that was to come except what "lies still in the freedom of Ilúvatar"; that is, his liberty to insert into the flow of history events without prior natural cause. Moreover Mandos as the Doomsman of the Valar pronounced "his dooms and judgments only at the bidding of Manwë" (p. 28).

Accordingly, there was a hierarchy in Valinor which ran from Ilúvatar to Manwë and through him to Mandos. And by means of this hierarchy was his holy Providence revealed and carried out, as it was later in the Doom declared by Mandos upon the rebellious Noldor Elves. For after the Ainur had descended into Eä, Ilúvatar withdrew himself and no longer spoke to them directly as he had during the Music and during his bestowal of Being upon the world they created together.

There was, however, one notable exception, in his dealings with Aulë. Tolkien, in his first mention of Aulë, described him as a Vala who delighted in making new things for the sheer pleasure of their making, not to hoard them for himself possessively but to give them away freely to any who might want them (p. 19). In this desire to create he resembled Melkor, who also strove to make new things, but Aulë differed radically from him in remaining faithful to Ilúvatar and in submitting in all that he did to the Father's Will.

This difference can best be seen in the remarkable episode which describes Aulë's attempt to create the hitherto unknown race of Dwarves (pp. 43–46). His motive in doing so was not to compete with Ilúvatar but to make pupils to whom he could teach his many skills. For, as the years passed and the Children of Ilúvatar failed to arrive, he became impatient and decided to make them himself. Not well remembering the forms of the Children as he had seen them briefly in the Vision of the World that was yet to Be, Aulë shaped them as he thought they were. But his simulacra missed the truth, being ugly and squat. Also because of Melkor's interferences in all that Aulë did he gave them extra strength of body, as well as minds with great power to resist. Seven such Dwarves he made in a secret cave, and began to teach them a new language he had composed for them.

But Ilúvatar knew all this and, remaining invisible, spoke to Aulë, asking why he had tried to do what he well knew was forbidden and, moreover, beyond his ability to perform. All that Aulë had been given at the time of his creation was his own Being,[2] and this he was unable to impart to the works of his hands. Only Ilúvatar could give it with the Imperishable Flame. Consequently, his Dwarves could be nothing more than automatons without any wills of their own, thinking what he thought, moving only when he moved them, and standing frozen when he did not. Did he truly want dolls of this sort for pupils?

By posing such questions Ilúvatar made Aulë realize that possession of an independent and free will was vital to all intelligent creatures who have life. He might have added that his Providence operated on that same premise and that he might have created the Ainur and his Children unfree, but did not. For he did not want mere dolls either but free beings who served him willingly, able to love him and be loved in return, and capable of judging the beauty and majesty of his works for themselves.

Aulë instantly learned his lesson. Confessing his impatience and folly, he assured the voice of Ilúvatar that he had been imitating him not in any spirit of mockery but in the manner of a young child who did whatever he saw his father do. Weeping, he offered to destroy the Dwarves, and raised his hammer to smash them.

But Ilúvatar had compassion on Aulë because of his humility and, saying nothing, gave life to the Dwarves so that they fell on their knees and begged Aulë not to kill them. Then the All-Father explained to Aulë that he had bestowed Being on them. But he would not permit them to be born before his Firstborn Children, the Elves, awakened to life. To do so would be to violate the order of things established by his Providential plan. Therefore, the Seven Fathers of the Dwarves must "sleep now in darkness under stone." And when the Elves had been born he, Ilúvatar, would awaken them. Then they would be like Children to Aulë, their father. However, let Aulë be warned. Strife would often erupt between Elves and Dwarves, "the children of my adoption and the children of my choice" (p. 44).

This episode shows much about Ilúvatar and hence about his Providence. Its scheme has been arranged since before the Beginning but, because he is merciful to those who are humble and repent of their misdeeds, he is willing to fit their actions into its design, yet only so as to change it as little as possible, for he is just as well as merciful. And justice in the case of Aulë's Dwarves requires that they do not take the place of the Firstborn but should come after them. Since this change somehow shakes the whole fabric of Eä, Elves and Dwarves will often be at odds. Nothing is said here about Men, the Secondborn, but presumably they will awaken after the Dwarves. Is justice done thereby? Tolkien does not answer. But we may guess, if we like, that in this case mercy for the Dwarves outweighs justice for Men, as mercy outweighs justice, though only up to a point which lies beyond human ken.

In many respects Tolkien's Dwarves were a race apart. They lived much longer than Men but were not immortal like Elves. Also, their beliefs about what happened to them after death were unlike those of the other two races. They believed that Aulë would set them in a special place in the Halls of Mandos, and that there "Ilúvatar would hallow them and give them a place among the Children in the

End." They would then become servants of Aulë "and aid him in the remaking of Arda after the Last Battle." (There may be a flavor of the Norse Ragnarök here.) Dwarves also were sure that their Seven Fathers were periodically reincarnated in their descendants and then bore the same names they had before death, as Durin did.[3]

Now when Aulë confessed to his spouse Yavanna Kementári, "Queen of the Earth," the story of his sin and of its pardon by the mercy of Ilúvatar, she agreed that he had in truth received forgiveness twice compounded. But she lamented that his Dwarves would exercise no care for the vegetation and the animals on Middle-earth which it was her task to love and cherish. She foresaw that their axes would cut down her trees and kill her beasts without pity. Such seemed to her the dilemma of mercy.

Aulë tried to pacify her by pointing out that the Elves and Men who were to be Ilúvatar's Children would do the same kind of damage when they were born, for the Father would give them dominion over all the Earth, and they would use her animals for meat and her trees for lumber to build with, duly thanking the Creator for them.

But finding small comfort in these comparisons, Yavanna went to King Manwë to ask whether it was true that the Children were to be given dominion over beast and tree as Aulë told her. Manwë confirmed that it would be so. Then she grieved that so many of her works already had been marred by Melkor, and now the Dwarves and the Children would mar yet others. And bitterly she exclaimed, "Shall nothing that I have devised be free from the dominion of others?" (p. 45).

Then Manwë, pitying Yavanna, asked which of all her works she would preserve from such domination if given the choice. She replied that since her beasts (kelvar) could flee or fight for their lives and her vegetation (olvar) could not, she chose the latter, especially the trees, which she loved best. And she crowned her plea with the wish that "trees might speak on behalf of all things that have roots, and punish those that wrong them!" In this she was asking, though not by name, for the Ents, who play a major role in *The Lord of the Rings* but in *The Silmarillion* only a minor one.

At first the idea of trees having life enough to speak and to punish seemed strange to Manwë, but Yavanna replied that this idea had been in the Music of the Ainur. And Manwë, reliving that Music, saw that it was there, as well as many other wonders he had not noticed before. Then, awaking as from a trance, he reported the decree of Eru-Ilúvatar that when his Children awoke then Yavanna's thought should awake also, and it would "summon spirits from afar," some of which would give life to both beasts and trees and "be held in reverence and their just anger . . . feared" (p. 46).[4]

In this way the Providence of Ilúvatar, after mercifully giving life to Aulë's Dwarves went on to give life to Yavanna's Ents to defend her woods against them. Thus the balance of life on Middle-earth was maintained and the dilemma of mercy equitably solved. Thus, also, two new races, both of them empowered to choose between Good and Evil, came to join its free peoples.

In fact *three* new races, for Manwë reminded Yavanna that they had sung together in the Music, their thoughts being of great birds soaring high. These, too, said Manwë, "shall come to be by the heed of Ilúvatar . . . the Eagles of the Lords of the West." Yavanna rejoiced with him and offered her tallest trees for their nests. But Manwë declared that none of her trees would be high enough. The Eagles must nest in mountains, where they could hear and report to Manwë the voices that called upon him. In *The Silmarillion* they have their eyries in the Crissaegrim, mountain peaks south of Gondolin, whence they observe what is happening within a wide radius, and act as Manwë's messengers. They appear also at crucial moments in *The Hobbit* and *The Lord of the Rings*, sent by Manwë at the behest of Ilúvatar.

*   *   *

After the Music and after Aulë's making of the Dwarves had revealed much about the nature of Ilúvatar and his Providence, came a third episode which gives still further insight into it. This occurred when Fëanor had swayed most of the Noldor into following him out of Valinor and into Middle-earth for the recovery of the three Silmarils stolen by Morgoth and carried off by him into Angband there.

Through Manwë's herald, Eönwë, Ilúvatar gave the departing Noldor in general, by way of advice and not by command, a warning not to go on a road where unseen sorrows awaited them. But he was careful to stress that they were at liberty either to go or to stay, whichever they chose, for "as ye came hither freely, freely shall ye depart." But as for Fëanor and his sons, specifically, they had sworn an Oath to pursue "to the ends of the World" anyone at all who kept a single Silmaril from them (p. 83). By this Oath they had sworn away their freedom to go or stay and had committed themselves in vain to exile from Valinor forever. For as mere Elves they had not the power to overcome any Vala, especially Morgoth, the mightiest Vala of them all (p. 85).

But Fëanor only laughed at Eönwë and led the Noldor on to the Kinslaying of the Teleri Elves at Alqualondë in order to seize their ships for transport across the Great Sea. By this grievous crime he compounded his guilt and fueled the wrath of Ilúvatar against him and his followers. So the next and last message was delivered to the Noldor by Mandos, the grimmest of the Valar and the one most closely associated with death.

Mandos made it clear that the option was still open to the Noldor to return to Tirion and stand before the Valar to be judged and to seek pardon. But he was not gentle to those who would not take that course, for Ilúvatar was no longer gentle of mood. On them Mandos pronounced a curse and Prophecy of Doom (pp. 87–88) which shut them out of Valinor irrevocably.[5] For slaying the Teleri many of the Noldor would themselves be slain on Middle-earth "by weapon and by torment and by grief." Those not so slain would grow weary of the world, and wane, and be supplanted by the race of Men. As indeed happened, according to *The Lord of the Rings,* at the end of the Third Age.

But, said Mandos, the special anger of Ilúvatar, acting through the Valar, would pursue the House of Fëanor and its liegemen wherever they might go. The evil Oath they had sworn would force them on and yet betray them in the end. All they did would turn out badly "by treason of kin unto kin, and the fear of treason." That is to say, the same kind of treason the House of Fëanor had perpetrated against their kinsmen, the Teleri, would be visited upon them by their Noldor kindred. Never would Fëanor and his sons be wholly trusted, nor would they ever wholly trust in return. Pariahs would they be among their own tribe.

To bring about these results Ilúvatar, it would seem, does not need to intervene in the events which ensue. They come about quite naturally by the very characters of those who enact them. The natures of Fëanor and his sons being what they are, the natures of the other Noldor princes being what they are, and the past between them being what it has been, the future can scarcely be otherwise. All that Ilúvatar needs here is foreknowledge of the natural workings of character to know what will happen. And this is another species of his Providence, allowing the free wills of all parties to operate as they will, even to their own destruction.

All who heard Mandos speak were shaken, but Finarfin alone, half-brother to Fëanor and married to Eärwen of Alqualondë, took advantage of the alternative offered by Mandos and returned to Tirion with his liegemen. There they were pardoned by the Valar, and Finarfin became that city's ruler. His four sons, however, especially Finrod Felagund (the eldest) did not go back with him, for love of the sons of Fingolfin, their cousins. Nor did Finarfin's daughter Galadriel, who longed for Middle-earth's wide lands "to rule there a realm at her own will" (p. 84). This longing she satisfied by founding Lothlórien in the Third Age, as told in *The Lord of the Rings*.

The treason of kin unto kin foretold by Mandos began to operate all too soon. Fëanor and those faithful to him secretly stole the captured ships of the Teleri and sailed away from the main host of the Noldor, now captained by his half-brother Fingolfin. And after landing safely on the northwestern shores of Middle-earth Fëanor did not send the ships back to fetch the other Noldor but burned them, in order that he and his host might first attack Morgoth and recover the Silmarils.

Fingolfin's array eventually managed to cross the Sea on the grinding icebergs of the Helcaraxë in the extreme north, where the distance between Valinor and Middle-earth was narrowest. Many of them perished there and all suffered. So never again did the survivors trust the good faith of Fëanor or his seven sons, although his eldest, Maedhros, was aghast at the burning of the ships, expecting that they would be sailed back to bring over his kinsmen, especially Fingon, his dearest friend, son of Fingolfin.

The other foretellings by Eönwë and Mandos likewise came true. Eönwë had warned Fëanor that he could never conquer Morgoth or any other Vala. And so it turned out. Even before the host of Fingolfin crossed the Helcaraxë, Fëanor, rushing far ahead exultantly in his berserk madness to attack Angband almost alone, was slain by Morgoth's demon servants the Valaraukar or Balrogs, with their whips of flame, as Gandalf was on the bridge at Khazad-dûm in *The Lord of the Rings.*

Then in the Five Great Battles, with lesser skirmishes between, the Noldor never succeeded in penetrating to Morgoth's lair in the depths of Angband. In the first three Battles they routed his armies of Orcs, but he was not with them, only their captains appointed by him, whom he governed safely from afar. In the last two Battles Morgoth overwhelmed the Noldor armies, breeding Dragons and bringing in Easterlings whom he had corrupted long since to serve him.

"For blood ye shall render blood," Mandos had prophesied, referring to the Kinslaying at Alqualondë. In their wars against Morgoth the Noldor did indeed render blood —far more than they had spilled among the Teleri. One by one the bravest and best of them were slain. Fingolfin died in challenging Morgoth to single combat. Finrod Felagund, and Fingon, and Turgon in their various ways all died violently. Worst of all, Morgoth's armies sacked the cities they had built, killing every innocent woman and child, until few of the Noldor remained on Middle-earth except in small groups huddled along the margins of the Sea.

But Ilúvatar did not leave Morgoth unpunished either. After his theft of the three Silmarils Morgoth set them in his iron crown, which he wore as a symbol that he was King over all of Middle-earth. There they pained him incessantly as with a searing fire. And unlike the Valar who did not rebel against Ilúvatar, he was perpetually haunted by fear—fear of the Noldor, fear of the Valar, fear of what Ilúvatar might send against him next. He did well to fear the Valar. For at last, upon hearing the plea of Eärendil, they conquered and captured Morgoth. And they shut him out in the Void, never to return to Eä.

His loss of one Silmaril to Beren bound the seven sons

of Fëanor by the unholy Oath they had sworn with their father "to pursue with vengeance and hatred to the ends of the World" anyone at all who withheld any Silmaril from them. In the context of the time the Oath bound them, reluctant though they were, to attack Doriath and then those who fled with its Silmaril to the shore of the Sea. In the series of murders which ensued, all of the brothers died except the two eldest, Maedhros and Maglor the minstrel. But they did not win thereby the Silmaril so dearly bought.

It went instead to Eärendil and lighted first his way to Valinor, then that of the ship Vingilot in which he was set to sail the heavens as the Morning and the Evening Star. Truly had Mandos said that "their Oath shall drive them and yet betray them, and ever snatch away the very treasures that they have sworn to pursue" (p. 88). Paramount among these treasures for Maedhros was the respect and trust of the other princes of the Noldor, and these he had now forfeited. As Tolkien describes the Oath when it was first sworn by Fëanor and his sons it was unbreakable and should never have been taken.

Yet Maedhros and Maglor *had* taken it, and because of it one more tragic scene remained for them to enact. At the overthrow of Morgoth the two Silmarils in his possession were put into the custody of Eönwë, Manwë's herald, who set a guard over them. So the brothers broke into his camp by night, slew the guards, and seized the Jewels. The camp being roused against them, they prepared to fight to the death. But Eönwë forbade his people to attack them, and they fled with the two Jewels they had come for.

But when the Silmarils scorched their hands they saw that their right to them, through Fëanor, had expired, and that they had done evil in stealing them. "In anguish and despair" Maedhros threw himself with his Silmaril into a fiery chasm and there died. But Maglor, throwing his far out into the Sea, lived on to wander alone on its shore where the waves broke, "singing in pain and regret." He never rejoined the Elves. And that, too, was a kind of dying. So, ignobly, fared those who kept the Oath they should never have sworn. Thus, by the decree of Ilúvatar, one Silmaril sailed the heavens, a second shone in the ocean's depths, and the third shed its light unblemished among the fires at the heart of the world. They had been a bane to their maker, Fëanor, and to all who possessed them after him, save only Eärendil.

III

The Valar and the Elves

IN RELATION TO ILÚVATAR himself the Ainur (Valar) were angelic beings who, having been created by him, were intended to love and obey their creator freely with the independent wills he gave them. And this they did, all save Melkor, who thought himself self-created and obedient to none. After helping Ilúvatar create Eä (our World) with their singing, the Ainur were given by him the major task of putting its tangled elements into order so as to make of it a fit dwelling place for the Children of Ilúvatar who were to come thereafter.

In relation to these Children (both Elves and Men) the Ainur were guardians, not masters. For it turned out that whenever they tried to force the Children to do anything they did not wish to do, the results were not good. By this the Valar came to understand that the wills given by Ilúvatar to his Children were as free as their own, and were not to be compelled. So the Valar became to them not rulers but elder brothers and sisters, and advisers. In their immortality, their wisdom, and their beauty Ilúvatar made the Elves, his Firstborn, "more like in nature to the Ainur, though less in might and stature; whereas to Men he gave strange gifts" (pp. 41–42).

The strangest of these gifts was that of death after old age, followed by immediate return of the soul to Ilúvatar. The inability of Men to accept death as a gift was to become the central theme of *Akallabêth*. But the spirits of the Elves

who died by wounds or by grief went to wait in the Halls
of Mandos for the ending of the World, and some mysterious aftermath.

About the Valar (Ainur), generically and individually,
most is told in *Valaquenta* but much also in *Ainulindalë.*
Tolkien's account of them is continued and completed in
the present chapter. Of the seven Ainur who descended to
Eä as Valar in male form, the preceding chapter tells much
about Manwë, Ulmo, Aulë, and Mandos but nothing about
the other three, Irmo, Oromë, and Tulkas. Similarly, of
those seven who went down as Valier in female form, only
Yavanna, wife of Aulë, has been mentioned. Yet certain it
is that each of the fourteen represented one element in the
mind of Ilúvatar and ruled those features of Eä most congenial to his or her given nature. Consequently, to fail to
speak of any one of the Valar or Valier would be to impov-
erish our conception of the manifold mind of Ilúvatar.

The spouse of Manwë was Varda, Lady of the Stars,
more commonly invoked by Elves as Elbereth, Star-kin-
dler. They dwelt together in Valinor on Oiolossë, the lofti-
est peak of the Pelóri Mountains. When she and Manwë sat
on their thrones together he could see whatever was happening on Middle-earth far across the Sea, and she could
hear the voices that cried to her from the darkness which
Melkor made there.[1] Of all the Valar and Valier the Elves
held her most in reverence and love.

Ulmo, Lord of Waters, had no spouse or fixed dwelling
place in Valinor but remained alone in the waters of the
rivers and seas and also in those that ran under the Earth.
He seldom walked on land or assumed a body like that of
Ilúvatar's Children, as did the other Valar. Seldom, too, did
he attend their councils unless some crucial matter was
under debate. He often frightened the Children by appearing to them in the form of a mighty wave. Yet he loved
them and never abandoned them even when the Valar put
the Noldor under the Curse of Mandos. In his streams and

lakes that ran far inland on Middle-earth he made such
music on his horns as aroused in those who heard it an
unquenchable longing for the Sea.

Mandos' Halls of the Dead lay empty in Valinor before
the Children awakened, for no Vala ever died. But after
Elves and Men had been born they were found to have been
constructed differently by Ilúvatar, and to have been assigned to different lots. Men were mortals, who must die,
but Mandos had no jurisdiction over their spirits, which
went not to his Halls but to some mysterious Elsewhere.
On the other hand, Elves were made for immortality but
could be slain by physical violence. It was the spirits of
Elves so slain that Mandos summoned and consigned to his
Halls, where they sat waiting. Waiting for what? The end
of the World? Some kind of Judgment? We are never told.

Mandos' spouse was Vairë, the Weaver, who wove into
her webs all the events that had ever happened. Unlike the
Norns in Icelandic mythology, however, she never wove in
events yet to come but only those already past. Thus the
future was not predestined in Valinor but lay hidden in the
free wills of Ilúvatar and of both Elves and Men.

Irmo, younger brother of Mandos, was Lord of Lórien,
fairest of gardens. To all who sought it in need of rest and
refreshment he and his spouse, Estë the gentle, gave restful
dreams, and healing. Hither came Fëanor's mother, Míriel
Serindë, called the Broideress because of her surpassing
skill in needlework, lovelier than that of any other woman
of the Noldor. She had been so weakened by Fëanor's
prodigious birth that not even Lórien could save her. There
she faded and died.

Galadriel, daughter of Finarfin and therefore a Princess
of the Noldor, evidently knew well these gardens and their
function, for in later ages she used them as her model in
fashioning Lothlórien on Middle-earth. Although *mallorn*
trees are not mentioned as growing in Valinor's Lórien it
is probable that they did and that Galadriel carried their

seeds with her when the Noldor left Valinor. How else to explain the *mellyrn* which were Lothlórien's chief glory? They grew nowhere else on Middle-earth until Galadriel gave Sam the Hobbit a single seed for the adornment of the Shire at the ending of *The Lord of the Rings*.

Nienna, sister of Irmo and Mandos, was the great Valië so sensitive to the suffering caused by the wounds which Melkor would inflict upon Eä that she wove her laments into her Music of the Ainur before the World received Being from Ilúvatar. Afterward she lived alone in halls "west of west," built into the very Walls of the World. Her sorrow was not selfish but was designed to teach pity and enduring hope. She seldom visited the happy city of Valmar. Instead she went to the Halls of Mandos, which were near her own, bringing to those spirits who waited there, and cried to her, strength of heart and wisdom born of tears. She it was who most profoundly felt the tragedy of life.

Tulkas and Oromë were the fighters among the Valar. Tulkas the Strong loved contests of all sorts from wrestling and running to battling against Melkor, the prospects of this latter sport being what attracted him to come to Eä in the first place. And he laughed always whenever he fought. He had a suitable spouse, Nessa, sister of Oromë, who could outrun any deer and was tireless in dancing.

Oromë, by contrast, was grim in battle. He was a dedicated hunter of the fiercest monsters and wild beasts to be found on Middle-earth, which he pursued on his steed Nahar, winding Valaróma, his great horn. When Melkor sent his evil creatures into the forests, Oromë trained the Maiar who followed him, and also his hunting dogs, to run them down and destroy them. The forests he hunted in he loved, every tree in them. His spouse was Vána, the Everyoung, sister of Yavanna. All flowers bloomed and all birds sang when she passed by.

But Melkor was no longer counted among the Valar. By

his arrogance and his violent undoing of their works while
he claimed sole kingship over them and over the whole of
Eä, he separated himself from them. And of course he never
married as they did, for there was none of like spirit who
would espouse him, even had he wished.

If it is asked why all the Valar married save Ulmo and
Nienna, perhaps the answer was that in their unions each
spouse strengthened the other in many ways, as did Manwë
and Varda. Certainly none ever had children, being creatures of spirit only. But perhaps the truer answer was that,
just as they wore the bodily forms of the Children of Ilúvatar in order to attract their love, so also they adopted their
custom of marriage for the same reason.

Now the Elves named the Valar "the Powers of Arda"
by reason of their rule over it, under Ilúvatar (p. 25), but
eight of them, headed by Manwë, they deemed the Aratar
or High Ones, who surpassed not only all the other Valar
and Maiar but also "any other order that Ilúvatar has sent
into Eä" (p. 29).

When Ilúvatar created the Ainur he simultaneously
created the Maiar "of the same order . . . but of lesser
degree" (p. 30) to be their servants and helpers. By his
repeated use of the term "order" Tolkien shows that he
knew and adopted the medieval notion that there were nine
"orders" of angels, as set forth in the highly popular book,
The Celestial Hierarchy by Dionysius the Areopagite (about
A.D. 500). But, not wanting to cumber his mythology with
widely different ranks of angels, Tolkien kept them all in
one "order," the Powers, yet allowed for variations of degree within it. Although the Maiar were numerous, he said,
their numbers, and even their names, remained largely
unknown to the Children of Ilúvatar.

According to Dionysius, Powers, along with Dominations and Principalities, occupy the second rank of angels,
below the first rank, which consists of Seraphim, Cheru-
bim, and Thrones, but above the third rank, whose mem-

bers are Virtues, Archangels, and Angels. Milton's *Paradise Lost* (Book 2) uses the same hierarchical structure when Satan addresses his fallen followers in Hell as "Thrones, Dominations, Virtues, Princedoms [Principalities], Powers . . ." Since Tolkien names the Ainur who descend to Eä "Powers," he shows us what their "order" is.[2]

Among the Maiar the chief was Manwë's herald Eönwë, mighty in arms. But the wisest was Olórin who, though he lived in Lórien, went often to Nienna, who taught him pity and patience. He loved the Elves well but preferred to walk among them unseen, putting into their hearts "fair visions or the promptings of wisdom." And later when Men joined the Elves in their struggle against Morgoth on Middle-earth he pitied their sorrows and encouraged them not to despair or yield to dark imaginings.

Ossë, Ulmo's Maia, whose allotted province was the waters breaking on the shores of Middle-earth and of all islands, delighted in storms. His spouse was Uinen, the Lady of the Seas, who loved all creatures, even the weeds that lived in these waters. She knew how to calm the billows raised by her husband. Mariners often cried out to her and they reverenced her as much as they revered any Vala.

Unable to rule the Sea, Melkor hated it. So he schemed to win Ossë, promising him Ulmo's place and power—a promise which he neither would nor could have kept. But Ossë believed Melkor and raised tempestuous seas which ruined many coastal lands. His spouse Uinen, however, persuaded him to go before Ulmo and to confess all. When Ulmo pardoned him Ossë resumed his former allegiance, though at times he still enjoyed raising a storm or two.

Ossë's union with Uinen shows that the Maiar sometimes married each other. And the long union between the Maia Melian and the Elf-king Thingol of Doriath, the only union of its kind, gave birth to Lúthien, who loved and married the man Beren, again the only union of its kind.

She died twice rather than lose him after death, as is told hereafter.

Melkor, too, had a great many Maiar, some drawn to his first splendor, others corrupted by him after he lost it. Most terrible among them were the Valaraukar or Balrogs, true demons of terror. Also dreadful was Sauron Gorthaur, originally a Maia of Aulë, who became in Morgoth's hands a master of deceit and an ally in all his works, "only less evil than his master in that for long he served another and not himself" (p. 32). Even that doubtful virtue he was to lose in the Second and Third Ages of Middle-earth when, after Morgoth's overthrow, he aspired to rule all the World for himself alone.

*   *   *

In the timeless ages before any flora or fauna could grow on the primeval Earth, Melkor was besting the Valar in the battle to control it, until Tulkas the Strong came down from far heaven to help them. Melkor was never one to meet any foe head on, preferring to undo him by secret lies and treachery. So, fearing the angry might of Tulkas, he fled from him into the darkness outside Eä, where he brooded and waited his time. His absence freed the Valar to regain control of the whole of Eä and to set in proper order all its seas, meadows, forests, and mountains.

This done, Aulë at the urging of his spouse Yavanna made two diminutive suns—one (Illuin) in Middle-earth's northern region, and the other (Ormal) in its southern. Both he set aloft on mighty pillars on the tops of mountains. Together they lighted almost all of Middle-earth, then flat. Not that the Valar needed light to see by, but Yavanna's seeds of vegetation and spawn of beasts "which she had long devised" could not grow without it. Conditions now being suitable, she planted what she had devised, and all the Earth was green.

The Valar were living then not in Valinor but on Middle-earth, on the island of Almaren in the Great Lake. In celebration of Earth's first Spring, Manwë proclaimed a feast to which all the Valar came. Wearied by their labors in shaping Eä, they kept no guard against Melkor. And, after eating, Tulkas fell asleep. Seeing his chance Melkor and his Maiar dug in the icy north a vast underground fortress, Utumno, from which flowed out his hatred, a blight withering every plant that grew and turning the beasts into "monsters of horn and ivory," slaughtering one another like mammoths or dinosaurs.

While the alerted Valar were away searching for him elsewhere, Melkor and his Maiar stole down upon the two lights Aulë had made, shattered their pillars, and broke their lamps. So huge was that overthrow that it convulsed both Sea and Earth and spewed fire far and wide. Then Melkor hid himself deep in Utumno. The Valar did not stop to dig him out, preoccupied as they were with efforts to subdue the destructive forces he had let loose, some of which had utterly demolished their own dwelling place on Almaren.

The Valar then made the momentous decision to leave the continent of Middle-earth and, instead, to occupy and fortify Aman the Blessed (soon to be called Valinor), a long island far across the ocean at the uttermost west of Eä. Beyond it lay only the Encircling Outer Sea, and beyond that the Walls of the Night. Their duty to Ilúvatar, as the Valar always remembered, was first to make Eä habitable for his Children, and then to foster in them a spiritual wisdom pleasing to him.

If they remained on Almaren they would be physically closer to the Firstborn Children, whose birth they rightly expected to take place soon in a region somewhere to the northeast of the Great Lake. But with Melkor on the loose, Almaren might not be safe for them. On the other hand, a fortified Aman would be much safer once the Children reached it, but reaching it would require a long march westward, followed by an ocean crossing, every mile of it vulnerable to Melkor. Perhaps the Valar foresaw that eventually they would have to capture and bind him while the Children were on the way. In any case, they chose Aman over Almaren.

To defend Valinor the Valar raised the Pelóri mountain chain along the island's length. And on its highest peak, Taniquetil "the holy," Manwë set his throne, whence he and his queen Varda could survey the whole of Middle-earth and could rule it as Ilúvatar decreed. West of the Pelóri, and protected by it, the Valar built first their houses and gardens, and finally Valmar, their city of many bells. In that loveliest and most sacred of lands nothing ever faded or died, and even its stones and fountains were hallowed.

Outside Valmar's western gate Yavanna sanctified a green mound and sat on its grass singing a song of power while the assembled Valar listened in silence on their thrones. As she chanted they saw sprouting from the mound two shoots which grew into saplings, and these into tall flowering trees, the Two Trees of Valinor—first, Telperion, silver in leaf and flower, then Laurelin, golden in both. Since there was as yet neither sun nor moon, the main function of these trees was to bathe Valinor in their varied, holy light.

The Norse gods likewise sat in council in a ring under the shade of Yggdrasil, the World Ash. Tolkien, always a lover of trees, puts his circle of the assembled Valar (the Ring of Doom) near the Two Trees which light their land, whereas Yggdrasil, though giving out no light at all, binds together the three-layered Norse world of Asgard, Midgard, and Niflheim.

Together the Two Trees shed over the land a lovely glow from their blossoms, but not at the same time. Telperion, being the elder, bloomed first and was seen by the Valar who watched it to give out its light over a period of seven hours, waxing from darkness to full splendor and waning back again to darkness in that span of time. Laurelin likewise had a cycle of seven hours. But it began to brighten an hour before Telperion became dark, shone alone during the other's dark period, and itself waned into full obscurity only after Telperion had been waxing for an hour.

Ever afterward the Valar reckoned the hour of Telperion's first blooming as the hour from which they began the Count of Time. Moreover, against future need, Varda hoarded in shining vats the dews of light which dripped down from the Trees. Later on, the descendants of Telperion were to have an eventful history both on Númenor and on Middle-earth (to which Isildur brought a seedling, as told in *Akallabêth* and in *The Lord of the Rings*).

At the time when both Trees burst into their first bloom under the chanting of Yavanna, Middle-earth as yet had for its illumination only those faint stars which Varda had made long ago in her labors to construct Eä in seemly fashion. And now that the Valar had moved away to Valinor, and seldom returned to Middle-earth, Melkor freely walked in its shadows wielding extremes of ice and fire there, unseen and unhindered. Although spirits in the forms of hawks and eagles kept reporting to Manwë what was happening above ground and under ground, even he on Taniquetil, whose eyes could see all else on Earth's surface, could not pierce the shadows with which Melkor surrounded himself.

Others of the Valar could not forget Middle-earth, or abandon it to Melkor. Ulmo moved everywhere in its rivers, lakes, springs, and other waters. His great and terrible music ran "through all the veins of the world in sorrow and in joy." So by his power life kept coursing through hidden lodes underground, and Earth's vegetation did not wholly die even under Melkor's darkness.

Oromë, too, continued to hunt down the monsters and

cruel beasts ruled by Melkor, sounding his mighty horn until Melkor himself quailed in Utumno and the shadows of evil fled from its sound. But as soon as he had passed they returned, more numerous than before, and more dreadful, as Melkor built his strength in the north and spread his dominion farther and farther southward. Moreover, he constructed a second fortress, Angband, near the north-western shores of the Great Sea closest to Valinor to guard against any assault from that quarter. Sauron as his chief lieutenant commanded this stronghold.

But Yavanna, who cherished all growing things, was the Vala who returned perhaps oftenest to Middle-earth to heal what Melkor had harmed, and this was much. She walked in the shadows, grieving. To her comfort, however, she found that the oldest living things still survived: weeds in the sea, great trees on the earth, and in the hills dark crea-tures not only old but strong. Many of these she put to sleep so that they would not die before Earth's next Springtime should come.

Fittingly, it was she who warned a council of the Valar that the hour for the birth of the Elves was approaching, and she asked whether they were to be born on a Middle-earth still in darkness and still ruled by Melkor. At the command of Manwë, spokesman for Ilúvatar, Mandos de-clared "it is doom" that the Elves, the Firstborn, should awake during a night which would cause them first to look up at the stars and to call, in time of need, upon Varda (Elbereth).

To fulfill this decree of Ilúvatar, Varda used the vats filled with the silver dew dropped by Telperion and made with it many new, bright stars which she strewed over the sky. The old stars she gathered in constellations which were signs. Menelmacar, the Swordsman of the Sky (Orion), foreboded the Last Battle, which was to be fought at the end of days; and Valacirca, the Sickle of the Valar (the Great Bear), challenged Melkor and foretold his defeat.

In that hour when Orion first climbed the sky the Elves, the Firstborn, awoke from the sleep of Ilúvatar beside the lake Cuiviénen, far to the north and east in Middle-earth. Clearly these Elves did not evolve from some prior race but were created all at once as a new race whom Ilúvatar shaped with bodies, minds, and independent wills. They "awoke" instantly when he gave them the Imperishable Flame of life, and from no long sleep like that of Aulë's Dwarves.

The first sound they heard was the tumbling of water into the lake, their first sight the starry heaven reflected in its calm surface. Silent at their birth, they began of their own accord to speak and to give names to all things. They had not yet met any other living thing that spoke or sang. They were singing, however, when Oromë on one of his hunting expeditions found them by chance and wondered at their beauty, greater than any other Ilúvatar ever made for Eä.

Carpenter's statement (p. 93) that Elves are "Man before the Fall which deprived him of his powers of achievement" seems misleading, and perhaps unintelligible. He goes on to argue that Tolkien's Elves, "though capable of sin and error, have not 'fallen' in the theological sense." But if Elves are capable of sinning, and in fact do sin often enough in *The Silmarillion*, it is hard to see how they can have done so without first "falling" from a state of innocence in a "theological sense," whatever the latter phrase means. It might be better not to differentiate between "theological" and other types of falls and simply to point out that, for whatever reason, Elves are as inherently capable of sin and error as human beings are. Witness Eöl, Maeglin, several of Feänor's sons, and even, in part, Feänor himself.

But Melkor had already discovered the Elves years before Oromë and had sent his Dark Riders on wild horses to seize any who wandered off alone. This he did partly to frighten them away from Oromë if he should ever come, but mainly to subject these captives to the most abominable of his crimes.

In his dungeons by "slow arts of cruelty" he broke their wills, tampered with them genetically, and bred these newborn, innocent Elves into a race of hideous Orcs. Moreover, they bred true. Their offspring were not Elves but Orcs directed toward Evil, so that they became Melkor's slaves. And he taught them hatred. They hated the Elves, their former kinsmen, and no less their Master who had transformed them into the brutes they were. Of them, being ripe for war, his armies were chiefly composed and, after Melkor, Sauron's armies in the War of the Rings.

Because of Melkor's false whispers against Oromë some of the Elves were terrified by the latter's coming, but the braver of them saw that he was no Dark Rider, since the light of Valinor shone in his face, and they were drawn to him. Oromë remained with the Elves long enough to witness Melkor's outrages against them. Then swiftly he rode over land and sea to report these tidings to the Valar, but himself returned at once to the Elves to protect them in Melkor's darkness.

After praying to Ilúvatar for wisdom Manwë announced to a council of the Valar at the Ring of Doom near the Two Trees the plan which the All-Father had put into his heart —to retake Middle-earth at all costs in order to save the Elves from Melkor. Accordingly the Valar landed there in full force, set a guard over Cuiviénen, and besieged Utumno. They fought at its gates battles so violent that the whole northern land mass of Middle-earth was laid waste, and the Sea between it and Valinor grew wider when billows overran many parts of the Middle-earth coastline. Utumno fell at last, its roof torn off. Then Melkor fled to its deepest pit, where Tulkas wrestled with him and bound him with the chain Angainor, forged by Aulë. Yet the Valar failed to find other deep caverns whence evil creatures fled into the gloom, roaming there and waiting for their Dark Lord's return (p. 51).

Taken to Valinor, Melkor lay prostrate on his face begging for Manwë's pardon. This was refused, and he was sentenced to imprisonment for three Ages in the prison of Mandos, from which not even a Vala could escape. At the end of that time his plea for pardon would be considered again.

Melkor being now safely out of the way for a while, the Valar faced another crucial question: whether to summon the Elves to Valinor or to let them walk freely wherever they wished on Middle-earth, using their "gifts of skill" to heal the lands disordered by the battles against Melkor. Ulmo and his party favored the latter alternative. Most of the Valar, however, feared the dangers threatening the Elves from the deceits of the evil creatures still wandering on Middle-earth. And, more selfishly, they eagerly desired the presence and love of the Firstborn. When Mandos heard this course prevail he said, "So it is doomed," expressing the concurrence of Manwë with it.

But Tolkien adds soberly, "From this summons came many woes that afterwards befell" (p. 52). He is referring to the longing to return to Middle-earth among those Elves, particularly the Noldor under the leadership of Fëanor, who were born in Valinor and had never had the chance to explore Middle-earth—a longing which begot among many of them a mistaken sense of imprisonment by the Valar.

At first the Elves were afraid to go to Valinor when summoned, and not until their leaders had been taken there and had seen its splendors did most of them agree to undertake the long venture to the home of the Valar. A number of them never went at all but stayed on Middle-earth. Those who were to go divided themselves into three tribes or "houses," each closely interlaced within itself by bonds of kinship and united by its own characteristic traits.

Led by Ingwë, High King of the Elvish race, the Vanyar were the people most loved by Manwë and Varda and most loving to them in return. So close grew this bond that later, when the other tribes had built the Elvish city of Tirion on Valinor, the Vanyar gradually left it and built their dwellings on Taniquetil to be near Manwë, spokesman for Ilúvatar. They may well be accounted the most religious of the three houses, and the holiest. Typically they were the first to set out on the westward trek, following Ingwë.

Under Finwë, next came the Noldor, or Deep Elves— Deep in the sense that they were the most intellectual and most profoundly searching of the tribes. Much about them is revealed by the fact that the Vala to whom they most closely attached themselves was Aulë the Smith, maker of the Dwarves, most skilled among the Valar in works of hand and mind.

On their long, slow journey westward one of the tribes of the Elves, almost certainly the Noldor, finding that the trees which then covered the land had a capacity for speech but no language, tarried long enough to teach them the Elvish tongue. Better yet, they inspired the Ents, the tree-herds, to develop in addition their own Entish way of speaking. In so doing they won the everlasting gratitude of Treebeard, the oldest of them (*Lord of the Rings* II, 67–71). Since he was himself one of the first living dwellers on Middle-earth, promised by Manwë to Yavanna, as told in the preceding chapter, Treebeard saw them affectionately as children still—"the Elf-children," he called them. He appreciated their quick sympathies and admired their invention of languages: "Elves made all the old words: they began it."

Among the Noldor, Fëanor had not been born yet; so the script he later devised was not the first. He had at least one predecessor, another Noldor Elf named Rúmil (*The Lord of the Rings* III, 395), who composed a Tengwar or written alphabet. In short, the Noldor had a tradition of interest in language and its written forms, of which there is no trace among either the Vanyar or the Teleri, and which was in keeping with their curiosity about everything learnable.

Last in the westward pilgrimage went the Teleri, third and largest of the Elf tribes, led by the brothers Elwë and Olwë. Being only half convinced that they should go all the way to Valinor, they tended to linger at places they liked, especially near water. So when they came to the great river Anduin, of which much is written in *The Lord of the Rings*, they hesitated on its eastern bank although the Vanyar and the Noldor had already crossed it. Then a portion of Olwë's host were led southward by a self-declared leader named Lenwë. They did not turn north again into Beleriand until Lenwë's son led them there. Meanwhile Elwë had brought the greater part of the Teleri across the Misty Mountains into the eastern region of that land. He had been one of the ambassadors taken by Oromë to Valinor and he longed to return there. Besides, he was a close friend of Finwë, King of the Noldor, and wished to rejoin him.

Searching for Finwë one day alone in the forest, Elwë came upon Melian, a Maia of the Vala called Lórien. Among his Maiar none was "more beautiful than Melian, nor more wise, nor more skilled in songs of enchantment." These songs were to play a major role in the tale of the love between her daughter Lúthien and the Man Beren, as will be seen hereafter. And the songs played their part also in the love that passed between Melian and Elwë. For he saw in her face the light of Valinor and "being filled with love Elwë came to her, and took her hand, and straightway a spell was laid on him," so that the two stood together, not speaking, for long years. Then Elwë forgot his people and remained to become King Thingol of Doriath with the aid of Melian his wife.

It remains to ask why and how Melian came to be in that forest on Middle-earth just at the right time and place for Elwë to find her. Being akin to Yavanna she loved the

living things of Middle-earth, especially its great trees and
its nightingales, which she taught to sing. As soon as the
Elves awoke at Cuiviénen she freely left Valinor to roam
the woods and fill them with song. Perhaps she wished only
in a general way to welcome and delight the Firstborn
Children of Ilúvatar. But when she met Elwë it was she
who cast the spell which enthralled him and ended by
enthralling her too.

It is not hard to see in their union the Providence of
Ilúvatar using them both for the best ends. For without
this union Lúthien would never have been born to love
Beren, and without those two who else would have been
capable of stealing a Silmaril from Morgoth—the very
Silmaril, moreover, which by devious descent came at
last to Eärendil? Through its help, that mariner reached
Valinor and only he, both Elf and Man, was ᴜ1e long-
awaited pleader who could bring the Valar to launch
the War of Wrath against Morgoth. Upon the love of
Melian and Thingol, therefore, hung the whole rescue
of Middle-earth.

But to return to the westward journey of the Elves. The
Teleri, having spent much time searching in vain for Elwë,
their lost leader, eventually accepted his brother Olwë as
their King and pressed on to the west. But meantime
Oromë had brought the Vanyar and the Noldor to the
seacoast of Middle-earth near the Mouths of the River Sirion. And looking out over the Great Sea they were so
terrified by its darkness and its depth that many of them
retreated from the coast and refused to embark upon its
restless waters. Oromë then went on to Valinor to seek
Manwë's counsel, which sent Ulmo to talk to the frightened Elves. By his persuasive words and the seductive
music of his horns he changed their fear of the ocean into
love of it. Then, uprooting an island far out to sea, Ulmo
and his Maiar towed it to the Bay of Balar. Upon this solid
land the Vanyar and the Noldor gladly embarked, and so

were drawn by Ulmo to the shores of Valinor, where the Valar welcomed them. Yet a fragment known as the Isle of Balar broke off and remained in the Bay.

The Teleri, however, were still too far inland to share in this passage. As soon as they heard of it they hastened down to the Mouths of Sirion, longing to be gone. There they lived for many years, taught by Ossë and his spouse Uinen how to make all kinds of sea-music. In this way the Teleri, who since their birth had loved water and had been the sweetest singers among the Elves, came to love the sea and to fill their songs with the sounds of waves breaking always on the shore.

Finally Ulmo yielded to the pleas of the Noldor and their King Finwë that he transport to Valinor the Teleri, whose friendship they missed. Most of them accepted Ulmo's offer eagerly. But his vassal Ossë, ruler of coastal waters, persuaded some to remain on Middle-earth, where they became its first mariners and, under Círdan the Shipwright, its first builders of ships. Also some of the followers of Elwë found him after long search and gathered round him in his new kingdom of Doriath. Yet, despite these defections, Olwë had the main host of the Teleri with him when he set foot on the Isle of Balar.

This Isle, nevertheless, was never to reach Valinor itself. At the plea of Ossë and the Teleri on it, Ulmo anchored it some distance offshore in the Bay of Eldamar, where it became known as Tol Eressëa, the Lonely Isle. For a long age the Teleri lived there, content under the stars and yet within sight of Valinor, from which the light of the Two Trees streamed out upon them through Calacirya, a gap in the Pelóri range. Slowly, however, their hearts were more and more drawn toward this light. Then Ulmo, at the will of the other Valar, sent them Ossë to teach them how to build ships. When all the necessary ships had been completed, Ossë gave them a gift of many strong swans, which drew the ships over the waters of the Bay to the shore of Valinor at last.

After this the Teleri could move freely anywhere in Valinor, but they preferred to walk in the waves that broke on the shore or to sail their ships on the waters of the Bay. The Noldor strewed their beaches with many bright and precious gems by way of welcome. And the Teleri built themselves their city of Alqualondë, where they erected mansions with halls of pearl and made a harbor for their ships. These they shaped like swans, "with beaks of gold and eyes of gold and jet," in memory of Ossë's gift (p. 61).

IV

Fëanor

BEHIND US NOW lie the giant works of Ilúvatar and his Ainur in creating and shaping our World. Behind, too, the long westward migration of the three Elf tribes to Aman at the summons of the Valar as told in the *Quenta Silmarillion*, Chapter 3, and likewise the settlement of each tribe in its preferred location there. But ahead looms the tragedy of the Noldor after their flight back to Middle-earth to recover the Silmarils stolen by Morgoth.

Before and during the *Quenta Silmarillion* account of this flight, Tolkien sketches a portrait of Fëanor, the Noldor Prince who instigates and controls it. Fëanor, the mightiest genius ever produced by the Elvish race, has a character more complex than that of any other person, be he Elf, Man, or Dwarf, who takes part in the war against Morgoth. Tolkien studies him carefully from many sides, for Fëanor while alive is the mainspring of the disasters that ensue. And after his death his influence is perpetuated by his seven sons, who have sworn to pursue and kill anyone who withholds from them even a single one of the three Silmarils made by their father. So the voice of Fëanor, long dead, may be said to echo down the tragedy to the very end.

*   *   *

Although Manwë loved the Vanyar Elves best, Aulë loved the Noldor and often came with his Maiar to teach them his lore. The more the Noldor learned the more they craved insatiably to learn, so that in some fields of knowledge they went further than their teachers. In language, for instance; they greatly loved words and kept always trying to find fitter names for all the things they saw or dreamed of. In this they resembled Tolkien himself. Again, while quarrying in the hills of Valinor for stone with which to build the city of Tirion and in it the Tower of their King, Finwë, the Noldor masons first discovered veins of precious gems. They devised tools for cutting these and for carving them into varied forms never seen before (p. 60). These works of art they did not hoard but gave away freely. Aulë taught them this selflessness.

So Curufinwë, the Skilled Son of Finwë, called by his mother Fëanáro, Spirit of Fire, did not spring suddenly full-armed from the soil of Valinor, but had behind him ruling Noldor traits and long traditions: in his boundless hunger for knowledge, in his love of language, and in his experiments with gems. For what were the Silmarils but Jewels more marvelous and holy than all others? The existence of these traditions takes nothing away from Fëanor's genius, for he transformed them into wonders which no other Noldor, indeed no other Elf, had the wit to imagine.

His position as eldest son of King Finwë also set him apart. His mother, deeply loved by Finwë, was Míriel Serindë, Míriel the Broideress, a woman of the Noldor. This title did not demean her. The Noldor highly valued skill in designing and executing fine needlework, and Míriel's hands were more "skilled to fineness" than those of any other even among that exacting race. Fëanor was her only child, for she did not long survive his birth. She told Finwë then that she could never bear him another child, "for strength that would have nourished the life of many has gone forth into Fëanor" (p. 63). In a word, Fëanor's vitality of spirit and strength of body were prodigious, like that of many a Northern hero from Sigurd to Grettir the Strong, to Beowulf, mightiest of the men of his time, and the rest.[1]

By the advice of Manwë, Míriel was sent to the gardens of Lórien to be healed. But even there, too drained to live, she faded quietly into death. After that, Finwë went often to Lórien to call out her name in sorrow, but he could not bring her back, and after a while ceased to go. Fëanor, therefore, had to grow up without the love and the training he would have received from his mother, but dearly loved by his father. He developed swiftly into a masterful adult, perpetually at work on some project or other, not welcoming advice about it from anybody. As Tolkien reports, "He became of all the Noldor, then or after, the most subtle in mind and the most skilled in hand"—that is, the most brilliant in formulating new ideas and then in finding the means for putting them into execution (p. 64).

Among other achievements Fëanor discovered how to make gems larger and brighter than those lying buried in the mines underground. By day they looked colorless, but under the stars they blazed with blue and silver—seemingly a step along the road to his fashioning of the Silmarils.

Also, improving on Rúmil's pictographic script, he invented what came to be called "the Tengwar of Fëanor," an alphabet whose letters, while owing something to Rúmil's, "were largely a new invention."[2] It was more flexible and more cursive than its predecessor, and therefore easier to write with brush or pen. These were the letters which the Noldor took with them into exile on Middle-earth and taught to the Edain, their human allies. By the Third Age, wherever the Common Speech was spoken it was written down in Fëanor's script. This almost universal adoption of his Tengwar shows the many-sided genius of its originator at work in a field far removed from the physical sciences, that of his other triumphs.

Still another wonder produced by Fëanor in Valinor was the seven "Seeing Stones," or *Palantíri. The Silmarillion* barely mentions them as a means by which it was possible to see objects, however small, at very great distances. That Fëanor bothered to make them at all testifies to his eagerness to learn as much as he could of Middle-earth and to his often expressed longing to found new kingdoms there, a possibility which appealed likewise to many of his people who followed him when he later left the Valar.

Long after Fëanor's death, however, it turned out that the seven *palantíri* he had made were much more than superb binoculars.[3] He had so constructed them that through any one of the seven a beholder, looking into its depths, could converse with the owner of any of the other six stones, however far in distance and in time, and could in fact read his thoughts. Like Sauron's One Ring they also exerted a hypnotic spell on those who were near them. And each could be so mastered by its possessor as to trap and enslave anyone weaker of will than himself who dared to look into it. If such possession was challenged it became a battlefield of wills. Aragorn, for one, contested Sauron's mastery of the *palantír* held by Saruman in Orthanc. What followed was a struggle of his will against Sauron's, long and bitter, which Aragorn was barely strong enough to win.[4] As a result an alarmed Sauron launched his armies against Gondor prematurely.

But none of this appears in *The Silmarillion,* possibly because Fëanor died so early in the war against Morgoth. After that war had been won, the Eldar gave the Stones to the human Edain who went to Númenor (p. 276). Thence Isildur rescued them before that island was overwhelmed by the sea, and brought them to Middle-earth. There the *palantíri,* controlled by Sauron, Saruman, and Denethor, became crucial factors in the War of the Rings. Considering all these powers, the Seven Stones must be reckoned high among the achievements wrought by what Gandalf called in admiration "the unimaginable hand and mind of Fëanor."[5]

So passed Fëanor's busy, productive years until worldly

affairs began to intrude upon the work in which he delighted. In his youth he had married Nerdanel, daughter of the Noldor smith Mahtan who was dear to Aulë. She was a strong-willed female, able at first to restrain Fëanor's tempestuous nature, but only for a time. After she had borne him seven sons, she found that in spite of all she could do he was growing ever more self-centered. So she left him. During the years when she lived with her family she managed to school the elder two of her sons, Maedhros and Maglor, to some degree of self-control, but not the younger five.

After her abandonment of them the seven clung all the more closely to their father and were seldom separated from him. Together with Fëanor they explored Valinor restlessly from end to end, even to the shores of the Encircling Sea, "seeking the unknown." Often they were guests of Aulë. Only the third son, Celegorm, preferred to frequent the house of Oromë, learning to become a hunter and to understand the language of birds and beasts.

At about this time Finwë married again, choosing Indis, a princess not of the Noldor but of the Vanyar, dearest to Manwë. She had the strong sense of morality and piety characteristic of her race. And these she encouraged in the two sons, Fingolfin and Finarfin, whom she bore to Finwë. These two were half-brothers to Fëanor, possessing none of his inventive genius but far excelling him in steadfastness and in the knowledge of right conduct.

This second wedding estranged Fëanor from his father for a time. Perhaps he was jealous, but without cause, since he remained dearer to Finwë than Indis and her sons. Perhaps also he feared that a dynastic struggle might arise with Fingolfin about the succession to the kingship over the Noldor. But even without these barriers, the temperaments of Finwë's two families were so utterly at variance that they had little in common except Finwë himself. Accordingly, Fëanor and his sons lived apart from their close kin,

continuing to explore Valinor and to acquire knowledge
and crafts. And, significantly, none of the seven ever married. By contrast, Fingolfin's two sons, Fingon and Turgon, and his daughter Aredhel the White all married and
had children, as did also Finarfin's four sons and their
sister, Galadriel. (See Genealogical Table, p. 305).

This breach within the ruling House of the Noldor came
about at the worst of times, when Melkor, having served his
sentence of three Ages in the prison of Mandos, was pardoned by Manwë, too blindly merciful. Melkor had always
hated the Elves for raising the Valar against him, and he
hated them still. Looking about him Melkor now devised
the scheme of separating the Valar from the Elves. Not
from the Vanyar, who were impregnable to his deceits,
nor from the Teleri, who seemed not worth his efforts, but
from the Noldor, whose internal rift invited him in to
widen it, each from each and all from the Valar. In particular he set out to entangle in lying tales Fëanor, who loathed
him and first named him Morgoth, the Black Enemy.

At this point a totally unforeseen event came to pass:
Fëanor completed, and exhibited to all, the three Silmarils
he had just made. Whether moved by sheer inspiration
only, or by some premonition of the death of the Two
Trees at the hands of Morgoth, he had long been considering how to preserve their light imperishably. And having
now come to the height of his powers he had worked alone
and secretly, as he always did, calling upon all he had ever
learned and upon all his skill of hand.

First he had compounded a new substance never before
known, by some called *silima,* harder than adamant, virtually unbreakable. Then he had contrived to enclose in it
"the blended light of the Trees," like a soul centered within
a living body yet acting also in all its parts. And indeed the
Silmarils resembled things that were alive, for "they rejoiced in light and received it, and gave it back in hues more
marvellous than before" (p. 67).

In effect, they were as close to living creatures as any things could be which lacked the sacred Flame of Ilúvatar, and they were the mightiest works ever wrought by Fëanor himself or by any other Elf before or since. This quality of the Silmarils was recognized by Varda when she "hallowed" them so that any hands mortal, or unclean, or evil, which might touch them would be scorched.

Morgoth, who always envied and hated the holy, lusted now for the Silmarils and all the more cunningly labored to breed enmity between the Valar and the Noldor, especially Fëanor. To this end he spread lies among them, hinting that the Valar had brought the Noldor to Valinor for fear that on Middle-earth they would establish wide kingdoms which the Valar could not control. Moreover, Morgoth whispered to credulous Noldor ears that the race of Men, soon to be born, would occupy these kingdoms in their stead, a weak and short-lived people whom the Valar could easily enslave.

Blinded by pride and forgetting how much of their knowledge they owed to the Valar, many of the Noldor began to murmur against them, Fëanor in the forefront because of his longing for freedom in wider lands than Valinor. Moreover he, who at the time of his making the Silmarils had loved them all too well, began to treasure them with growing greed. He locked them "in the deep chambers of his hoard in Tirion," showing them only to his father and his seven sons, and seldom remembering that their light did not belong to him alone. As Tolkien stressed over and over in *The Lord of the Rings*, "possessiveness" was at the root of much evil.[6] This was the trap into which Fëanor was now falling. Tolkien's use of the word "hoard" is a warning of his danger.

Morgoth then set Fëanor and his half-brothers at odds. He gave out rumors to Fëanor that the latter were scheming to supplant him in his succession to the kingship, while at the same time warning Fingolfin that Fëanor was plotting to drive him from the city of Tirion. The transition from that state of mind on both sides to the forging of swords, axes, and spears by both was all too easy. And Fëanor, brilliant though he was, yet the fool of his passions, first advocated in public a return to Middle-earth to escape slavery under the Valar.

At a council of the Noldor summoned by King Finwë this ugly quarrel between the half-brothers came out into the open (pp. 69–70). Fingolfin, speaking first, begged Finwë to restrain Fëanor from issuing pronouncements "as if he were King," reminding Finwë that it was he who ordered his people to journey from Middle-earth to Valinor. Fingolfin offered to support that command to remain on Valinor. But Fëanor then drew his sword and threatened to kill him if he continued maneuvering "to usurp my place and the love of my father." Fingolfin gave no answer but left the meeting to consult with Finarfin.

This council having settled nothing, the Valar called before them in the Ring of Doom all parties to the quarrel. Fëanor they questioned most closely, holding him to be the chief advocate of discontent. But Morgoth's primary role in inciting the quarrel soon became clear, and Tulkas went to seize him and bring him to the judgment of the Valar. For drawing his sword against Fingolfin, however, Fëanor was sentenced by Mandos to twelve years of banishment from Tirion. When these had elapsed the case against him would be considered closed "if others will release thee" (p. 71).

Then and there Fingolfin declared, "I will release my brother." But Fëanor did not thank him and, instead, went silently into exile, taking with him his seven sons. At Formenos, north of Valmar, they built a stronghold to which they transferred all they had in the way of weapons and gems, including the Silmarils. King Finwë joined them there because of his love for Fëanor, leaving Fingolfin to rule the Noldor in Tirion.

Morgoth knew that he was being sought, and hid himself

for a time on Middle-earth, but then he returned to tempt Fëanor at the gate of Formenos. The Silmarils, he said, would never be safe from the Valar as long as they were kept in Valinor. He therefore offered to help Fëanor if he would flee with the Great Jewels to Middle-earth. But Fëanor had eyes to pierce through Morgoth's pretenses and to discover lurking behind them his lust for the Silmarils. Therefore he slammed shut the gate of Formenos in his face. Like a thundercloud Morgoth passed away in wrath from Valinor, leaving behind him dread—even among the Valar.

Manwë believed that he had returned to his fortresses on Middle-earth and increased the watch on Valinor's northern regions, closest to the mainland, but in fact Morgoth had doubled back and landed on Avathar, a southern region of Valinor dark with many shadows. There he sought out Ungoliant, formerly a Maia of his, who had disowned his lordship, bent on doing her own will, not his. She had taken on the form of a monstrous spider, hungry for light but hating it. Having sucked up all the light she could find she spun it out into so thick a gloom that no more light could penetrate it to feed her.

When Morgoth came to her in the form of a great Dark Lord and proposed that she should help him in stealing the light of the Two Trees and killing them, she was eager to accept, yet reluctant to face the power of the Valar. To bribe her further Morgoth vowed that if she was still hungry after feeding upon the Trees' light he would give her "whatsoever thy lust may demand. Yea, with both hands" (p. 74). Thereupon she accepted the enterprise, having her own notions of what she would do afterward, as he had his.

Ungoliant's spun darkness was Unlight, not the mere absence of light but a positive thing in itself which no eyes could pierce. Wrapped in this cloak the two conspirators crept northward upon the Trees, unnoticed because Manwë was holding in his halls on Taniquetil a harvest

festival to celebrate the crops reaped from Yavanna's plant-
ings. He meant to use this occasion to heal the griefs of the
Noldor. Besides the Vanyar, all the Noldor from Tirion
were present. But from Formenos came only Fëanor, and
he by express command. For King Finwë had declined to
come, saying that so long as Fëanor remained banished
from Tirion "I hold myself unkinged" (p. 75).

Standing before Manwë's throne, Fëanor and Fingolfin
were reconciled, at least in word. Fingolfin, who felt himself in a false position as ruler of the Noldor in Tirion, did
his utmost to mend the breach. First he sought to end
Fëanor's banishment by releasing him from blame, as required by Mandos. Then, since Fëanor proudly made no
reply, Fingolfin went further still by accepting Fëanor's
right as heir to the throne of the Noldor saying, "Thou
shalt lead and I will follow. May no new grief divide us."
This assurance Fëanor accepted, but in words that lacked
warmth: "I hear thee . . . So be it." And Tolkien added
ominously that "they did not know the meaning that their
words would bear."

Even while this ceremony was in progress Morgoth's
spear smote each of the Two Trees to its core. Sap poured
out of the wounds like blood. Ungoliant drank it. Then she
inserted her poisonous beak into the wounds, draining and
poisoning them so that, root and branch, the Two Trees
died. Next she drank dry the vats kept by Varda filled with
their dew, until she swelled to a size so huge that it terrified
even Morgoth.

Upon all the land of Valinor then fell the Cloud of Ungoliant, "a thing with being of its own" able to pierce heart
and mind, and Manwë alone had eyes to see Morgoth
fleeing northward. Oromë and Tulkas pursued him but
were blinded by the Cloud and lost his tracks utterly.

The unnatural Darkness of Ungoliant having been
swept away by Manwë's winds, the Valar and their followers gathered around the Two Trees, now so dead that their

branches fell to pieces under the touch of Yavanna, who had sung them into life. And she told her watchers that having once brought their light into being she could never do so again. But if she had only a little of their light, still preserved in Fëanor's Silmarils, she could "recall life to the Trees" and make them again what once they were. All looked at Fëanor expecting him to offer her his Silmarils. But he cried out that, like Yavanna, having once made the Jewels he could never make them again. In order to give her the light she needed he would have to break them open and so break his own heart.

Fëanor had not yet said "yea" or "nay" and, brooding upon his answer, remembered Morgoth's lie, which to him was no lie, that the Silmarils could never be safe in Valinor if the Valar wanted to "possess them." It seemed to him, looking round him in his paranoia, that the Valar were enemies who now indeed wanted to take *his* Silmarils from him. So his answer was a veiled refusal coupled with an insult. He would not give up the Silmarils of his own free will, he said, and if the Valar forced him to, they would be acting like Morgoth.

This was Fëanor's moment of truth, and he failed the test. Although the mightiest genius of the Elves, he had sunk so far into the greed of "possessiveness" that he could not give away to others the work of his hands as was the custom in Valinor the Blessed. Aulë never kept for himself any new thing he had made but freely shared it with all who asked. The Noldor smiths and masons, too, kept nothing secret. Nor, of course, did the Valar. Yavanna planted her crops for all to eat, and Varda her stars for all to enjoy and to see by. And so with all the rest.

Tolkien remarks of Fëanor's "nay" that "had he said 'yea' at the first . . . it may be that his after deeds would have been other than they were. But now the doom of the Noldor drew near" (p. 79). In other words, had Fëanor given Yavanna the light of the Silmarils by breaking them open, that would have been an act of love, obedience, and self-sacrifice, after which he would never even have dreamed of defying the Valar and leading the Noldor back to Middle-earth, with disastrous consequences for them all.

The future which Fëanor had chosen began to unroll itself immediately. News came from the Noldor at Formenos that Morgoth and a blinding Darkness had stopped there on their way north. King Finwë had been slain while trying to defend the gate alone. Then Morgoth had broken in, had taken the Silmarils and all the other jewels "hoarded" there, and had gone on, none knew where. Hearing these bitter tidings, Fëanor cursed Morgoth, and even cursed Manwë to his face for issuing the summons which had drawn him away from Formenos in its fatal hour. Mad with rage and grief he raced back there for, says Tolkien, "his father was dearer to him than the light of Valinor, or the peerless works of his hands; and who among sons, of Elves or of Men, have held their fathers of greater worth?" (p. 79).

Fëanor now had two driving motives for pursuing Morgoth to Middle-earth, love for his Silmarils and love for his father. Whatever may be said about his too-selfish love for the three Jewels, Tolkien assures us that his unselfish love for Finwë was the greater. And, considering how intense was his possessiveness for the Silmarils, it stands much to his credit that this filial affection exceeded it.

Meanwhile Ungoliant and Morgoth crossed the ice of the Helcaraxë together into the northern wastes of Middle-earth near the ruins of Angband, his former fortress. Ungoliant, seeing Morgoth's desire to escape her by entering it, demanded fulfilment of his promise to give her whatso-ever she lusted for, "Yea, with both hands." Fearful, he gave her all the jewels stolen from Formenos except the Silmarils which, he said, "I name unto myself forever." Thereupon she enmeshed him in a clinging web which began to strangle him. He uttered a cry of anguish so loud that it was heard by Balrogs still lurking in the hidden depths of Angband. They came to his rescue, severing Ungoliant's web with their whips of flame.

She fled then to Nan Dungortheb, the Valley of Dreadful Death, where she mated with other spiders still surviving from Angband's wreck, and ate them. Then she herself fled on, always southward, but her offspring stayed at Nan Dungortheb, making that valley a place of terror in after years. Nor was this all. Thousands of years later, far to the southeast, one of Ungoliant's descendants, the great spider Shelob almost devoured Frodo and Sam on their way into Mordor via the Pass of Cirith Ungol.[7]

Freed from Ungoliant, Morgoth hastened to rebuild and strengthen Angband. Above its main gate he piled the three peaks of Thangorodrim, for he still had the strength of a Vala. Its deepest regions he expanded and peopled with his former servants and with his new race of Orcs, which multiplied rapidly at his command. And he forged for himself an Iron Crown in which he set the three Silmarils, in token of his being King of the World, as he boasted. They burned and pained him without pause according to Varda's decree, since they were hallowed and he was evil. Yet he never took them off, nor did he ever leave Angband, save once at the challenge of Fingolfin. From his throne there he directed his armies in the world above, spending his spirit to keep them bound to evil. He expected war from Valinor and was preparing for it.

Fëanor, suddenly appearing in Tirion, was to be its instigator. His appearance there was in itself a defiance of the Valar in that his twelve years of banishment from that city had not yet expired. Finwë being dead, he claimed the Kingship over the Noldor. He called them all to council and all came. Now Fëanor was a lord of language, an orator superbly skilled in swaying an audience to his cause. On this occasion his cause was to persuade his people to accept him as their King, and so to follow him back to Middle-earth to avenge Finwë's death on Morgoth, and to recapture the Silmarils from him. Yet, as Tolkien remarks, almost all he said "came from the very lies of Morgoth himself" (p. 82). This ironical comment seems to mean that although Fëanor always explicitly rejected Morgoth's deceits they remained deeply implanted in his mind, and his unconscious use of them signified symbolically their appeal to the evil side of his nature.

Fëanor spoke first of his duty as Finwë's son, and the Noldors' duty as his people, to avenge Finwë's death upon Morgoth.[8] Moreover, he declared that the Valar being kin to Morgoth, Finwë's slayer, neither he nor the rest of the Noldor could continue to live with them. This was a plausible but perverse and false appeal to the code against Kinslaying, which Fëanor himself broke later on in his attack on the Teleri Elves at Alqualondë.

What Tolkien does in bringing this and other Norse codes of conduct into *The Silmarillion* is to treat them as normative for Elves in the First Age. Some codes he had to give them and the Norse seemed primitive enough, yet viable and familiar, too, for his purposes. Similarly when writing *The Lord of the Rings*, set in the Third Age, he called upon the Norse view that a solemn oath is so strong a bond that an oathbreaker cannot escape it even in death. Therefore Aragorn, by treading the Paths of the Dead, was able to summon up the unresting spirits of the men who swore to give aid to his ancestor Isildur and did not keep their word. Once they had helped him by terrifying into flight Gondor's enemies coming up from the south he released them to their rest.

The dilemma posed by the Oath of Fëanor and his sons to kill anyone at all who refuses to yield them possession of even one of the Silmarils is that, once sworn, the Oath cannot be broken even though it is evil in requiring murder. The universal condemnation of oath-breaking in Norse mythology is expressed, for example, in William

Morris' translation of *Volsunga Saga* and in several of the lays in *The Elder Edda*. In these lays, however, as in Aragorn's calling up the spirits of the dead to fulfill their oath in *The Lord of the Rings*, the fulfillment of the broken oath requires help in battle but not murder. Fëanor's Oath sets no limit to the means used in keeping it. So the attempt to keep it leads his sons from one horrible killing to another, and eventually to Maedhros' despairing suicide and Maglor's self-exile from his own kind.

Fëanor next proposed that all the Noldor return to Cuiviénen where they were born and where wide lands stretching under fair stars lay ready for the taking. But they must not delay. A new race of Men, Children of Ilúvatar like themselves, were soon to be born, and they were the ones who would rule Middle-earth if the Elves allowed the Valar to keep them captive in Valinor. He warned them frankly that war awaited them, and many hardships, and a long road. Let them travel light. "After Morgoth to the ends of the Earth!" was Fëanor's battle cry. Once they had won back the Silmarils they alone would have the Light of the Two Trees radiant in them and would be the rulers of Middle-earth.

So far he had his audience with him. Fëanor had said nothing, except the underlying premise of abandoning Valinor for Middle-earth, which most of them might oppose. But quite suddenly, as if by prearrangement, he and his seven sons all swore the dreadful Oath "which none shall break and none should take" (p. 83), vowing to pursue with vengeance anyone who should keep a Silmaril from their possession. This Oath has already been considered in Chapter II.

It was a mistake on Fëanor's part, for it seemed to make the Silmarils the exclusive possession of him and his sons. It was too "possessive." Fëanor and his sons might consider the three Great Jewels their private property whose ownership was enforced by so terrible an oath. But as his audience saw it, the Silmarils belonged to all, as had the Two Trees from which they derived their sacred Light.

So the Oath caused anger and division among those who heard it. Fingolfin, ruler of the city of Tirion *pro tem* in Finwë's absence, together with his son Turgon, spoke against it vehemently, almost reopening the old breach with Fëanor. On the one hand Finarfin, Fingolfin's brother, acted as a peacemaker, urging a pause to let tempers cool. His second son, Orodreth, did the same. But Finrod, Finarfin's eldest, joined Turgon in opposing Fëanor. On the other hand, Finarfin's daughter Galadriel sided with Fëanor because, like him, she wanted a realm of her own, and later achieved it in Lothlórien. With her agreed Fingolfin's son Fingon, although he disliked Fëanor personally. And with Fingon silently sided Angrod and Aegnor, Finarfin's younger sons, as was their custom. This was the kind of debate which Ulmo foresaw when he advised that the Elves not be summoned to Valinor but be left to find their own places on Middle-earth.

Finally, Fëanor won over the majority of the Noldor to his purposes. So when Finarfin tried to speak again in favor of delay they shouted him down. Immediately, without due preparations, Fëanor and his sons started to lead the march northward, fearing changes of opinion among the fickle crowd, or perhaps some word of prohibition from the Valar. But the latter still adhered to the principle they had laid down for themselves when the Elves first came to Valinor, that Elves might freely come and freely depart without any pressure from them. For in this principle lay their recognition that the Elves had freedom of choice from Ilúvatar. Of all the Noldor, now a numerous people, only one-tenth decided to stay in Valinor.

But when Fëanor began to marshal the others for departure, he found that only a few, relatively speaking, accepted him in Finwë's place as King. With these he set forth as a vanguard. Most of the Noldor had come to approve Fingolfin and his sons while he ruled in Tirion and still looked upon him as their preferred leader. Fëanor's smaller band, therefore, was followed by a much larger host led by Fingon under the overall command of Fingolfin.

But just as the Noldor in their several bands were emerging from the gates of Tirion, Manwë's Herald, Eönwë, appeared at last with a message from Manwë which he was charged to deliver—a message of "counsel only," not of command. To the Noldor generally Manwë's advice was not to join in "the folly of Fëanor" but to remain in Valinor. Down Fëanor's road many unforeseen sorrows awaited them, he warned, and the Valar would neither help nor hinder them in their distress. As for Fëanor specifically, his own choice exiled him from the land of the Valar. But no Elf, or Elves, could ever overcome a Vala, whether good or evil, even if the Elf had received from Eru powers three times greater than those Fëanor already had. Fëanor's whole mission therefore was hopeless.

This statement by Manwë left Fëanor permanently self-banished from Valinor and at the same time committed him to a battle on Middle-earth which he could never win. Fëanor was himself not abashed, but he was concerned lest the Noldor, many of them already dubious, should take Manwë's message as a pretext for turning back.

His high spirits had already carried him through the crisis of the Oath. Now he laughed! Then, first addressing the Noldor as a whole as the Herald had done, Fëanor asked whether they would allow him, their King's heir, to be sent off into banishment with his sons while they returned to bondage in Valinor. Of course Manwë had threatened them with sorrow, but had they not known it already in Valinor, falling from joy to woe? Let them now try on Middle-earth to reverse the sequence, to find, through sorrow, joy and certainly freedom.

Then to the Herald he gave a reply for Manwë, saying that if Fëanor could never conquer Morgoth at least he did not sit idle, as did the Valar. He would inflict upon him so much harm that even they in the Ring of Doom would marvel, and in the end they would follow him. These final words, at least, were to be realized, as the final chapters of *The Silmarillion* report.

So impressive were Fëanor's words that the Herald bowed to him with respect and the Noldor leaders opposed to him were silenced for a while.

Hardly had Fëanor surmounted this crisis than he encountered another even more serious because of its moral implications. As he led the Noldor northward to that region of Valinor which lay nearest the coasts of Middle-earth, Fëanor realized for the first time that the long Noldor columns must somehow acquire a fleet of ships to transport them across the Great Sea. Their departure from Tirion had been so hasty that they had had no time even to foresee the problem, much less to take measures to solve it in some way. Fëanor would never have dared to begin any of his researches in so haphazard a manner. But in the leading of armies Fëanor was not Fëanor.

Resolving to persuade the Teleri to join the rebellion against the Valar, Fëanor hastened ahead and spoke to them in Alqualondë as he had spoken to the Noldor in Tirion. But he misjudged his audience. Morgoth had written off the Teleri as unfitted for his schemes. Consequently he had not spread his lies among them to stir up divisions and enmities, and they were uncorrupted. They did not yearn for new kingdoms of their own on Middle-earth but were content where they were, looking for no better place and no better leader than their prince, Olwë. Above all, they had not lost faith in the Valar but trusted Ulmo and his kinsmen to redress the hurts of Morgoth in due time.

Angered now, Fëanor rebuked them for renouncing their friendship with the Noldor who had been their friends for so long. When the Teleri had arrived belatedly in Valinor, he reminded them, the Noldor had carved out a harbor for their ships and had worked side by side with them in building their city of Alqualondë.

Prince Olwë then spoke for his people. The Teleri were not renouncing their friendship but like good friends were rebuking the Noldor for their folly in leaving Valinor. He then examined the possibility of lending or renting their ships to the Noldor as proposed (probably) in Fëanor's speech to the Teleri. To this request he gave a flat "No." He reminded Fëanor that the Teleri had never learned shipbuilding from the Noldor but rather from the Lords of the Sea, Ulmo's Maiar. All the Teleri, even their wives and daughters, had a share in that enterprise. Finally, Olwë turned against Fëanor his own words of refusal spoken to the Valar when they proposed that he smash open the three Silmarils to provide Light needed to rejuvenate the Two Trees. The Teleri ships, declared Olwë, were to the Teleri as his Jewels had been to Fëanor, "the work of our hearts, whose like we shall not make again" (p. 86).

This plea did not move Fëanor, who, brooding alone as always, decided to take the ships by force. As soon as his Noldor vanguard arrived he had them board and seize the white swanlike ships which lay at anchor in the Haven of the Swans. A fierce struggle against the Teleri ensued, with many dead on both sides. Finally the outcome was decided by the unlooked-for arrival of Fingon, eldest son of Fingolfin, with the forefront of the main Noldor host. Seeing many of their kinsmen falling, these warriors dashed in to save them, not stopping to ask the causes of the strife.

Thus many of the Teleri mariners, armed only with slender bows, were "wickedly slain," as Tolkien puts it. Such was the Kinslaying at Alqualondë, which was to haunt and hurt the whole Noldor tribe in their battles on Middle-earth over untold centuries. The importance accorded to kinship was always great, whether on Valinor or Middle-earth. Its reciprocal obligations outweighed most other duties. All Elves were held to be kinsmen of all other

Elves, no matter what their tribe. So what Fëanor had done, without consulting any of the other Noldor princes, was to set kin against kin in lethal warfare over the ships which belonged, by every test, to the Teleri alone.

Not all of Fëanor's seven sons approved of their father's actions at Alqualondë. His second son, Maglor the minstrel, composed a lament called "Noldolantë, the Fall of the Noldor," whose title implies that he regarded the victory over the Teleri as no true victory but as a moral Fall. And this view of the episode was soon reinforced by the Doom of Mandos, uttered at the northernmost confines of Valinor (pp. 87–88). This Curse and Doom he laid upon all the Noldor who would not stay to sue for and win the pardon of the Valar, as detailed before in Chapter II.

Looming high and dark upon a cliff, Mandos spoke for all the Valar and, through them, for Ilúvatar. He imposed a Curse of retribution in kind upon the Noldor, and on the house of Fëanor in particular, for the wrongs they had committed against the Teleri at Alqualondë. Upon the Noldor as a tribe he pronounced a Doom of "tears unnumbered" on Middle-earth and banishment from the Blessed Realm forever. But for Fëanor's house he prophesied in addition dire consequences of the Oath they swore to recover the Silmarils: betrayal, and an evil outcome of all their undertakings, caused "by treason of kin unto kin, and the fear of treason." Having spilled the blood of their kinsmen unrighteously, they must pay for it with the spilling of their own, and perish on Middle-earth "by weapon and by torment and by grief." Those who did not die would grow weary of the world, and wane like shadows as the younger race of Men supplanted them.

So many of Fëanor's people quailed before the horror of this Curse that he saw the need to strengthen their purpose to go onward. He strongly affirmed that those who swore the Oath to recover the Silmarils were bound to keep it. Mandos had threatened them with many evils, but not with cowardice. Therefore they would hold to their course and do such deeds as would give minstrels matter for their songs until the world ended.

But Finarfin, long dubious about the desperate enterprise against Morgoth, now grieved also for his brother-in-law, Olwë of Alqualondë, and seized the final chance of return offered by Mandos. He marched back home to Valmar, where the Valar pardoned him and set him to rule the remnant of the Noldor in Tirion. But his four sons, notably Finrod, did not return with him; neither did his daughter Galadriel. It seemed to them shameful to desert the children of Fingolfin, their cousins and friends, who remained loyal to Fingolfin despite the perils of the way.

At its extreme north the coast of Valinor, there called Araman, was separated from the coast of Middle-earth only by a narrow strait filled with grinding icebergs, the Helcaraxë, never yet crossed by any Elf and deemed by Fëanor impassable. Yet the ships he had seized were too few to transport the whole host of the Noldor, grown to its full numbers now that Fingolfin's folk had caught up with Fëanor's vanguard. Each of the two bands distrusted the other and looked for treachery from it. Here the Doom of Mandos first began to work. Without warning, Fëanor and his sons quietly embarked their men and sailed away eastward across the sea, leaving their Noldor kin stranded on the shore of Araman.

The eldest son, Maedhros, thought that the ships would surely be sailed back to Araman when empty, to pick up and transport Fingolfin's people. Fëanor, however, "laughed as one fey" (p. 90) and ordered that the graceful vessels be set afire. Maedhros alone refused to take any part in the vile arson. Seeing the red light of the flames in the eastern sky, Fingolfin knew that he had been betrayed. All the more fiercely, then, did he determine to catch up with Fëanor on Middle-earth somehow to pay off the score. And finding no other route he and his followers dared on foot

the shifting ice of the Helcaraxë. Many died but most survived to set foot at last on the solid ground of Middle-earth.

Fey, as used by Tolkien above and later repeated (p. 107)
to describe Fëanor's condition, is a Norse word widely
found in the sagas to betoken the state of mind in a warrior
who knows he is doomed to die soon, and welcomes death.
It implies a mood of high excitement coupled with some
degree of foreknowledge. Often it appears in conjunction
with another Norse term, *berserk*, to describe a man who
throws himself into the battle, summoning all his resources
of strength in one wild surge and therefore able to fight on
without feeling the pain of wounds, even mortal wounds.
In short, it signifies a kind of battle-madness.

It is enlightening, I believe, to see Fëanor as driven in
some degree by both these fevers as he receives first
Manwë's message declaring that he can never defeat a Vala
like Morgoth, and then the Doom of Mandos, prophesying
the failure of all his undertakings by treason of kin unto
kin. Gradually he has come to accept the idea that he is
marked for an early death. But what of it? He and his
warriors will first do such deeds as minstrels will celebrate
in ages yet to come.

Certainly there is not much common sense about his
actions during this period. To inflame the Noldor against
Morgoth is one thing, wild and daring in itself, but to
deride the Valar is not only madly presumptuous but quite
unnecessary. Then to precipitate the slaying of the Teleri
at Alqualondë, whom he knows to be kin to every Noldor
including himself, is to take upon himself a guilt which can
never be erased. The theft of their swanlike ships might
have been a necessary evil but it is, at the very least, un-
worthy of Fëanor. Then, to cap it all, his abandonment of
the whole host of Fingolfin, his own Noldor tribe, to hard-
ship and death on the Helcaraxë is so incredible as to turn
even his eldest son against him.

What can Fëanor expect to gain by these crimes and

follies? He seems to think that he can avenge his father and snatch back the Silmarils with his own small vanguard alone. And why the haste which hurries him on from one moral disaster to another? Apparently he wants to be sure to get his hands on the Silmarils first, lest others have a share in their recovery and therefore a claim upon them. His "possessiveness" for *his* Jewels causes him to believe that they belong solely and completely to him alone. But this form of greed has turned back upon itself and now possesses him.

It has wiped out all his generous feelings, all his sense of right and wrong, all his practical common sense and, not least, his thirst for new knowledge which has made his past brilliant and beneficial to his race. By manipulating Fëanor Morgoth has succeeded in his strategy of separating the Noldor from each other, and all of them from the Valar. The marring of Fëanor, with its consequences, is one of the major tragedies of *The Silmarillion*.

The last days and deeds of Fëanor are soon related. After landing at the Firth of Drengist he leads his forces inland to the northern shore of Lake Mithrim, where they begin to fortify a camp. But Morgoth, well aware of their coming, sends against them a large army of Orcs which takes them by surprise. Although outnumbered and unready, the Noldor quickly rout them and pursue their remnants across the Mountains of Shadow to the plains near Angband. In his eagerness Fëanor draws far ahead of the other pursuers, laughing as he wields his sword, "for he was fey, consumed by the flame of his own wrath" (p. 107). Seeing that he is almost alone, the Orcs turn on him, and Balrogs issue from Angband to aid them.

Long Fëanor fights on against their whips of flame, until at last Gothmog, Lord of Balrogs, fells him, covered with mortal burns. His sons come up then to carry him to the Noldor camp.

Looking back at the peaks of Thangorodrim over Angband, Fëanor knows "with the foreknowledge of death that no power of the Noldor would ever overthrow them." Nevertheless he has his sons swear again to honor the Oath they have all taken together. Then he dies. Prodigious in his birth, he is prodigious also in his death. For his body has been so consumed by the fiery spirit within it that only a little ash remains, blown away by the wind.

Tolkien gives him this epitaph: "Thus ended the mightiest of the Noldor, of whose deeds came both their greatest renown and their most grievous woe."

The Valar too, Tolkien adds, grieved for the marring of Fëanor as much as they did for the death of the Trees. "For Fëanor was made the mightiest in all parts of body and mind, in valour, in endurance, in beauty, in understanding, in skill, in strength and in subtlety alike, of all the Children of Ilúvatar" (p. 98).

Manwë alone could partly conceive the works of wonder that Fëanor might otherwise have wrought for the glory of Eä. He wept when his herald brought back Fëanor's defiance of his counsel but took some comfort from Fëanor's boast that the Noldor would do on Middle-earth deeds which would live in the fame of song forever. Such gain would indeed come from Evil, Manwë reflected. But Mandos balanced the scales by reminding him that Evil was evil still.

V

The First Two Battles of Beleriand: Dagor-nuin-Giliath

BELERIAND, the westernmost region of Middle-earth where the Noldor landed, proved to be no barren and un-peopled waste but a prosperous kingdom ruled by the Elven King Elwë (soon to be known as Thingol—Grey-cloak) and his Queen, Melian. Elwë, one of the two Princes leading the Teleri on their migration westward, had wandered away one day into the woods where he and Melian met and loved each other. He lost all desire to return to his people, and she to go back to Valinor, where she served as a Maia in Lórien, that haven of healing and of rest. Gradually they were joined by all the Elves of Teleri stock who preferred to remain on Middle-earth rather than venture across the Great Sea. So in time King Elwë found himself ruling the whole fertile, well-watered area stretching from the Blue Mountains (Ered Luin) westward to the Sea. As the maps of Middle-earth in the Third Age show, at the time of *The Lord of the Rings* this entire area had been buried by an onrush of the Sea because of the convulsions befalling it in the War of Wrath waged by the Valar against Morgoth at the end of the First Age.

In King Thingol's time the Teleri settled in Beleriand called themselves the Sindar, or Grey-elves. As a Maia Melian had so much knowledge and powers so great, not possessed by any Elf, that although most of Middle-earth

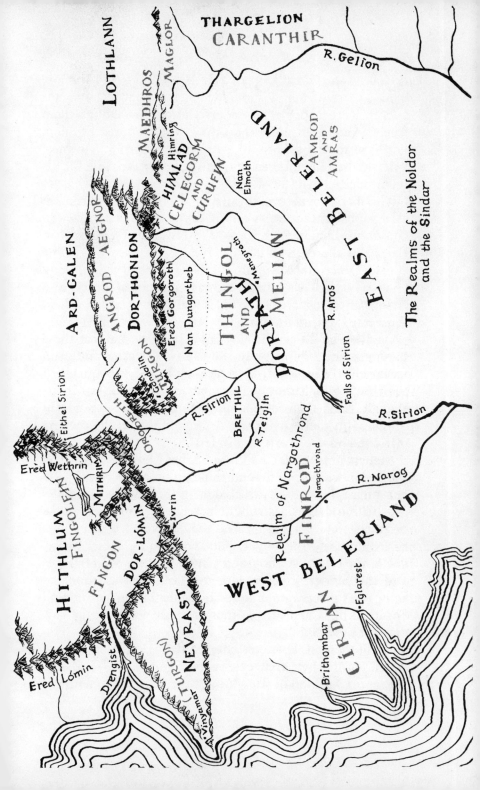

lay asleep she was able to awaken Beleriand to life and joy. Those parts of her wisdom which her husband and her people were capable of understanding she taught them freely. And, even more than they, her daughter Lúthien, fairest of maidens, both inherited and learned at her knee.

It will be remembered that Ilúvatar forgave Aulë for his unauthorized making of the Seven Fathers of the Dwarves but in his Providence stipulated that they must remain asleep until after the awakening of the Elves, his Firstborn Children. The appearance of the Dwarves (Naugrim) in Beleriand therefore followed that of the Teleri by some considerable interval. Also, the Dwarves had paused long enough on their way westward to build their underground cities of Belegost and Nogrod, dug into the eastern side of the Ered Luin mountains.

At first the Teleri did not know what to make of these hardy, stunted beings with their muscular arms and grim faces. They were a secretive race who spoke a language of their own which they were reluctant to reveal to others, though they themselves quickly learned the Sindarin tongue. But they turned out to be wonders in the carving of stone and the working of metals.

Melian, as a Maia, could foresee that Melkor's release by the Valar would put an end to peace on Middle-earth. By her advice Thingol contracted with the Dwarves of Belegost to build him a stronghold secure against attack. In exchange for lustrous pearls, they delved for him, in a rocky hill protected by forest and flowing river, Menegroth, the city of a Thousand Caves. In these the Dwarves and the Sindar Elves together carved reproductions of things and places remembered by Melian from Valinor, all beautiful but especially so those she had loved in the gardens of Lórien.

From then on, Dwarves entered Beleriand from time to time to trade their artifacts for those of the Sindar. But as the freeing of Melkor drew near, they reported to Thingol that fell beasts, wolves and werewolves, and Orcs from Angband increasingly roamed woodland and mountain. The Naugrim did not fear them, being warlike and lusting for battle. But Thingol, knowing that his Sindar had never fought, bought chain mail and such weapons as swords, spears, and axes from the smiths of Nogrod, who excelled in the tempering of steel. And he welcomed into his kingdom that fraction of the Teleri, the Nandor, who had followed Lenwë away from the main body. Becoming a woodland people, they were lost to sight for long years, until fear of the evil creatures from the North caused Denethor, son of Lenwë, to lead them into Beleriand seeking the protection of Thingol, their kinsman. He gave them a home in Ossiriand in the southeastern part of his realm where the six tributary rivers flowed into the River Gelion. They came to be called Green-elves.

As Melian had foreseen, after Morgoth had rebuilt Angband he suddenly sent two armies of Orcs against Thingol, one to the east of Menegroth, the other to its west. So began the First and Second Battles in the Wars of Beleriand. And in these battles the Noldor vanguard unwittingly played a decisive part, though only near the end.

Against the Orc host to his east, Thingol called Denethor to send all the Green-elves he could muster, while he himself led out his own army of Sindar from Menegroth. They planned in this way to attack the enemy from north and south simultaneously. But Thingol, having farther to go, reached the battlefield only after Denethor, too rashly, had already launched his assault. The Green-elves, much more lightly armed than the Orcs, suffered heavy losses. Moreover, Denethor, with all his nearest kin, had allowed himself to be separated from the main body of his troops and had taken refuge on the hill of Amon Ereb, where the Orcs slew them all. Thingol avenged his allies by falling upon the enemy's rear with great slaughter. Fleeing north, their remnants were ambushed by the warlike Naugrim from the Ered Luin, whose axes left few alive to return to Angband. This victory ended the First Battle.

Meantime the Orcs west of Menegroth had defeated Círdan's Sindar and driven them far south, cutting them off from all contact with Thingol, who then summoned all his neighboring folk to the safety of Doriath. Around it Melian threw her Girdle, "an unseen wall of shadow and bewilderment" (p. 97), not to be pierced against her will. It was this western Orc army that Celegorm, Fëanor's third son, with a small part of the Noldor vanguard waylaid and drove into the Fens of Serech, whence only the lucky escaped. Thus triumphantly ended Dagor-nuin-Giliath, the Battle-under-Stars, the Second Battle in Beleriand.

So, counting the Orc battalions slain in their attempt to surprise the Noldor at Lake Mithrim, Morgoth lost three Orc armies in the First and Second Battles for Beleriand. On the other hand, he put out of action permanently the Green-elves, who never again sent an army into the field. And Morgoth's Balrogs had killed Fëanor, that enigmatic genius whose value to the Noldor in the subsequent Battles of Beleriand, had he lived to take part in them, cannot be assessed. He might have been a dangerous divisive element. Or, turning his thoughts to the *palantíri*, for instance, he might have used them as a helpful means of communication between military positions and actions widely separated by distance.

In his First and Second Battles Morgoth used the Orcs as his heavy infantry, but he learned that they were no match for the Noldor in any open conflict. On the other hand the Balrogs, his former Maiar, were invincible even by the Noldor swords, but they were few, to be reserved for special missions. These results of Morgoth's findings were to appear in the later Battles of Beleriand.

All the fighting in Beleriand so far had taken place under the stars, for as yet there was neither Sun nor Moon. Not that any of the combatants could not see perfectly well by starlight, for they were accustomed to nothing brighter. But psychologically the dimness favored Morgoth and the dubious shadow-creatures congenial to his dark nature. Besides, the vegetation on Eä, and the animals which it would feed, could not grow without the warmth and nutritive beams of a Sun. Moreover, Manwë knew that the hour for the coming of Men, the Hildor, was nearing. And remembering the harms worked by Morgoth on the Elves when they awoke, he decided to send Light to Middle-earth to hinder the evils Morgoth would try to visit upon these mortal, and weaker, Second Children of Ilúvatar.

Accordingly Manwë asked Yavanna to put forth all her powers of growth upon the Two Trees, seemingly dead long since. She succeeded in singing into existence on Telperion one flower of silver and on Laurelin one fruit of gold. These Manwë hallowed, and Aulë contrived vessels to contain and preserve their light. Then they were given to Varda (Elbereth), who made of them lamps to illumine all Middle-earth. Telperion's flower became the Moon, Laurelin's fruit the Sun. Their courses she set to traverse Earth's equator in the upper reaches of the atmosphere below the stars, proceeding from east to west, then returning underneath the Earth to rise in the east again.

Inasmuch as the Moon and the Sun could not guide themselves, the Valar chose two of their Maiar for that work, Tilion for the Moon and Arien for the Sun. Appropriately, Tilion was a Maia of the hunter Oromë and owned a silver bow. In fact he loved silver in all its forms. When he wearied with hunting he used to go to Lórien and there lie dreaming in the beams of Telperion. So he begged for the privilege of tending the Moon, which was that Tree's last Flower of Silver.

Arien, on the other hand, had long tended the golden flowers in the gardens of the Valier, watering them with the shining dew of Laurelin the Golden and basking in its heat. For she was innately a spirit of fire who had nevertheless rejected Morgoth, as the Balrogs had not. She was stronger than Tilion, with eyes so blinding that no Elf could look into them. Sloughing off the human form which, like all the Valar, she assumed on coming to Eä, she became what she truly was, "a naked flame, terrible in her splendour" (p. 100).[1]

The Moon was ready first and rose in the west (not the east) above Valinor, whence Varda sent it up to begin its coursing through the heavens, as was proper because Telperion was the elder of the Two Trees. Morgoth, loving darkness, took no joy at all even in the Moon's mild light, but the Elves took much. As it happened, the Moon ascended for the first time just when Fingolfin with his host won through the Helcaraxë to set foot on Middle-earth. He welcomed its appearance by sounding silver trumpets.

After seven Moon-nights the Sun was completed and dawned above the Pelóri crags, lacing with fire the clouds over Middle-earth. Varda tried to have the Sun and the Moon mingle their lights at times as had the two Trees while they lived. But Tilion proved to be so wayward and so easily attracted by Arien that Varda tried other timings of their lights, such as never allowing the two to be in the sky together. But by reason of Tilion's uncertain pace and his love of Arien this did not work either. So she finally put up with the vagaries of Tilion, even to the extent of allowing eclipses, as happen today.

Tolkien's handling of the whole matter of the making of the Moon and the Sun is of particular interest because it illustrates one of the central distinctions between myth and physical science. In science events are caused by the interaction of inanimate forces, although some of us still feel the need to trace them back to a Creator. In myth, however, everything is done at every level by living beings. Modern science may tell us that a Sun (neither male nor female, of course) is formed by the compaction of hot gases, usually hydrogen. But Tolkien tells us that the Sun of our Earth, at least, was made from the light of a certain kind of Tree sung up by a Vala (Yavanna), put into a transparent vessel by another Vala (Aulë), and set upon its course by yet another Vala (Varda), who in turn has it "guided" by a Maia fitted by her nature to do so. Again, science teaches that the paths of Sun and Moon are governed by the laws of gravitation. But Tolkien has it that their general pattern is set by Varda, with variations brought about by male-female loves.

Tolkien well knows these scientific explanations, of course, but finds no juice in them. The universe of myth runs on the doing of beings who have powers and sorrows and wisdom and folly like our own, but magnified. And none is more aware than he that the two kinds of worlds must never mix, or both will explode.

Be that as it may, due to the irregularities of Tilion (the Moon) and the regularity of Arien (the Sun), the Valar counted the number of the passing days by the Sun. Morgoth, however, so hated and feared her that he only wished her gone. Tilion he dared to attack with spirits of shadow, which Tilion beat back. But to Arien Morgoth now lacked the power even to go near. For he had poured much of his innate strength into his creatures to make and keep them evil, thereby binding himself and them ever more closely to the depths of Angband, which he seldom left.[2] There he hid from the Sun with perpetual clouds and fumes.

The Valar, for their part, having witnessed Morgoth's attempt against Tilion, and remembering his ruin of their first dwelling at Almaren, made Valinor secure against any threat in the future. This they did by raising the height and steepness of the Pelóri, posting on them a constant watch, and backing them up with a permanently armed encampment. Only the pass at the Calacirya they kept open to permit the Elves there to breathe freely the winds blowing from Middle-earth, where they were born. But they fortified it strongly. And in the Great Sea between Aman and the mainland they set a string of enchanted isles to trap all mariners, and waters haunted by shadows and bewilderment after the manner of Melian's Girdle. None of the messengers sent westward by the Noldor later on, in the days of their desperation, ever got through to Valinor until, at last, Eärendil.

The Sun's warmth over Middle-earth brought to it a Second Spring, awakening all the seeds of vegetation that waited in the Sleep of Yavanna. Everywhere life teemed on the land and in the waters, being born, growing old, and dying in its brief span, for all were mortal. In Beleriand, too, flourished beauty that faded into death. And in Hildórien far to the east was born the long-awaited race of Men, the younger Children of Ilúvatar. They were mortal too, and brief of life besides. They awoke at the very rising of the Sun in the west, over Valinor. Seeing it, many Men were drawn westward. Others wandered in other directions.

Not to them, as to the Elves, came any Vala to lead them to Aman. In fact, Men were forbidden to come to that sacred land. As a result, says Tolkien, surveying the state of his time, Men have feared the Valar and have not loved and understood them as they should. Yet Ulmo was always present, speaking to Men mysteriously in the streams they crossed and drank from (p. 103).

Only three main human tribes entered Beleriand: the House of Bëor the Old, first to arrive; second, the House of Haladin; and last, the House of Hador the Golden-haired. These Edain, or Atani as they came to be called, were taught much by the Sindar, and served them and the Noldor as faithful allies in the war against Morgoth.

Those earliest Men were equal to the Elves in body but inferior to them in skill, in beauty, and especially in wisdom, which the Elves could accumulate in their unending lives. For Elves were born capable of immortality, although they could be killed by physical wounds and might also die after untold ages as their spirits gradually consumed the bodies which enclosed them. Men, however, were born to die not only by wounds but also by age, sickness, and many nameless frailties. The futures after death of Elves and Men also differed.

As told in *The Lord of the Rings*, those Elves still remaining on Middle-earth after the Third Age waned and faded into a forgotten folk, mere memories of what they once had been. For that reason almost all of them preferred, if permitted, to sail in Círdan's ships to Valinor the Blessed where their original splendor could still be theirs.

But to return to the First Age and the first two Battles in Beleriand. Counting his losses in those Battles, Morgoth immediately schemed to oust the victorious Noldor by some means other than war. He therefore sent them an embassy which proposed a meeting to sign a treaty of peace on the most favorable of terms and baited the trap with an offer to surrender one Silmaril. Maedhros, eldest son of the dead Fëanor, persuaded his brothers that recovery of even one Silmaril was worth any risk and that he himself should go to the appointed meeting place with a strong force (p. 108).

This he did, but Morgoth sent Balrogs who slew all except Maedhros. Him they captured and took with them back to Angband. Morgoth now had what he wanted, a hostage, whom he agreed to free if the Noldor would depart. But the other six brothers refused, well aware that Morgoth would not keep his word, and bound also by their Oath never to give up the war against him. Morgoth retaliated by hanging Maedhros on a sheer cliff of Thangorodrim by a steel band around his right wrist, fastened into the rock. Like Prometheus he hung there in pain.

At this point the Sun first rose, frightening Morgoth and his creatures into the depths of Angband. Fingolfin and his host on their way to Mithrim were enabled to cross his territories without hindrance and even to batter at its gates while their trumpets sounded in challenge. After this gesture, which the cautious Fingolfin knew to be nothing more, he traveled on to Lake Mithrim where he made camp on the north shore.

Fëanor's sons had been encamped there but withdrew to the south shore, knowing that they were not exactly loved by those whom they had betrayed on the shores of Araman by first stealing and then burning all the ships. Indeed, they thought themselves in danger of attack. Referring to that part of Mandos' Curse which pronounced that "by treason of kin unto kin, and the fear of treason" all things attempted by the House of Fëanor would turn out badly (pp. 88, 109), Tolkien observes that because of the Curse the Noldor frittered away by their feuds an opportunity, which never came again, to take Morgoth at a grave disadvantage.

Realizing this fact Fingon, son of Fingolfin, who had long been a friend of Maedhros, determined to end the feud, if possible, by finding him and bringing him back. Fingon knew that his friend was in the hands of Morgoth but not where. Hidden by the dark fumes sent up from Angband, he managed to climb high on Thangorodrim, where he sang with his harp an old, old song of Valinor known to both friends. Presently he heard the voice of Maedhros singing the same lay. Fingon traced it to a precipice he could not climb. Maedhros begged him to kill him with an arrow from his bow. While he prepared to shoot, Fingon cried to Manwë to let his shaft fly true and to have pity on the Noldor in their need.

Manwë the merciful bettered the prayer. He had long since ordered his Eagles to nest in the crags near Angband, from which they could watch what Morgoth did. And now their mighty King Thorondor carried Fingon on his back up to where Maedhros hung. But Fingon found that he could neither loosen the band that bound him nor sever it. Maedhros begged for death, but Fingon cut off his hand above the wrist, and Thorondor carried them both back to Lake Mithrim.

All the Noldor united in praising Fingon's great deed and forgot their enmity. As soon as his wound had healed sufficiently, Maedhros went to Fingolfin and begged forgiveness for the desertion of his host in Araman, although Maedhros had opposed it and had refused to take any part in the burning of the Teleri ships. These truths he did not mention lest he should seem to be asking pardon only for himself. And he surrendered all claim to the kingship, declaring that it belonged to Fingolfin as "eldest here of the house of Finwë, and not the least wise." Not all Maedhros' brothers agreed with these words and actions, but those who did not held their peace.

Strengthened by their new unity, the Noldor set watchers to the east, the west, and the south of Angband to report what Morgoth did. They also sent messengers far and wide over Beleriand to map it and, wherever possible, to win allies among its scattered peoples. Thingol, who regarded himself as King over all of Beleriand, gave but a frosty welcome to these newcomers and admitted to Doriath only the Princes of Finarfin's House, his blood kindred since their mother, Eärwen of Alqualondë, was the daughter of his brother Olwë.

The Realms of the Noldor

THIS MAPPING of Beleriand was highly characteristic of the Noldor, for many of them had been born in Valinor and had never set foot on Middle-earth. Ever inquisitive and eager for knowledge of every kind, they came to be known as "the Deep Elves, the friends of Aulë" (p. 53). Of the three Elf tribes they were the most active in intellect and in skill of hand. For the Vanyar gave themselves to holiness, building their dwellings ever closer to the Halls of Manwë on Oiolossë, whose love for them they returned. And the Teleri loved the Sea, never wearying of sailing on it their swan-like ships. Seldom did they leave their city of Alqualondë, set well back from the shore and fashioned of glowing pearls.

Rightly were the Noldor named friends of Aulë, who governed all things on the surface of the Earth and under it. From him they learned much and even "added to his teaching, delighting in tongues and scripts" (p. 39) such as the alphabet of Rúmil and, later, the Tengwar of Fëanor. Also, in building their own city of Tirion on the hill of Túna they found many gems in the earth, some of which they scattered on the beaches near Alqualondë as a gift for the Teleri. With the remainder they experimented until they learned how to devise new gems, a skill used and greatly enhanced by Fëanor in his making of the Silmarils.

The Noldor fascination with words stood them in good stead when they came to live in Beleriand with the Teleri, who had developed from the common Elvish speech a new tongue called Sindarin (p. 348). Desiring to know the Sindar better, and also to win them as allies in the war against Morgoth, the Noldor came to use Sindarin in all their public dealings, and to reserve their own Noldor speech for private conversation among themselves.

To win the support of King Thingol of Doriath, Finrod sent his brother Angrod, third son of Finarfin, as emissary to Thingol to win his friendship by giving him a better understanding of the Noldor and their purposes. Angrod accordingly told Thingol all the military details about his people—their deeds in the north, their numbers, and the disposition of their forces. But letting the past bury itself, he said nothing that might offend the King, mentioning neither the manner in which the Noldor were exiled, nor the Kinslaying of the Teleri at Alqualondë, nor the Oath of Fëanor.

Thingol in reply gave the Noldor permission to live in Hithlum to his northeast; likewise in the highlands of Dorthonion, which lay to his north between Doriath and Angband; and, finally, in the unsettled areas to his east. Upon Doriath itself they were not to trespass. Neither were they to take over any areas other than those specifically assigned to them, since these were populated by his subjects, who must not be disturbed. In sum Thingol asserted his kingship over the whole of Beleriand and made of the Noldor his tenants by permission only.

When Angrod told the Noldor Princes about Thingol's claims as King over all Beleriand, dispensing to them as vassals his permissions and prohibitions and warnings, they were aghast but most of them said nothing at that time. As will be seen, the exigencies of defense against Morgoth compelled them later to establish strongholds in strategic spots all over Beleriand and to control the regions round about in ways which amounted to a carving out of separate kingdoms by each of the Princes.

Only some of the sons of Fëanor were openly angry. Maedhros tried to moderate their wrath by pointing out, laughing, that a King is a king only over the region he can rule, which in Thingol's case was Doriath only. When the Orc armies came down upon him the Noldor, not he, drove them out of the lands they had occupied to his west and south. There and elsewhere outside Doriath the Noldor had the right to settle as they pleased.

But Caranthir the Dark, fourth son of Fëanor and harshest of the seven, mistook his proper target, which was Thingol, and lashed out instead against Fingon and Angrod, demanding to know who made them spokesmen for the Noldor. Angrod, affronted, stalked out of the council. Maedhros rebuked Caranthir, but most of the Noldor began again to fear and dislike the cruel sons of Fëanor, so prone to rashness and violence. As always, these Noldor unfairly lumped Maedhros indiscriminately with the worst of his brothers. Yet Maedhros at this juncture, when the unity of the Noldor was threatened, once more restrained his brothers and led them far northeastward to the lands around the Hill of Himring where they could have little communication with the other Noldor. There he kept them busy fortifying and otherwise strengthening the whole of that frontier called the March of Maedhros against future attacks by Morgoth. But Maedhros himself maintained friendship as well as he could with the Houses of Fingolfin and Finarfin by traveling the long journey around Doriath to share counsel with them from time to time.

Caranthir and his followers held the easternmost end of the March nearest to the Ered Luin mountains. There they encountered the Dwarves, who since the First Battle had ceased trafficking in Beleriand. The chief obstacle to amity between the two races was the quick resentments of the Naugrim and the disdain of Caranthir for them. Nevertheless their mutual hatred of Morgoth led to an alliance profitable to both sides. From the Noldor the Dwarves learned "many secrets of craft" (p. 113); and they in turn channeled all the busy products of their minds and forges through Caranthir, making him rich.

Twenty years later Fingolfin, as High King of the Noldor, held a great Feast of Reuniting at the pools of Ivrin, just south of the Mountains of Shadow, which protected his realms of Dor-lómin, Mithrim, and Hithlum. To it came Maedhros with his most trustworthy brother, Maglor, second son of Fëanor and a great minstrel, escorted by a band of their warriors. Also bidden were Círdan the Shipwright with many of his Grey-elves. And there were even some representatives of the Green-elves from Ossiriand. But from Doriath came only Mablung, chief captain of Thingol, and his minstrel Daeron, with greetings. Thingol himself wanted no reunion with the pre-emptors of his lands.

All present at Ivrin swore oaths of friendship and alliance with enemy as well as with friend. The Noldor took care at that gathering to speak chiefly Sindarin as a mark of their desire for a permanent citizenship in Beleriand. And to many of them the advice of Fëanor seemed good, to seek fair kingdoms in Middle-earth. Thirty years of peace ensued, while Morgoth remained shut in Angband.

But Turgon, second son of Fingolfin, with his friend Finrod, eldest son of Finarfin, feeling the need for a change of scene, went southward along the River Sirion, and they slept one night on its bank at the Meres of Twilight, where the River Aros flowed into it. There Ulmo gave both Elves warning dreams that they should look for "places of hidden strength" (p. 114), in case Morgoth, surging out of Angband, should break through the Noldor forces fencing the northern Marches against him. Then Finrod remembered the visit he and his sister Galadriel had paid to their kinsman Thingol at Menegroth, where Finrod so admired the security and beauty of Menegroth's thousand caves that he determined to build for himself a similar stronghold.

Thingol advised him to examine a deep gorge in the

River Narog, with caves already dug into its steep western shore. Aided by Dwarves from the Ered Luin he dug "deep halls and armories" in imitation of Menegroth, naming them Nargothrond. And he paid his workmen well, having brought more treasure from Tirion than any other Noldor Prince. In gratitude the Dwarves made for him their masterpiece, Nauglamír, a necklace richly set with gems from Valinor yet, despite its weight, resting lightly on any wearer.[1] Hence the Dwarves gave him the name Felagund, Hewer of Caves, and Finrod Felagund he was titled ever after.

But Galadriel remained at Thingol's court, for she had fallen in love with Celeborn his kinsman, and he with her. There she learned much from Melian, until she became in after years "greatest of Elfin women," to use Tolkien's praise of her.

Unlike Finrod, his cousin Turgon nostalgically took as his model Tirion, city of the Noldor, built by them on the hill of Túna in Valinor. Unable to find a site which satisfied his yearning, he wandered far to the west until he rested for a while at Vinyamar on the shore of the Great Sea. Ulmo told him there to search in the Vale of Sirion. This he did. At last he chanced upon the hidden Vale of Tumladen, encircled by steep mountains, and in its midst a hill which reminded him of Túna, the mount on which Tirion stood. Intending to keep it secret, he told nobody of it but returned home to Nevrast to plan the city of his heart's desire.

At this time, hearing from his spies of these wanderings of the Noldor leaders, Morgoth determined to take them by surprise, if possible. After swift forgings of weapons and armor (which caused fire from his smithies to break out from the earth's cracks near Angband and to erupt from the Iron Mountains round about) he sent armies of Orcs pouring down from the Pass of Sirion in the west and, in the east, through that segment of the March of Maedhros guarded by Maglor between the hills of Himring and the outcroppings of the Ered Luin. Fingolfin and Maedhros, however, were prompt in attacking the main host of Orcs simultaneously from west and east as they were trying to seize Dorthonion. This Noldor onset utterly defeated and killed most of the invaders. And pursuers of remnants retreating northward slew the remainder, every one, even in sight of the Gates of Angband. So ended the Third Battle of the Wars of Beleriand. Dagor Aglareb, the Glorious Battle, it was named.

Taught by this and previous battles, the Noldor tightened the siege of Angband and increased their watchfulness. So confident were they now that even Fingolfin the cautious boasted that never again could Morgoth burst their siege. But, remembering the Curse of Mandos on the Noldor, he added the proviso "save by treason among themselves" (p. 115).

Militarily, however, the situation was at best a stalemate and, more realistically, a war of attrition which the Noldor could never expect to win. Angband they could never break into by arms, as the dying Fëanor had foreseen. And the Noldor siege was itself incomplete because they were unable to cross the icebound peaks of the Iron Mountains to contain it from the north. Over that route Morgoth's spies kept on entering Beleriand, and the Orcs had standing orders to capture every Elf they could and to bring him, bound, to Angband. After overcoming their wills, Morgoth sent such captives back to Beleriand, where they did *his* will in everything. Too, there was no limit to the number of Orcs Morgoth could breed, whereas the Noldor birthrate seems to have been very low—too low to replace their inevitable losses in the constant skirmishings which went on, in addition to the larger battles. We seldom hear of children being born to them, perhaps because of the perils of the times.

For example, a hundred years after the Glorious Battle,

Morgoth tried to take Fingolfin off guard, "for he knew the vigilance of Maedhros" (p. 116), and sent a relatively small band of Orcs northward from Angband, then west, then south along the coast to the Firth of Drengist, then west again into Hithlum, where Fingolfin lay. But Fingon, discovering the move in time, fell upon them at the head of the Firth and drove the majority into the Sea.

This minor engagement, besides all the major Battles, convinced Morgoth that, the Orcs alone being no match for the Noldor, he must make some new type of creature to help his Orcs. The result was Glaurung, the first fire-drake, who emerged from Angband prematurely, only half-grown, against Morgoth's orders. Even so, the Elves fled from him until Fingon rode out of Hithlum against him with mounted bowmen, whose darts pierced Glaurung's as yet unhardened armor and drove him back into Angband.

Dragons mature slowly. For two hundred years after that first appearance Morgoth mounted no assaults save feints against the Marches. That was a good time for Beleriand. The Noldor not only built dwelling places but also turned to making "poems and histories and books of lore." In many districts the Noldor and Sindar became one people, speaking one tongue, Sindarin. Only inherent tribal differences remained. The Noldor were stronger in war and wisdom. They preferred building in stone on unforested land. The Sindar surpassed them in music, all except Maglor, best of minstrels, and loved the woods and rivers. Some of them delighted to wander without any fixed home, singing as they went.

Broad and varied were the regions of Beleriand for any who chose to roam through them. However, such a one had better not venture too far north, for there, on the very edge of the Arctic cold, Morgoth had long since erected Ered Engrin, the Iron Mountains, to encircle and protect his two fortresses, Utumno in the north and Angband southwest of it. He had honeycombed each with underground furnaces.

And from Angband he had driven a tunnel southwest through Ered Engrin which issued on the plain of Ard-galen and was barred by a mighty gate. Over this entrance he piled the ash and slag of his smithies and his tunnelings in vast heaps. In time these grew into the high and massive peaks known as Thangorodrim.

To the west of these, and luckily safeguarded against Angband by their own Ered Wethrin, Mountains of Shadow, lay the pleasant lands of Hithlum. The most feasible pass through these mountains to the east was Eithel Sirion, well watched by Fingolfin, whose territories stretched behind it. In the west, at the head of the Firth of Drengist, lay Cirith Ninniach, the Rainbow Cleft, leading on into Dor-lómin—the realm of Fingon, his eldest son. Father and son together kept watch on Ard-galen with cavalry patrols. The sires of these horses had been transported from Aman in the ships seized from the Teleri by Fëanor and had been given to Fingolfin by Maedhros in atonement.

Southwest of Hithlum, Turgon the Wise, second son of Fingolfin, held the country of Nevrast, the Hither Shore, so-called because all along its western boundary the Great Sea beat. When Turgon led his Noldor into Nevrast he found many Grey-elves already settled there; but they accepted him as their lord. In consequence, the mingling of the Noldor and the Sindar came about most quickly in that realm. Turgon had his capital at Vinyamar beside the Sea. So Fingolfin had his sons close about him and was the happier for it.

Turning eastward from Nevrast, any traveler would find himself facing the highland of Dorthonion, situated ominously between Angband to the north and Doriath to the south. If wise, he would enter it from its northern side, which sloped gradually up from Ard-galen through pine forests to a treeless plateau, dotted plentifully with lakes standing in the shadow of bare peaks higher than those of

Ered Wethrin. Had he chosen to tackle its southern side he would have been confronted by the sheer cliffs of Ered Gorgoroth, the Mountains of Terror, where footholds were few. Dorthonion was defended with a scanty troop by Angrod and Aegnor, third and fourth sons of Finarfin, as vassals of their eldest brother Finrod, now King of Nargothrond.

Finrod was also responsible for holding the Pass of Sirion between Dorthonion and the Ered Wethrin, where that river flowed southward through a narrow valley between abrupt walls. Here he built on the island of Tol Sirion the watch-tower called Minas Tirith, a name to be used again in the Third Age to describe the tower of Gondor in *The Lord of the Rings*. Command over this watch-tower he gave to his brother Orodreth, second son of Finarfin.

Additionally, Finrod's kingdom of Nargothrond extended not only east of the River Narog, on whose bank the capital lay, to the plains between it and Sirion, but also westward to the River Nenning and thence to the Sea. But it did not include the region called the Falas, the western coasts of Beleriand south of Nevrast, where Círdan the Shipwright held sway. Círdan's subjects were the Sindar, who delighted in helping to build his ships. In friendly conjunction the Noldor under Finrod and the Grey-elves under Círdan rebuilt the harbors of Brithombar and Eglarest, where mighty cities grew up. Finrod also set up near Eglarest a tower to watch for possible landings by Orcs from the Sea—needlessly, as it turned out, for Morgoth and his servants hated water and avoided it. Wherever water was, there also was Ulmo the Vala, their enemy. From Círdan's coastal Elves the Noldor learned how to build ships and, in these vessels, explored the Isle of Balar, far to the south, to see whether it might serve as a refuge in extremity. But they were destined never to live there.

All told, Finrod's realm ran, from north to south and

from east to west, over many a square league of varied country, far larger than that held by the other "great lords of the Noldor, Fingolfin, Fingon, and Maedhros," although he was the youngest of them all (p. 121). Perhaps not unfittingly, since Finrod was the eldest son of Finarfin, who remained in Valinor; he therefore stood as the head of his House on Middle-earth. Kingship, of course, was not measured by acreage. So, although Fingolfin and his sons ruled only the relatively small province of Hithlum, he remained recognized by all as the overlord of all the Noldor. Moreover, his troops guarded the western wing of Beleriand's border against Morgoth and, hardened by constant fighting, became the Noldor most feared by Morgoth and his Orcs.

Sirion was so large and long a river that, beginning from its sources near the Mountains of Shadow in the north and flowing through many mouths into the Bay of Balar in the south, it divided the country almost equally into East Beleriand and West Beleriand. Anyone floating south on it from its beginnings would arrive before long at that foulest of regions, between Dorthonion and Doriath, known as Nan Dungortheb, the Valley of Dreadful Death. This was the quickest way east for the traveler who dared to take it and who contrived to come out at its other end alive. Its western approach passed by the peaks of the Crissaegrim, where Manwë's eagles had their eyries.

Farther on lay the ravines to which Ungoliant fled from the Balrogs and where she remained long enough to beget her poisonous brood. She herself had long since crawled away southward but her offspring remained, spinning their sticky nets for prey. And the streams trickling down the steeps from Dorthonion filled with "shadows of madness and despair" the hearts of those who tasted them. The best course for anyone passing through was to hug close to the woods of Doriath to the south, for round them rested the Girdle of Melian, which at least never hurt anyone who did not try to enter them against Thingol's will. After crossing the rivers Esgalduin and Aros, the survivor would enter the lands garrisoned by the sons of Fëanor.

But any traveler whose business lay in the south rather than in the east gladly remained on Sirion and floated on past the Valley of Dreadful Death. By so doing he would traverse Thingol's realm of Doriath. To his left would lie the forests of Neldoreth and Region, divided only by the River Esgalduin, on whose southern bank stood Mene-groth of the Thousand Caves. On his right would be the Forest of Brethil. Thus the whole of Doriath consisted of forests flowed through by several rivers, all of it lying within the protective Girdle of Melian, which none might pierce without her permission. In these rivers dwelt also Ulmo, whom she revered and loved.

Where the River Aros joined Sirion the voyager would do well to land and carry his boat, making a portage round the Twilight Meres, a place of marshes and mists to which the Girdle's enchantment extended. Below the Meres, Si-rion plunged in a massive fall under Andram, a line of hills known as the Long Wall, and emerged in tumult farther south at what were named the Gates of Sirion. So the Sirion was not navigable from the Meres to the Gates but, below them, would give no more trouble to a traveler who set his boat upon its waters for the remaining distance to the Bay of Balar.

Many leagues to the east and roughly parallel to the Sirion flowed the River Gelion. Its springs began just south of the March of Maedhros, fed chiefly by the rains which fell in the Blue Mountains. And during its long course southward through Thargelion and Ossiriand these moun-tains fed it still, with six tributaries so large as to deserve the title of large rivers in their own right. Unlike Sirion, the Gelion had neither marshes nor falls.

Yet, even by this roundabout route, travel from Sirion to East Beleriand was not easy. The Andram, the Long Wall of hills, had to be crossed. South of it waited Taur-Im-Duinath, an area of tangled trees greater than all of Doriath, and empty of folk except for a few Dark Elves, who were neither Noldor nor Sindar, wandering through it. And anyone wishing to proceed north from Andram to the March of Maedhros had many long leagues to cover.

There he would find that the geography rendered Beleriand most vulnerable to attack by Morgoth through the March. Only small hills, and in some places none at all, barred the way to invaders. Yet the sons of Fëanor, backed by "many people" and directed by Maedhros, had portioned out this frontier among themselves for defense. Their cavalry often scoured the northern plain of Lothlann, watching for signs of any onslaught from Angband.

Maedhros himself set up his chief citadel on the bare, cold Hill of Himring at the western end of the line. Between him and Dorthonion ran the Pass of Aglon, which gave access from Lothlann to Himlad and thence to the inhabited lands of East Beleriand. Celegorm, a burly huntsman like Oromë, who had proved himself an able strategist in the First Battle, and with him Curufin, had fortified this Pass with great strength, and likewise the province of Himlad. To his east Maedhros had positioned Maglor, to whom he entrusted defense of the Gap where no hills reared up to bar the way, and where the Orcs had burst through in the Third Battle. To Maglor's east, Caranthir had fortified the foothills of the Ered Luin in front of Mount Rerir. He dwelt at Lake Helevorn behind Rerir.

So the sons of Fëanor under Maedhros were lords of the whole of East Beleriand, but at Maedhros' urging they seldom left their duties at the frontier except occasionally to hunt in the greenwoods to the south. In these woods lived Amrod and Amros, youngest of the sons, too inexperienced as yet to be assigned to the defense of any portion of the March. Seldom did they go north to it. Now and then, too, some of the Noldor from West Beleriand came to visit these fair lands, especially Finrod Felagund, who loved to roam. Being sociable and loving by nature, he made friends of the shy Green-elves in Beleriand. But none of the Noldor ever thought to climb over Ered Luin to learn what was going on in the rest of Middle-earth; so they heard of it only by hearsay, and late.

Nargothrond had already been built and peopled by Finrod for many a year while Turgon in Nevrast planned, detail by detail, how best to fashion in the hidden vale of Tumladen a city as fair as Tirion in Aman, and resembling it. After the Third Battle had been won, and the fortunes of the Noldor had reached their peak, he secretly sent his master masons to fashion, according to his design, a city on the hill that rose in the midst of the plain. Ondolindë he called it in the Elvish tongue of Valinor, but the Sindarin name of Gondolin prevailed. One entrance it had, and one only, a tunnel worn deep under the encircling mountains by a stream flowing to join the River Sirion.

When the new city stood ready for occupancy and Turgon was about to leave Nevrast with all his people, Ulmo came to him again. As lord of the Sirion, Ulmo promised Turgon to prevent the discovery of the secret entrance against his will. Gondolin, he warned, would be the last of Beleriand's realms to be overthrown by Morgoth, but overthrown it would be by treason within its walls, for Turgon, like all the Noldor in exile, lay subject to the Doom of Mandos. This, originating in the Will of Ilúvatar, not even the Valar could revoke. But, Ulmo said, when the end was near he would send a messenger to warn him. Let Turgon leave in Vinyamar arms and a sword for the message-bearer which would identify him. Turgon complied.

Then he began dispatching to Gondolin his Noldor followers, amounting to a third of Fingolfin's host, and an even greater number of his Sindar. Over a length of days they left in small companies, marching under the shades of Ered Wethrin, the Mountains of Shadow. And last of all,

Turgon and his household. None saw them as they marched or as they entered the one entrance, shutting its gates behind them. For over 350 years they seemed to vanish, and were not seen again until they emerged to take part in the Fifth Battle and its grievous defeats.

During those years they grew in number and prosperity, laboring all the while upon white-walled Gondolin and, especially, upon the Tower of the King. There fountains played and images of the Two Trees, sculptured by Turgon himself without the aid of Dwarves, stood as if alive. At last Gondolin came to be a shining city on a hill. Many timeless treasures it held but none so precious as Turgon's daughter, Idril Celebrindal, "Silver foot."

Meanwhile in Thingol's court Galadriel of the House of Finarfin lingered on, for love of Celeborn and for the wisdom she garnered from Melian the Maia. There came a day, however, when Melian in return sought to learn what had happened in Valinor after the murder of the Two Trees by Morgoth, and why and how the Noldor had come to Middle-earth. Broaching these subjects to Galadriel, she guessed aloud that the Noldor were driven out from Valinor as exiles, and that some evil haunted the sons of Fëanor which made them "so haughty and so fell" (p. 127).

Here again she assumed, as did so many others, that all the sons of Fëanor were the same, unaware that Maedhros had humbled himself before Fingolfin, surrendering his own claim to the kingship of the Noldor, giving him gifts in atonement for wrongs suffered, and doing all he could to rule those of his brothers who were truly proud and cruel. Likewise Maglor the minstrel, a glorious singer of tales, was no villain but a companion worthy of trust.

In reply to Melian's guesses Galadriel answered that the Noldor were not driven out but came of their own free choice to avenge the death of Finwë and to recover the Silmarils. Of these events she told the whole tale, but without divulging the Oath, the Kinslaying, or the burning of the ships. Melian sensed that Galadriel was hiding from her other events which took place along the road to Middle-earth and tried to probe further. But Galadriel refused to be probed, showing by her refusal the strength of will which was to make her a great Queen of Lothlórien in the Third Age.

Melian of course told Thingol what she learned from Galadriel. And, as a Maia, she foresaw that the Silmarils could never be recovered by the power of Elves alone, and that Beleriand would be broken in battles yet to come. Thingol at first merely took this news as an assurance that the Noldor would never make any separate treaty of peace with Morgoth, and would therefore be all the better allies for him. When warned by Melian, "Beware of the sons of Fëanor!" because they had done evil both to the Valar and to their own Noldor kindred, Thingol answered that although he had heard little to like about them "they are likely to prove the deadliest foes of our foe" (p. 128).

Almost as though he could hear what Melian told Thingol, across the long leagues from Angband, Morgoth spread abroad among the Sindar whispered lies about the misdeeds of the Noldor before they came to Beleriand. And the Sindar believed them, not knowing Morgoth and his ways. Círdan the Shipwright sent messengers to tell Thingol the tales he was hearing.

At that time the sons of Finarfin had come to see their sister Galadriel in Doriath. Thereupon Thingol bitterly reproached Finrod for hiding from him the misdeeds of the other Noldor princes. Finrod pointed out that neither he nor they had thought, or done, any ill against Doriath. Thingol then accused Finrod of coming to his table "red-handed from the slaying of your mother's kin," the Teleri, without confessing the deed and asking pardon.

Finrod said no more, lest defense of himself entail making charges against the other Noldor. But not so Angrod, who had once exchanged quarrelsome words with Caranthir. He burst out angrily against "fell Fëanor" himself, then against all his sons, sparing no detail about the Kin-slaying at Alqualondë, the Doom of Mandos, and the burning of the Teleri ships. He ended with an account of the crossing of the Grinding Ice.

In consequence, Thingol forgave his kindred, the sons of Finarfin, and promised to remain a friend of the house of Fingolfin. But he decreed that nevermore should the Noldor tongue be spoken in Beleriand by Noldor or Sindar, on penalty of the speaker's being held guilty of slaying and betraying his kin without repentance. For this crime the sentence could be severe, even unto death.

So it happened that Thingol of Doriath cleaved a chasm between the Sindar and the Noldor, most pleasing to Morgoth, and likewise between the seven sons of Fëanor and all the other Noldor. On this occasion, at least, the old breach was reopened not by any of the sons of Fëanor but by the intemperate rage of Angrod, Finarfin's son.

His completion of Nargothrond Finrod celebrated with a feast for the House of Finarfin only, inviting neither those of Fingolfin's House nor the sons of Fëanor. This exclusiveness was a sign of the worsening times, in marked contrast with Fingolfin's Feast of Reuniting, which had excluded nobody, as related earlier in this chapter. Galadriel came with the rest of Finarfin's House to stay for a time with her brother in his new city but, troubled that Finrod had no wife, she asked him why. With foresight of the future he replied that he expected to die and to leave Nargothrond so ruined that nothing of it would be left for a son of his to inherit. Such cold thoughts were unlike Finrod, but they showed the decline of hope spreading among the Noldor as they faced the times to come.

*   *   *

Also doomful was the tale of how Aredhel, the White Lady of the Noldor, brought treachery into Gondolin unwittingly (pp. 131ff). Being Turgon's sister she went with him into that hidden city from the first and lived there quietly for some centuries. But slowly she wearied of being shut inside its walls, and she longed to walk outside, over the plains and through the forests, free. Finally Turgon yielded to her entreaties to be allowed to leave, although foreboding evil both for her and for the city he loved. He admonished her, however, that she must go only to their brother Fingon in Hithlum.

This inhibition Aredhel resented and said proudly that, being his sister and not his slave, she would go wherever she pleased. Turgon reminded her that she must at all costs keep secret the entrance to Gondolin, and he sent with her three of his lords with orders to escort her to Hithlum if they could persuade her to go there.

In this they failed. At the Ford of Brithiach the White Lady decided to go eastward to the sons of Fëanor, her friends, and naively asked leave to pass through Doriath. Long secluded in Gondolin from the events happening outside, she was unaware of Thingol's policy of admitting no Noldor save the children of Finarfin, especially not those who were friends of the sons of Fëanor. Warned by the march-wardens that the Nan Dungortheb, the Valley of Dreadful Death between Doriath and Dorthonion, was filled with perils, Aredhel chose nevertheless to take that route. There she shook off her escort. They lost their way and, pursued by Ungoliant's brood, barely managed to return to Gondolin alive.

She fearlessly rode on alone until she came safely to the people of Celegorm, who welcomed her. But Celegorm, trained by Oromë the hunter and dearest to her among the seven sons, was away hunting in Thargelion. At first Aredhel enjoyed wandering freely, but after a year of waiting for his return she grew restless again and rode farther and farther alone, looking for new paths, new sights, new experiences, until she found herself entangled in the forest of Nan Elmoth.

There dwelt Eöl the Dark Elf,[2] also alone, where no sunlight could penetrate the tall, dark trees, loving darkness and the stars. He was kin to Thingol but preferred the company of Dwarves to that of Elves. He often visited them in their deep cities of Belegost and Nogrod. Thus he learned from them much lore, and himself invented a new metal, *galvorn*, strong as steel but malleable. No weapon could pierce it.

Seeing Aredhel afar, Eöl set his spells to draw her to his halls where his smithy was. And desiring her he married her. Since they had much in common she was content to stay with him. When their son was twelve years old, Eöl named him Maeglin, signifying Sharp Glance, for the son's eyes were more piercing than the father's own and could read thoughts "beyond the mist of words."

Maeglin grew up with his father's fierce, terse temperament but with the Noldor desire to know all things. He often went with Eöl to the Dwarf cities in the Ered Lindon, learning their crafts, but above all he treasured the skill of finding metallic ores, like any typical Noldor. Maeglin loved to listen to his mother's tales about the deeds of Fingolfin and his sons, especially Turgon. And, perhaps already scheming for the future, he heard gladly that Turgon had no male heir but only an unmarried daughter, Idril. However, Aredhel would never tell Maeglin where Turgon ruled or how to get there. He hoped in time to wheedle the secret from her or read it in her mind. But first he wanted, as did his mother, to speak to the sons of Fëanor, his kin, whose border posts lay close at hand.

When he broached the subject to his father, Eöl furiously forbade him to have any dealings with the Noldor, who had slain their kindred, the Teleri, and now had usurped their lands. In this way mistrust was born between father and son. So when the Dwarves of Nogrod invited Eöl to a midsummer festival he went alone. In his absence Maeglin easily persuaded Aredhel to go with him to look for the sons of Fëanor, as she had long wished to do anyway. Riding northwest, they crossed the Fords of the River Aros and, abandoning all thoughts of a visit to Fëanor's sons, turned westward into Nan Dungortheb, the Valley of Dreadful Death. This was duly noted by the scouts protecting the Pass of Aglon under Celegorm and Curufin the Crafty. Eöl, pursuing his wife and son, was seized by the riders of Curufin and brought before him. The two Elves held no love at all for each other. So the exchange which ensued between them was laced with insults on both sides, covert or open, in keeping with their natures (p. 135).

Curufin began by asking sarcastically what urgent errand could have brought "sun-shy" Eöl there by daylight. Eöl responded with the lie that he was merely joining his son and his wife, the White Lady, in their visit to the sons of Fëanor. Curufin laughed and uncovered the lie, informing Eöl that those he pursued had already ridden west without visiting any of the sons. Eöl might follow them as soon as he pleased—indeed, the sooner the better.

Eöl thanked him ironically as "a kinsman . . . kindly at need."

The word "kinsman" angered Curufin, who denied that anyone stealing a daughter of the Noldor "without gift or leave" could thereby gain kinship with the Noldor. He added the advice that Eöl had better go back to his dark woods because he foresaw that if Eöl continued his pursuit he would never return alive.

Eöl, nevertheless, did continue it with all speed, guessing that his quarry were heading for Gondolin. He would never have discovered the secret entrance had not the fugitives abandoned their horses at the Brithiach, as was necessary. By some "ill fate," says Tolkien, these neighed at the approach of the horse Eöl rode (p. 136). So he was able to discern far off which way his wife and son went, and to follow them stealthily. Meantime, passing through the Seven Gates across the entrance, Aredhel was warmly welcomed by King Turgon. And Maeglin, too, his "sister-son," he deemed worthy to be counted among the Princes of the Noldor and given high honor in Gondolin. Then Maeglin took Turgon as his lord, but his eyes strayed often to the golden beauty of Idril, the king's daughter.

At that point the Guard at the Gates captured Eöl, who told them that Aredhel was his wife. She lamented his coming but verified his claim on her and asked that he be admitted to receive Turgon's judgment. So Eöl was brought before the throne, full of sullen hatred for the Noldor. Turgon honored him as a kinsman and offered the Dark Elf his hand, saying that he might enjoy all the pleasures of Gondolin but not leave the city, as the law required. But Eöl would not take the proffered hand or acknowledge any law of the Noldor. He launched into his usual diatribe against them for seizing the lands of the Teleri. Aredhel they might keep, he added contemptuously, but not his son Maeglin. And thereupon he ordered Maeglin to come with him under penalty of a curse if he did not. By his silence Maeglin refused his father's command.

Turgon now spoke with the sternness proper to a King. His judgments, he declared, were law in Gondolin. Eöl, and Maeglin also, had only two choices, "to abide here or to die here." Crying out that Turgon should not have his son, Eöl suddenly drew a spear hidden under his cloak and hurled it at Maeglin. But Aredhel sprang to guard her son with her own body and received the spear in her shoulder, while Eöl was overpowered. That night she died of her wound. Turgon therefore had Eöl thrown down from the precipice of Caragdûr. With his last breath he cursed Maeglin, predicting that he would fail in all his designs in Gondolin and, in the end, die the same death as Eöl's.

Thenceforth Idril always mistrusted Maeglin, although

he grew great in Gondolin, second only to Turgon. With his Noldor skills he organized the smiths and miners of the city and found in the mountains around it many ores but, most valuable of all, hard iron with which he forged keener and keener weapons for its armies. Moreover, he was both wise in counsel and brave in battle during the Nirnaeth Arnoediad, the calamitous Fifth Battle of Beleriand.

One thing only he could never attain or even speak of openly—the love for Idril which he cherished secretly without hope. For the custom of the Elves forbade the marriage of first cousins, as they were. Also, even without that ban, Idril had no love at all for Maeglin. She well knew his passion for her but thought it all a crooked consequence of the Kinslaying of the Teleri by the Noldor, which brought down upon them the Curse of Mandos.

So, as the fruitless years went by, Maeglin's love became transformed into a lust for power in all other matters. And thus hidden treason came to flourish in hidden Gondolin.

VII

Of the Coming of Men

IT HAS BEEN TOLD in Chapter V how at the first rising of the Sun the race of Men, the Second Children of Ilúvatar, were born in Hildorien in the eastern regions of Middle-earth. They received no such summons to Valinor as the Elves had received many years before. Perhaps that minority of the Valar who had then counseled against such a summons now had their way, pointing to the discontent and rebellion of the Noldor which would never have come to pass without that decree. Whatever the reason, the Noldor, who were too busy fighting Morgoth ever to explore Middle-earth east of the Ered Luin mountains in the First Age, became aware of the existence of Men only after they entered Beleriand.

Finrod Felagund it was, who, while hunting in Ossiriand, encountered the first human tribe, led by Bëor the Old, to be seen by Noldor eyes. Finrod looked upon them with love and wooed them with the music of a harp. They in return revered him for his wisdom, for he told them in song the whole wonderful tale of Middle-earth since its creation, and also of Valinor across the Great Sea. Bëor replied that he and his people had left darkness behind them and come westward believing that here "we shall find Light" (p. 141). Literally, what he meant was the light of the Sun in the west on the day when he and his people were born. But the capitalization of the word "Light" here carries with it also a more sacred, spiritual meaning: they had been drawn westward by the brightness of Aman, abode of the angels of Ilúvatar.

Bëor did not say, because he himself did not know, that the darkness they fled was Morgoth's, and was an inner darkness. Learning quickly of the birth of Men, the Black Enemy himself had come from Angband to corrupt them, who were new and fair. Although soon called back to his fortress, he had time enough to implant in their hearts feelings of guilt and fear without cause, like those many of the Noldor still bore from the Kinslaying and the Doom of Mandos. More dangerously still, Morgoth sullied with terror and bitter grief Men's anticipation of Death, which Ilúvatar had given them as a special gift after the sufferings and many ills of their brief lives. Thenceforth Men did not look upon death as a release from sorrow and old age but as an event mysterious, painful, and in every way terrible. And, for the most part, they feared it more than any other event in their lives, longing for immortality like that of the Elves.

Yet it is certain that Ilúvatar did not intend his Second-born Children to be inferior to his Firstborn Elves in this respect (pp. 41–42). The Elves, perhaps even the Valar, would eventually grow weary of perpetual life, which binds them to Middle-earth, and would long for the freedom of Men, whose hearts "still seek beyond the world and . . . find no rest therein." True, Men would always fall within the Providential scheme of Ilúvatar. But their spirits will not, like those of the Elves, have to sit waiting after death in the Halls of Mandos for an unknown doom. Rather it is said that "the fate of Men after death, maybe is not in the hands of the Valar" (p. 105). If not, then it must be in the hands of Ilúvatar. Who else is capable of disposing of the fates of Men? So it seems that the spirits of human beings proceed immediately back to their Maker, where, probably, they are subjected to his Judgment. Tolkien's Catholicism seems to be active here.

Finrod soon found himself confronting an emergency. He learned from Bëor that another human tribe, the Haladin, differing from his own in speech, was about to enter Beleriand. At the same time he received from the Greenelves a demand to remove all newcomers from Ossiriand because they were "hewers of trees and hunters of beasts," which belonged to the Elves who lived there. Desiring always both justice and peace Finrod advised Bëor to gather together all the members of his tribe and take them to Estolad, a thinly populated region on the banks of the River Celon just south of the forest of Nan Elmoth. Bëor willingly did so. When the time came for Finrod to return to Nargothrond, Bëor had become so loyal to him that he left also and served him all the rest of his days. Rule over his tribe Bëor conferred upon his eldest son Baran.

Soon afterwards the Haladin came, but they turned north to settle in Thargelion, the country of Caranthir, whose Elves received them peacefully enough but without much attention. Behind the Haladin marched in ordered array the House of Hador the Golden-haired, a race of warriors led at that time by Marach. Being close friends of Bëor's people they went to dwell in lands a little to the southeast of Baran.

These three tribes of Men were much visited by both Noldor and Sindar Elves from West Beleriand, who were curious to see the Second Children of Ilúvatar, and who gave them collectively the title of Edain, Elf-friends. Fingolfin as High King of the Noldor sent them messages of welcome. And many young men of the Edain went to serve in the courts of the Elf lords for a term.

So, as the two races grew closer together, the kings of the Noldor Houses of Fingolfin, Finarfin, and Fëanor invited any of the Edain who wished to settle in their territories. In this way began the dispersal of the tribes of Men throughout Beleriand. Bëor's people migrated to Dorthonion, ruled by the House of Finarfin. Many of the House of

Hador moved to Hithlum, where Fingolfin reigned, but others of that House went farther south, below the Ered Wethrin mountains. The Haladin, however, remained in Thargelion.

Alone among the Elf Kings, Thingol of Doriath neither welcomed the arrival of Men nor was much consulted about their dispersal. Because he still considered himself the sole rightful monarch over all of Beleriand he resented this neglect and reasserted his claim by commanding that Men should dwell only in its northern parts, and that the lords they served must be responsible for their good behavior. As for Doriath, Thingol forbade any Man at all to enter it, even one of the tribe of Bëor who served Finrod. But Melian in her foresight confided to Galadriel that a Man of Bëor's House would nevertheless enter Doriath despite her Girdle, "for doom greater than my power shall send him" (p. 144). By this she meant Beren, of course.

Meanwhile among the Men still living in Estolad dissensions broke out, stirred by Morgoth in order to separate the Edain from the Elves. Chief fomenters of discontent were Bereg of the House of Bëor and Amlach, grandson of Marach, leader of the House of Hador. They argued that instead of the Light which they had come so far to find here, and which in fact shone only far across the Sea, Beleriand offered them nothing but perpetual war between Morgoth and Elves as cruel as he. Topping all was the command issued by Thingol that they must live in the north, closest to Angband. This they should refuse to obey.

When, finally, a council of Men was held at Estolad, those friendly to the Elves agreed that Morgoth was the source of all their ills because of his ambition to rule the whole of Middle-earth and all alive in it. But if Men left Beleriand, to what other place could they go where he could not pursue them? Better to stay here where the Elves kept him in check and Men could stand with them against the common foe.

Then spoke one who seemed to be Amlach but was actually a figment decked out by Morgoth in his shape. He
denied the existence of any Valinor, any Valar, even any
Morgoth. It was the Elves, he said, who craved dominion
over all of Middle-earth and, greedily digging into its en-
trails, had aroused the Orcs who had always lived there. Let
the Orcs keep their realm underground while Men lived
peacefully on the surface. And let the Elves not interfere.

Those who listened to these persuasions of the false Am-
lach resolved to go away, far from the Elves. But the true
Amlach returned, assuring them of his identity. And the
Elf-friends used the illusion as an example of Morgoth's
lies. He must fear Men and the help they could bring to
Elves, they said, if he had to resort to such blatant trickery.

Most of the Men present were convinced by the Elf-
friends, but others maintained that Morgoth hated them,
not feared them, and that they would do well not to meddle
in his quarrel with the Elves. So Bereg led away southward
a thousand of Bëor's people, diminishing their strength.
And, adds Tolkien, "they passed out of the songs of those
days" (p. 145). By frequent allusions of this kind to the songs
of the minstrels Tolkien keeps reminding us that everything he is writing about Elves and Men in the First Age
derives from minstrel accounts of these events. The glee-
man stands ever present as the source of the tales in *The
Silmarillion*.

After Bereg left, Amlach declared that he now had a
personal lifelong quarrel with Morgoth. And going north
he took service with Maedhros.

Enraged by his failure to separate Men from Elves, Morgoth sent out Orcs, who passed down the eastern side of the
Ered Luin, then crossed back over the mountains and fell
upon the Haladin in Thargelion. Since the Haladin did not
live together in towns but preferred scattered homesteads,
a number of these were taken by surprise. But one fearless
man, Haldad, rallied all the adults and children he could

find and with them retreated to the confluence of the Rivers Ascar and Gelion, where he built a stockade between the two waters. There Haldad and his son Haldar died in sorties, but his daughter Haleth maintained the defense until Orcs were pouring through a breech in the stockade. In the nick of time Caranthir and his host, riding down from the north, drove the Orcs into deep waters where they drowned. Praising Haleth, he offered her protection and free lands if she would bring her people farther north.

Haleth, however, wanted no protection from anyone, being independent and strong of heart, as were her people. So, after thanking Caranthir, she led them westward to Estolad, long the chief gathering place of the Edain. Under her rule the Haladin did not permit themselves to be absorbed by the other two tribes of Men mingled there but lived apart, until Haleth led them west again through Nan Dungortheb, the Valley of Dreadful Death. Although suffering much in that cruel passage, they were virtually carried through it by the strength of her will to the woods of Talath Dirnen, the Guarded Plain of Nargothrond. There they returned for a while to their old practice of living in separated homesteads. Then her following broke up, some drifting farther south to Finrod's realm of Nargothrond, whereas others went with Haleth to live in the Forest of Brethil.

These woods were claimed by Thingol as part of his kingdom of Doriath although they lay outside the Girdle of Melian. But through Finrod's intercession Thingol allowed the people of Haleth to stay there on condition that they defend the ford at the Crossings of Teiglin against Orcs and have no friendship with them. Whereupon Haleth was moved to remark that the proviso was peculiar, as if she, whose father and brother had been killed by Orcs, would become friendly with their slayers. When she died, her people buried her in a barrow, heaping a green mound over her.

Thus for a time Men lived dispersed among Elves in many places and in many fashions, without distinction between the two races. Then the Elf rulers recognized that this should not be. Men, having their own natures and customs, could develop as Men only in separate societies under human rulers. And in war, even though they allied themselves with Elves against Morgoth, they must fight under captains of their own race.

Accordingly Fingolfin in Hithlum gave to the House of Hador under Hador Lórindol, Goldenhead, the lordship of Dor-lómin, a province in the southern part of Hithlum. There Hador assembled most of his tribe and, ruling a fearless warrior people, became the most powerful of the chiefs of the Edain.

Similarly, in Dorthonion Boromir, grandson of Bëor the Old, received the lordship of his people and the district of Ladros in the northeastern section of the land. Angrod and Aegnor, sons of Finarfin, granted it to them. And the Haladin under Haleth, as seen before, occupied the Forest of Brethil by permission of Thingol, although a portion of that people put themselves under the jurisdiction of Finrod Felagund, the much loved, on the Guarded Plain of Nargothrond.

Between the three tribes of Men there were intermarriages, of course. One of the most significant for the future was that between Galdor of the Hador and Hareth of the Haladin. This was to produce in later generations Húrin and Túrin in one branch of the family and, in another branch, Tuor husband of Idril and father of their son Eärendil. But Beren was to be the child of a union between Barahir and Emeldir, within the tribe of Bëor.[1]

Notwithstanding the sameness common to all Men, each of the three tribes of the Edain had traits all its own. The Hador, being hardy and bold, were of great help to Fingolfin. They traveled north into the regions of deep cold beyond Angband to keep watch over it. Strong in mind and body, steadfast, as quick to laughter as to wrath, in many respects they outdid their kin in the other tribes. From their speech came the common tongue of Númenor (p. 148).

On the other hand, the men of Bëor's House most resembled the Noldor and were dearest to them: eager for knowledge, skillful in craft, intelligent, and tenacious in remembering the past in order to govern the present and the future. Also they were given to pity rather than to injurious laughter. Like them, but less eager to know, were the Haladin, who followed Haleth to the Forest of Brethil. That folk spoke little and were not comfortable in crowds or in cities. Many of them loved to wander alone in the woods. Their days in Beleriand were to be few and, alas, unhappy.

When Bëor the Old died of sheer old age after living for ninety-three years, the Elves at Finrod's court truly realized for the first time how short were the lives of Men, so unlike their own. This close view of human mortality caused them to wonder about the purpose of these brief lives of Men and the meaning of their death, which Elves found incomprehensible. Yet while their lives lasted, the Edain learned much art and knowledge from the Eldar, until they were far wiser than the tribes who remained east of Ered Luin and never had any contact with those who, at first or second hand, had known the Light of Valinor.

* * *

Shortly before Morgoth began the Fourth Battle of Beleriand, Fingolfin as High King of the Noldor, surveying the strength which had accrued to them from their alliances with the Sindar and the Edain, urged an attack upon Angband now, before Morgoth could devise new engines for their destruction. This would have been wise counsel had not Fingolfin and his allies forgotten the Doom of Mandos. This prophesied that nothing the Noldor did on Middle-earth would succeed and, consequently, that "their war

unaided [by the Valar] . . . was without final hope, whether
they hasted or delayed" (p. 150).

But it would appear that this Doom was too terrible, too
intolerable to bear remembering; so the Noldor suppressed
it and forgot it. In its stead they turned to the enjoyment
of their wide, fair realms in peace, hoping for the best. Nor
were they eager to die in an assault upon Angband, as many
must surely do, whether in victory or defeat.

For his part Morgoth was overconfident and struck too
soon, blinded by hate, expecting to wipe out his foes totally
and to defile their lands as well. Also he misjudged the
desperate bravery of both Elves and Men when facing disaster. Had he waited until his preparations were more
nearly complete, he might well have won the war utterly
there and then.

On a dark moonless winter night when frontier guards
were few and lax, Morgoth sent out from Angband and
from volcanoes in the Iron Mountains streams of lava so
swift that many of the Noldor perished in them before they
could reach high ground. Although the heights of Dorthonion and the Ered Wethrin surrounding Hithlum kept
back the flames, their trees burned and smoked, confusing
the defenders. In the forefront of the fire sped Glaurung,
father of dragons, grown to his full powers. After him
raced Balrogs. And after them, Orc armies in multitudes
never seen before. They overran Noldor strongholds and
slew Elves and Men alike wherever they could find them.

So began Dagor Bragollach, the Battle of Sudden Flame,
and sudden it truly was, for in it Morgoth achieved complete surprise and never let slip the initiative once he had
it. In its earliest days he succeeded in breaking up the
Noldor forces and separating them from one another, so
that in the hurly-burly they were swept aside and did not
know where to rally. But at least they did not flee. Most of
the Sindarin lacked staying power in battle and fled south,
away from the fighting. Many took refuge in Doriath, still

protected by the Girdle; others went as far away as the fortresses on the seacoast; others, to Nargothrond. Still others hid in Ossiriand or crossed the Ered Luin mountains and wandered aimlessly in the eastern wilds, taking with them rumors of war. Thus, except in Doriath, the Sindar were knocked out of combat. And there they were safe for a while, for Thingol took no part in the Fourth Battle but stayed in his caves of Menegroth. Nor did King Turgon of Gondolin come out to fight, deeming the time as not yet ripe.

As for the Noldor, the sons of Finarfin, Angrod and Aegnor, were slain in the defense of Dorthonion, as were most of the warriors of Bëor's people. But Barahir, one of their chiefs who was fighting in its northwestern region, saw King Finrod with a small company penned by Orcs in the Fen of Serech. He had been hurrying north with his host to give what help he could to his beleaguered brothers in Dorthonion and had become separated from the main body of his soldiers. With his best spearmen, Barahir was able to rescue him, but at a high cost in lives. Finding that it was too late to save Angrod and Aegnor, and anxious to see to the safety of Nargothrond, Finrod took his army back south to beat off the attacks which he expected to come soon. But not before swearing an oath of friendship with Barahir, who returned to the struggle in Dorthonion. However, most of Barahir's tribe, led by his wife Emeldir, took refuge in Hithlum, or in the Forest of Brethil.

Fingolfin and his son Fingon and their human auxiliaries, the Hador, were too busy keeping the Orcs out of Mithrim and Dor-lómin to help the House of Finarfin on Dorthonion or anybody else. Driven back from the plains of Ard-galen to the Ered Wethrin, they made a successful stand at the stronghold of Eithel Sirion, where many of the Hador died.

So Hithlum was saved, but Fingolfin's nearest Noldor allies, now that Dorthonion was lost, were the sons of

Fëanor, hundreds of miles to the east. They too had suffered serious reverses. Maedhros in his fortress on the Hill of Himring performed prodigies of valor in repelling the Orcs. But Orcs did force the pass of Aglon to his west and put to flight Celegorm and Curufin, who took their defeated force with them to Nargothrond, whereas they would have done better to join Maedhros, as the sequel showed.

To Maedhros' east, Maglor the minstrel, assailed by the great dragon Glaurung as well as by overwhelming masses of Orcs, could not hold the gap which bore his name. He betook himself with his remnants to the Hill of Himring to strengthen Maedhros. And on the eastern extreme of the March a humbled Caranthir was obliged to retreat southward to his youngest brothers, Amrod and Amras the hunters, in Ossiriand. Together they were able to station a small body of troops in the mount called Amon Ereb to watch for Orcs. And they were helped, too, by the Green-elves. So the Orcs did not venture into Ossiriand. But, led by Glaurung, they devastated Caranthir's province of Thargelion and purposely befouled Lake Helevorn.

Learning of this long, sad register of defeats, Fingolfin concluded that all was lost. In a madness of anger and despair he rode at full tilt on his horse Rochallor to do what hurt he could to Morgoth before he died. At the very gates of Angband he sounded his horn and smashed at them with his spear butt, crying aloud that he challenged Morgoth to single combat. The Black Enemy feared to emerge. But in front of his captains he could not refuse the duel lest they think him craven, as indeed he was. Black-armored, sable-shielded as by a thundercloud, and wearing the Crown of Iron which bore the three Silmarils and symbolized his claim to rule all of Eä, Morgoth towered as he came. In contrast, Fingolfin in silver armor shone like a star, and his sword Ringil, like ice.

In the duel that followed, Morgoth, resembling the

Norse god Thor, wielded Grond, a huge hammer, with which he struck at Fingolfin, tearing pits in the ashen plain as the Noldor King dodged aside.[2] Seven times did Ringil wound the foe, and seven times drew from him cries of pain. But when the King tired, Morgoth knocked him down repeatedly with his vast shield until in the end Fingolfin stumbled and fell backward into an unseen pit near Morgoth's feet. With his last strength the Elf-king slashed the foot of the corrupted Vala, spilling a stream of his dark blood and leaving him lame ever after.

So died Fingolfin, "most proud and valiant of the Elvenkings of old" (p. 154). The tale of his death, and its manner, was brought by Thorondor, King of Eagles, to his sons, Fingon in Hithlum and Turgon in Gondolin. And when Morgoth tried to feed Fingolfin's dead body to the wolves, Thorondor the servant of Manwë ripped Morgoth's face open with his claws and bore the body to a mountain top near Gondolin, where Turgon built over it a cairn of stones.

Morgoth was thus deeply marred, but Fingolfin's death marred the cause of the Noldor in Beleriand more deeply still. As their High King, respected and loved by Eldar and Edain alike, he was the linchpin which held them all together. Without him they had no true leader, for his son Fingon, who followed him in that office, was far from being his equal. And they needed him more than ever now that darkness was closing in.

Although Morgoth hunted Barahir and his tribe relentlessly and wove dark enchantments in the trees on Dorthonion's northern slope, Barahir fought on with lessening numbers. His wife Emeldir the Man-hearted at last led all the remaining women and children down from the plateau. Some of them were taken in by the Haladin in Brethil and the remainder, by the Hador in Dor-lómin. But Barahir had no thought of retreat, though his men were slain one by one until he had only a dozen left, led by Beren his son.

Outlaws they then became, without hope and without fear, wandering on the barren highlands above the enchanted forest with no fixed shelter.

For a time Maedhros, reinforced by many refugees who came to him, succeeded in seizing and holding the Pass at Aglon to his west, but not the Gap of Maglor, which continued to give the Orcs easy access into East Beleriand. In the west, for two years after the Fourth Battle the brother of Finrod, Orodreth, managed to hold for the Noldor the citadel of Minas Tirith on an island in the River Sirion, which controlled the narrows between Dorthonion and the Ered Wethrin. But then Sauron, "greatest and most terrible of the servants of Morgoth," took the island by assault. Having become a sorcerer mighty in evil, a lord of werewolves and a master of dreadful phantoms, he set so dark a cloud of fear upon the defenders that they fled with Orodreth to Nargothrond. Under Sauron's hand Tol Sirion came to be known as the Isle of Werewolves. Now that he controlled through Sauron that pass in the west, Morgoth sent bands of Orcs through it to harry Beleriand and, joining those of their kind that came down in the east through Maglor's Gap, they surrounded Doriath and spread desolation steadily southward.

Moreover, Morgoth hit upon the scheme of capturing as many Sindar and Noldor as possible, making them his thralls in Angband, and then releasing them, seemingly unharmed. These slaves of his did not what they themselves willed but what Morgoth willed. He used them to spread lies, setting the Sindar against their Noldor leaders, accusing them of treachery to one another. These lies many of the Sindar believed because they were of the same stock as the Teleri, against whom the Noldor launched the Kinslaying in Alqualondë. And particularly now, when the minds of the Sindar were clouded by fear as a consequence of defeat in the Fourth Battle, which they attributed to the bad leadership of the Noldor. But what the Noldor feared most was the treachery not of the Sindar but of their own kin who had been captured, taken to Angband, and set apparently free. For they knew well that often these freed Noldor were no longer themselves but were still bound to the service of Morgoth against them. So even those few who were truly unbroken and free were suspect and unwelcome.

Having had little success in corrupting the Edain, Morgoth sought out farther east a race of Men, later known as the Easterlings or Swarthy Men, who were more accessible to his temptations. These he called into Beleriand. Some of their many tribes he had already won over, and the others he expected to gain soon. In appearance they were altogether unlike the Edain to whom the Eldar had become accustomed. All were dark of eye and hair, short and broad of stature, long and strong of arm, and dark or sallow of skin. Expectably enough, they proved to be of dubious value in the defense of Beleriand. Some of them even preferred Dwarves to Elves.

But Maedhros, alarmed by the fewness of the Eldar and the Edain as compared with the inexhaustible hosts of Morgoth, allied himself with two of the greatest chiefs of these Easterlings, Bór and Ulfang, and gave them his friendship. To this alliance Bór and his sons were faithful. But when Caranthir accepted Ulfang and his sons, they betrayed him.

The Easterlings remained for many years in East Beleriand and seldom met the Edain, who had found homes in West Beleriand. The two races of Men did not like each other much, and neither of them wished to multiply their meetings. After the Fourth Battle the Hador kept close to Mithlum, and with them the pitifully few survivors of Bëor's House. The Haladin in the Forest of Brethil, however, saw themselves threatened by an Orc legion coming down from the western pass. Having won the friendship of the Sindar marchwardens of Doriath, the Haladin sent through them to Thingol an urgent warning of the threat.

Thingol responded by dispatching to their aid Beleg Strongbow, chief of his marchwardens, with a strong force of axmen. Together the Haladin and the Sindar axmen surprised the Orcs and wiped them out. Once more Morgoth learned the old lesson that unsupported Orcs could not overcome Elves, nor their Edain allies. So for years thereafter he sent no more Orcs alone down the western pass. This peace gave Finrod time to muster his strength in Nargothrond.

It happened that in the triumphant clash with the Orcs the brothers Húrin and Huor of the House of Hador took part. They were being fostered in Brethil at the time by their uncle, Haldir of the Haladin, as was the custom. Separated from the main battle the two young men were pursued to the ford of Brithiach, where they were saved only by a mist raised by Ulmo, and thence escaped into Dimbar under the cliffs of the Crissaegrim, where they wandered about, bewildered by the illusions of that land. At length Thorondor sent two of his Eagles to fly them over the peaks into hidden Gondolin, the first Men ever to see it.

King Turgon received them warmly, having been told by Ulmo that the House of Hador would help him in woeful times to come. But the King cherished Húrin and Huor not merely on this account but because he loved them. After they had stayed with him for nearly a year they told him that they wished to go home to their own people to share in the griefs which now beset them. And, knowing of Turgon's law against egress for any who had entered his secret city, Húrin pleaded that, human life being so short, he and Huor could not afford to spend more years there. So Turgon consented to their going in the same way, if Thorondor was willing.

But Maeglin, Turgon's nephew, did not love the race of Men and taunted them with favoritism in being set above the King's law. Húrin and Huor then swore an oath never to tell anyone where they had been. But when the Eagles that bore them away by night set them down not in Dimbar but in Dor-lómin many leagues to the west, they were subjected to much curious questioning, especially by their father Galdor. He wished to know where they had spent the year and how they had obtained the fine clothes they were wearing. Húrin pleaded their oath of silence. Then Galdor and many others guessed near the truth. And in due course these guesses came to the ears of Morgoth's agents.

Meditating on the events of the Fourth Battle, which had broken the siege of Angband, Turgon came to believe that it meant the downfall of the Noldor "unless aid should come" (p. 159). And whence could come aid strong enough to save them? Only from Valinor. So Turgon secretly sent shipwrights from Gondolin to build ships at the Mouths of Sirion and the Isle of Balar, as the Elves there had taught them to do long ago. Thence the mariners of the hidden kingdom sailed far westward to beg pardon and help from the Valar. But across the wild, enchanted Sea none managed to reach their goal, and few came back. The time for a successful crossing was still years away. First a Silmaril must be stolen from Morgoth's Iron Crown by Beren and Lúthien. And after that Eärendil, half Elf, half Man, must be born to sail the Great Sea by its light to win the help so needed.

Meantime the war did not cease. Morgoth, in spite of his victories in the Battle of Sudden Flame, feared Finrod Felagund and Turgon, whose whereabouts he could not discover. Of Nargothrond he knew nothing but the name, and of Gondolin not even that. He sent out his spies questing for them, but withdrew most of his Orcs to Angband to preserve them for a Fifth Battle which must be not merely just another victory but a final, total crushing of all his foes. For this he now prepared.

Seven years later Morgoth sent two great hosts of Orcs against Hithlum, one striking at it from the east, the other from the north. The Hador of Dor-lómin held the eastern fortress of Eithel Sirion against siege, but with heavy losses, until Húrin, grown to full manhood, sallied out and drove the besiegers with dire slaughter away from the Ered Wethrin and far across the ashen plains of Anfauglith. King Fingon's army, fighting outnumbered on the very plains of Hithlum, barely held back the invaders from the north. Then Círdan sailed up the Firth of Drengist with his Elves of the Falas and fell upon them unexpectedly from the west. The Orcs broke and fled toward Angband, pursued even to the Iron Mountains by a cavalry armed with bows. Thereafter, Húrin ruled the Hador in Dor-lómin as a vassal of King Fingon. And Morgoth, having failed in the opening moves of Nirnaeth Arnoediad, postponed the Fifth Battle for a while.

The constant succession of battles against Morgoth produced within the three tribes of Men, especially the Hador and the people of Bëor, seasoned warriors as skilled in arms and high in valor as the Noldor Elves at whose side they fought. Beren, Húrin, and Huor are examples. But of these three, Beren had the most shining future in store for him, and Húrin the darkest.

VIII

Beren and Lúthien

TOLKIEN first conceived the Beren-Lúthien story, probably, in 1918 (Carpenter, *Tolkien,* pp. 97, 107). Then between 1923 and 1927 he wrote it in rhyming eight-syllable couplets, calling it first "The Gest of Beren and Lúthien" and later "The Lay of Leithian." By 1926 it was more than 4000 lines long and, dissatisfied with its couplet form, Tolkien seems to have experimented with the idea of rendering it in more complex stanzas like those sung by Aragorn and Bilbo in *The Lord of the Rings* I, 204–05 and 246–49, respectively. Finally, however, he gave it the prose form we now have in *The Silmarillion.* These many rewritings suggest that it meant a great deal to him personally and that he kept groping for a form that would best express his feelings.

For possibly relevant biographical facts we may look again to Carpenter (esp. pp. 38–40, 68, 78–79, 252, 256). In brief, Edith Bratt, Tolkien's future wife, was an Anglican, whereas Tolkien was Roman Catholic. For his sake she became a Catholic in 1914, and they were married as such in 1916, shortly before he was sent by the British army to fight in France. After he had been invalided home, the two used to go on walks, on one of which Edith danced and sang for him in a woodland glade, as Lúthien did for Beren. When she died in November, 1971, Tolkien asked that the name Lúthien be put on her tombstone. "She was (and knew she was) my Lúthien," he said. When he followed her in death two years later he was buried with her and the name Beren was added to hers at his request above their common grave. Carpenter (p. 97) writes that the tale "Of Beren and Lúthien" was the one "most loved by Tolkien, not least because at one level he identified the character of Lúthien with his own wife." It was also a favorite with the gleemen who sang it, as well as with those Elves to whom they sang. For it told how, out of the tragedies of those days before the Fifth Battle, could and must be born both joy and light.

* * *

Beren's father Barahir and his companions, reduced to twelve, fought on in Dorthonion as a band of outlaws. A small lake, Tarn Aeluin, whose clear waters had been hallowed by Melian the Maia in days gone by, became their headquarters. And from that base they performed such feats of valor against Morgoth's servants as resounded among the peoples still free. Unable to track down the valiant band himself, Morgoth ordered Sauron to find and destroy them.

Gorlim, one of Barahir's men, had joined him upon finding his house plundered and his wife Eilinel gone. Always hoping that she would return, he used to go back secretly from time to time to his empty house, and this habit became known to Sauron. One evening at dusk, Gorlim found the house lighted and saw Eilinel inside, just as Sauron's hunters seized him. Long they tortured him to betray Barahir and long he resisted, yet not long enough, for finally he gave in and told all in exchange for Sauron's promise to release both him and his wife. After the betrayal was complete, Sauron mockingly revealed that Gorlim had seen only "a phantom dressed by wizardry" (p. 163), for Eilinel was dead. Speedily Sauron sent him to join her in death, thus jauntily keeping his promise to set them both free from his service.

Orcs dispatched to Tarn Aeluin surprised Barahir and

his company and killed them all except for Beren, who had left to perform a spying mission for his father. Warned by the wraith of Gorlim in a dream, Beren sped back to camp but arrived too late. First building a cairn over his father's body, he pursued the murderers to Rivil's Well, where he killed their captain. From him Beren took his father's hand and on its finger the ring given him by Finrod Felagund for rescuing him in the Fourth Battle. Beren escaped unhurt, "being defended by fate" (p. 164).

During four years more Beren stayed in Dorthonion carrying on his father's work of resistance to Morgoth and doing such deeds as became admired even in Doriath to the south. Then Sauron brought an army of Orcs supplemented by werewolves, "fell beasts inhabited by dreadful spirits that he had imprisoned in their bodies," and they forced Beren to flee elsewhere. But where? From a peak in Ered Gorgoroth, the Mountains of Terror, he saw Doriath far away and "it was put into his heart" to go into that Hidden Kingdom.

His journey thither was so terrible as to age and weaken him: clambering slowly down the sheer precipices of Ered Gorgoroth, crossing Nan Dungortheb, where the sorcery of Sauron clashed with Melian's power and ancient monsters hunted their prey with many eyes, and at the last traversing the mazes of the Girdle as Melian herself had foretold, "for a great doom lay upon him" (p. 165).

Looking and tottering like an old man, Beren came in the summer season into the woods of Neldoreth. There at dusk before the moon came up he saw Lúthien dancing, the daughter of Thingol and Melian, "the most beautiful of all the Children of Ilúvatar." She was the Morning Star of her race, as Arwen, Elfin bride of Aragorn in *The Lord of the Rings,* was to be its Evening Star. But Lúthien was not the child of a Maia for nothing. Seeing Beren watching her with yearning eyes, she cast a spell upon him which let her vanish from his clouded eyes, made him unable to say any

word, and lessened the swiftness of his pursuit. All summer
he sought her, and all autumn and winter too. She let
herself be glimpsed at a distance from time to time, during
autumn among leaves twirling in the wind, during winter
like a star upon a hill. But her spell was like a chain upon
his legs and he could never catch up with her.

At dawn one morning when Spring was ready to burst,
she allowed him to hear her sing for the first time. Her song
melted the bonds of winter in the streams and in the frozen
earth; and also her spell upon Beren. Within himself he had
called her Tinúviel, the Nightingale, not knowing her
name. Now he was able to cry "Tinúviel!" aloud and to go
close to her.

When she looked full upon the love in his face, what had
been a maiden coyness in her gave way to a love strong as
his, as was her doom. But frightened by the storm of the
new passion in her heart she vanished again, leaving Beren
groping for her, like one suddenly made blind, and overwhelmed by joy mixed with grief. Such was to be his fate
and hers throughout the long course of their love.

Scarcely daring to hope that Lúthien would come back
to him, Beren waited, and she came. Thereafter the lovers
often met in secret through the spring and the summer
which followed, until Daeron, the minstrel of Doriath, in
his jealousy told Thingol of their meetings. The King, to
whom Lúthien was dearest in the world, questioned her
about this mere Man Beren and about his presumption in
entering Doriath unbidden and wooing her without her
parents' leave. Knowing well her father's dangerous
ways, Lúthien would reveal nothing until he swore an
oath not to kill Beren or throw him into prison. Then,
before his guards could seize him, she herself brought
Beren with all honor before the King's throne. And when
Thingol asked him who he was that came like a thief into
Doriath, Lúthien it was who identified him publicly as
the son of Barahir, whose exploits against Morgoth were

already being sung by minstrels throughout the land.

Charged by the King to explain why he had come un-bidden and to show cause why he should not be heavily punished for his insolence in coming, Beren proudly de-clared that his "fate" obliged him to flee from Dorthonion to save his life. But now he sought much more, the hand of Lúthien. Thingol would then have had him slain at once, had not the oath exacted by Lúthien's care pre-vented that penalty. But, moved by his suspicious nature, he accused Beren of being a baseborn mortal who was one of Morgoth's spies.

Beren rejected these accusations and held up for all to see the ring given by Finrod Felagund to Barahir for saving his life in the Fourth Battle. And Melian counseled Thingol to have a care what he did to Beren, "for far and free does his fate lead him," and Thingol's fate was entwined with his (p. 167).

But Thingol paid her no heed. Looking upon the immor-tal loveliness of Lúthien and comparing her with Beren, the mortal son of a brief and little lord, Thingol determined that a union between them must not be. He therefore told Beren that only if he brought back a Silmaril from Mor-goth's crown could he marry Lúthien. He did not expect Beren to return alive from this quest. For he knew that throughout all the centuries of their siege of Angband none of the Noldor (save only Fingolfin) had ever seen, even from a distance, the shining light of the Silmarils, which lay hidden deep in Angband, guarded by the full might of Morgoth's legions and by Morgoth himself.

By dispatching Beren on this errand to steal one of the Silmarils wrought by Fëanor long ago, King Thingol ended the independence of Doriath and exposed it to all the evils from which the Noldor suffered, including the Curse of Mandos and the Oath sworn by the sons of Fëanor never to let anyone but themselves own even a single one of the Great Jewels. As Melian put it, he caused Doriath to be "drawn within the fate of a mightier realm" (p. 168), to wit, the whole realm of Beleriand. No longer could Doriath live unto itself. The Girdle could no longer isolate it. Whatever happened to the rest of Beleriand would happen to Doriath also.

Leaving Doriath with a proud promise to return with a Silmaril from Morgoth's crown, Beren had at first no idea how even to set about this formidable task. It occurred to him, however, to seek counsel from Finrod Felagund, whose ring he wore and who ruled Nargothrond. The road to that city lay through the Guarded Plain, where its Elves lay in wait unseen for all, friend or foe, who might travel it. This plain Beren crossed, shouting aloud that he was Beren son of Barahir, a friend of the King, coming to speak with him. To the King, therefore, he was taken by a band of watchful Elves who waylaid him. Beren then had his chance to tell Finrod of all that had befallen him on Dorthonion, of his meetings with Lúthien in the woods of Doriath, and of the heavy mission Thingol had laid upon him.

Finrod well remembered his oath of friendship to Barahir and felt bound to honor it by going along with Beren, even though he foresaw that to do so would bring death on himself. So he described to Beren the Oath taken by the sons of Fëanor, who "would lay all the Elf-kingdoms in ruin" rather than allow anyone else to win a Silmaril, as Beren's quest bound him to do. Moreover, Celegorm and Curufin were now in Nargothrond, said Finrod. They had been helping him whenever he needed them, acquiring many followers in the process, but they would bitterly oppose Beren if his purpose became known. Celegorm and Curufin, be it remembered, were the two sons who should have rallied to Maedhros during the Fourth Battle but fled to Nargothrond instead.

Finrod's forecast was fulfilled all too soon. While he was addressing a meeting of his people, Celegorm rose, drew his sword, and repeated aloud the words of the Oath he and his brothers had sworn with their father Fëanor, ending with the claim that the Silmarils belonged to them alone, forever. Curufin also spoke, but more craftily, foretelling the ruin of Nargothrond if Beren was allowed to divide its forces, one against another. So badly did Curufin frighten the people of the city that thereafter they pursued all strangers, even their own kin. And, besides, they turned away from Finrod their rightful King, denying his power to rule them and turning instead to Celegorm and Curufin, who began to think darkly of exiling Finrod and usurping his throne.

Finrod, in order to keep his oath to Barahir and yet prevent civil conflict, unkinged himself and threw his crown upon the floor. Ten faithful subjects he found ready to go with him and Beren into danger. And at the suggestion of their leader, Edrahil, Finrod gave the crown of Nargothrond to his brother Orodreth to act as Steward over the kingdom until he himself returned.

The twelve companions headed north along the River Narog, bound for Angband, and arrived at the Falls of Ivrin, where they met and killed a small band of Orcs. Carrying their war gear and transmuted in body and face into the likeness of Orcs by the arts of Finrod Felagund, they ventured into the pass between Dorthonion and Mithrim, hoping to deceive Sauron in his tower of Tol Sirion. But since they did not stop to report to Sauron, as Morgoth required of all his Orcs in that region, Sauron became suspicious and had them stopped and brought before him. Then ensued a contest between Sauron and Felagund "in songs of power" (p. 171). This contest Tolkien describes in rhymed couplets, but with a very loose meter, taken from the Lay of Leithian.

In the Riddle Game between Gollum and Bilbo in *The Hobbit*, each contestant put to the other puzzling descriptions of objects or persons whose identity he must guess.

The loser was he who first failed to guess his opponent's riddle correctly. In Anglo-Saxon times that game was common enough. The same does not seem to have been true of the Contest of Songs of Power. This genre did not flourish in Anglo-Saxon England, and its antecedents must be looked for elsewhere. Tolkien drew the tale of Kullervo from Finland's national epic, *Kalevala*. Why not seek there also the prototypes of the Contest of Spells in which Felagund and Sauron engaged? *Kalevala* is full of spells of all sorts and its heroes (Väinämoinen, Ilmarinen, Lemminkainen) are continuously searching for new spells with which to best their foes.[1]

This form of combat may be compared to a verbal wrestling match in which each wrestler tries to overthrow his opponent physically by the greater strength of his spells. In *The Silmarillion* Sauron begins with a chant about his magical arts, his treachery, and his betrayals. Of these misdeeds Sauron is proud, not conscience-smitten, for he has no conscience and therefore feels no shame.

His chant sways Felagund but does not fell him. Felagund retorts with a song depicting resistance to evil power and escape to freedom from its traps by observing fidelity and trust to others who fight against it.

As the clash of song against song continues, Felagund weakens, "reeling and foundering." But he fights back with chants about bird song at his home in Nargothrond and, moving on westward, about the sighing of the waves of the Great Sea on the sands of Middle-earth and on the sands of pearl in Eressëa, where the Teleri first beached their ships. By these memories of the beauty of sound and sight he had known in the past, Felagund hopes to strengthen himself against the hideousness of Sauron's voice and theme.

But he has in fact trapped himself. For Sauron immediately uses Felagund's good memories of Valinor to evoke the bad ones which over the years have been assailing his conscience: the Kinslaying by the Noldor at Alqualondë, the theft of the Teleri ships, the crossing of the Helcaraxë ice by Fingolfin's betrayed host, and the subsequent defeats of the Noldor which have brought capture and torture to many an Elf in victorious Angband. His own unresting guilt in these matters, recited by Sauron with his usual horrible jocularity, is too much for Felagund and throws him prone before Sauron. With him fall all his companions.

Sauron stripped off their disguise as Orcs but failed to wring from them their designs against Angband. So he put them into a dungeon under Tol Sirion and each night sent a werewolf to devour one of them. But none of the company would reveal the secret he sought.

Across the long leagues Lúthien was so attuned to Beren that she sensed his danger and, asking her mother, learned of his whereabouts and his despair. She resolved to go to him and trustingly sought help again from jealous Daeron, who again betrayed her to her father. So Thingol had a small house built for her in the upper branches of Hírilorn, tallest of beeches in the forest of Neldoreth, and set guards round about to keep her from descending.

However Melian, while in Valinor, had been a Maia in Lórien, that place of healing and of rest, and from her Lúthien had learned the arts of bringing sleep. She let her hair grow to a great length, like Rapunzel in Grimms' *Tales*. From some of its strands she wove a dark, covering robe which carried a spell of sleep, and from the remainder a long rope which, swaying over the guards' heads, brought them slumber. Then she climbed down it and, wrapped in her cloak, escaped unseen.

At that time Celegorm and Curufin were hunting Sauron's wolves on the Guarded Plain with the aid of Huan, a hound bred in Valinor by Oromë and given by him to his disciple Celegorm, to whom Huan remained faithful even in exile. Enmeshed in the Doom of the Noldor, Huan was to die on Middle-earth, but only after he had fought against the mightiest of its wolves. He understood all that was said to him but was himself permitted to speak words no more than three times before his death. It was he who scented Lúthien fleeing from Doriath and brought her to Celegorm. And she, learning that Celegorm was an enemy of Morgoth, trustfully revealed her beauty, which enchanted him. Too often did she give her trust to those who did not deserve it.

The brothers took her to Nargothrond, where they kept her wholly to themselves like any prisoner. And most shamefully they plotted how to force Thingol to give her in marriage to Celegorm so that he, as heir, might add power over Doriath to power over Nargothrond and so make himself the strongest of all the Noldor princes.

Fortunately the hound Huan was wiser and nobler than his master. Lúthien, kept immured, often spoke to him of Beren. Understanding her plight and deeply devoted to her, Huan gave her counsel. One night when all was still, he brought her dark, concealing cloak and led her out of Nargothrond secretly. Once free of the city he took her on his back and sped to Tol Sirion, where Beren lay.

Meantime Sauron's werewolves had devoured all the companions of Felagund and Beren, one by one, on succeeding nights.[2] When Beren's turn came, Felagund broke the chains that bound him, wrestled with the wolf bare-handed and killed it. But he was mortally wounded in the fight. Before he died, he took his last farewell of Beren, saying that he did not know whether they would ever meet again even after death "for the fates of our kindred are apart" (p. 174), Beren being a Man and Finrod an Elf. Thus, concludes Tolkien, King Finrod Felagund, "fairest and most beloved of the house of Finwë, redeemed his oath" to Barahir, while Beren mourned.

Even as he did so, Lúthien arrived at the bridge of Tol Sirion with Huan and sang a spell, able to pierce any wall, which came to Beren's ears like the singing of nightingales. In reply he chanted a song of his own composition praising the stars of the Great Bear, that Sickle of the Valar, hung in the northern sky by Elbereth as an assurance to all on Middle-earth that Morgoth would fall some day. Lúthien then intoned a rune of such power that the whole island shook.

Sauron recognized it as coming from Lúthien. The situation was now ripe for a Contest of Spells like that in which Sauron overcame Felagund not long before. But Sauron feared to undertake it against so powerful an enchantress as Lúthien. So he refused her challenge and set out to capture her for Morgoth by means of his werewolves. He assaulted her with wolf after wolf but Huan silently killed them all, even Draugluin, father of werewolves, although Draugluin was able to report to the wizard before he died that his slayer was Huan.

Sauron knew that Huan would die if assailed by the strongest of all wolves on Middle-earth. Therefore he himself took on wolf's shape, accounting himself the strongest wolf that had ever existed, and he sprang at Lúthien. Before she swooned at the horror of him, she managed to throw over his eyes a fold of her cloak, whose spell of sleep made him stumble drowsily for a moment. Huan then sprang in his turn and seized Sauron by the throat, holding his fierce grip while his victim shifted his shape from wolf to serpent and then back to that of his usual body. Without some sort of body which he could enter and possess, Sauron would not have been able to continue living on Eä. Huan's teeth in his throat were about to slay the body he always wore, thus driving him out of the world. But Lúthien mercifully intervened, promising to let him go free if he would surrender to her his control of Tol Sirion.

Sauron gladly yielded it and flew away to Dorthonion in the form of a vampire dripping blood, where he darkened the land with horror. Rid of him, Lúthien uttered a spell so strong that it undid the spell which Sauron had used to bind together the stones that made up his fortress. So the whole of it collapsed—walls, gates, and dungeons. Many captives emerged from the rubble, but not Beren. Seeking him, Lúthien searched everywhere among the ruins until she found him in a swoon of mourning near the corpse of Felagund. She thought him dead and, taking him in her arms, slipped into oblivion. But Beren, reviving, lifted her up to life. And their reunion was like a sunrise to them both.

Together they buried Felagund in a green grave on Tol Sirion, now cleansed of evil. It remained green until the invading seas flooded all of Beleriand, when, at last, the Valar overcame Morgoth and shut him out into the everlasting Void. Meanwhile Beren and Lúthien wandered in the Forest of Brethil freely, and unhurt even by Winter, for wherever Lúthien went there also went Spring.

Many of the prisoners released from Tol Sirion returned to Nargothrond telling of Felagund's heroic death. That tale turned the hearts of its citizens away from the treasons of Celegorm and Curufin the Crafty, and back to loyalty for the House of Finarfin and, specifically, for Orodreth, the brother whom Felagund had set over them as Steward. Orodreth did not order the death of the two sons of Fëanor because, after all, they were his kin and he had no wish to attract the Curse of Mandos to himself and his city. But he did exile them to their brothers in East Beleriand. Only Celebrimbor, who repudiated the deeds of his father Curufin, did Orodreth allow to remain. In the Second Age this youth was to become the splendid smith who made for Sauron the Rings of Power.

Accompanied still by Huan the hound, until then faithful, Celegorm and his brother rode through Dimbar, being minded to dare the dangers of Nan Dungortheb to reach Maedhros on the Hill of Himring. It happened that they came upon Beren and Lúthien walking and talking unwarily in the Forest of Brethil. Celegorm, still lusting after Lúthien's beauty, as he had when Huan first brought her to him on the Guarded Plain, treacherously tried to rid himself of a rival by riding Beren down with his horse. At the same time Curufin, bending over, lifted Lúthien to his saddle as he swept past her. But Beren, with a leap which became renowned, avoided Celegorm and jumped up behind Curufin, grasping him around the neck. They both fell off the horse, and Lúthien also.

While Beren was throttling Curufin on the ground, he was saved from a death on Celegorm's spear by Huan, who then for the first time turned against his former master and kept him at bay. Unhurt by her fall, Lúthien in her mercy would not let Beren kill Curufin, although Beren did confiscate his horse and his weapons, including the knife Angrist. Celegorm took up his brother to ride behind him on his horse. But Curufin's vileness was not yet over. As he rode away he snatched Celegorm's bow and shot an arrow at Lúthien, which Huan caught in his mouth. Then he shot another shameful arrow at her which Beren, ever willing to sacrifice himself for others, and stepping in front of her, received in his own breast.

Wise Huan brought to Lúthien from the woods a healing herb (perhaps the *athelas* later used by Aragorn in *The Lord of the Rings*) which she applied to the perilous wound. With her medical arts and with her love she cured him. And he led her into the Forest of Neldoreth.

Before the unlooked-for attack by the two sons of Fëanor, Beren had been so enjoying the happiness of Lúthien's presence by his side that he had been putting off, and indeed half-forgetting, the execution of his pledge to steal a Silmaril from Morgoth. From this exploit, he had always been sure, he could never emerge alive. But he had promised himself that after bringing Lúthien to the safety of Doriath he would attempt the task. And she had told him that, whether he did or not, she would refuse to be separated from him. But Beren had resolved secretly in his

heart that separated they must be, for he would not take her
with him into death.

So, after he had been healed of his wound in the Forest
of Neldoreth, which was within the confines of Doriath,
Beren rode away early one morning on Curufin's horse to
the Pass of Sirion, leaving Lúthien asleep in Huan's care.
From the Pass he could see the peaks of Thangorodrim
soaring above the ashen plain of Anfauglith. There he set
the horse free and, knowing himself about to die, composed
and sang a *Song of Parting* (p. 178) to the Earth on which
Lúthien had danced, an Earth made worthy of existence by
her presence on it, even were it now to vanish back into the
abyss from which it came. Presumably this Song, couched
in iambic rhyming couplets, came from the Lay of Leithian, although Tolkien does not expressly say so. Lúthien,
however, was not to be left behind so easily and, mounted
on Huan, had been pursuing Beren. She heard his Song and
answered it.

As yet neither of the lovers had devised a way of getting
inside Angband, much less stealing a Silmaril. But Huan
had. Turning aside to Tol Sirion, he clothed himself in the
hide of Draugluin the master werewolf he had killed there.
And Lúthien put on the skin of Thuringwethil, the vampire bat used by Sauron as a messenger between him and
Morgoth.

Catching up with Beren, they cast off their disguises and
Lúthien ran to his embrace. Beren's love for Lúthien gave
him joy at her coming but made it seem to him all the more
wrong to take her with him into the power of Morgoth. So
he tried again to dissuade her.

Then Huan spoke for the second time, warning Beren
that by loving him, a mortal, Lúthien had already made
herself subject to mortality too, and would die with him
no matter what course he chose. The real question was
what Beren would choose. He might "turn from his

fate" and take Lúthien with him, wandering the world in exile and seeking inner peace in vain until they died. Or he might "challenge the fate" that lay before them by taking her with him to confront Morgoth. The outcome of such a challenge, Huan added cryptically, was "hopeless, yet not certain," that is, it might look completely hopeless yet be in fact only uncertain, and not without hope (p. 179).

Obviously the confrontation of Morgoth was what Huan recommended. And when the choice was put in that light Beren saw immediately that it was the only honorable course, as well as the one assigned to him by Providence, which Huan called Fate or Doom. It remained only to reassume the disguises, but this time it was Beren who decked himself out in the werewolf hide of Draugluin. Lúthien assumed the vampire pelt as before. Huan, remaining behind, needed no disguise.

Passing by chasms full of serpents and cliffs where carrion birds nested, the two came to Angband's impregnable gates surmounted by topless precipices. What gave them pause there was the vast werewolf guarding that gate. Morgoth, expecting Huan, had reared one of Draugluin's whelps, hand-feeding him with living meat, and had "put his power upon him" until a devouring spirit filled the monster Carcharoth, the Red Maw, with "the fire and anguish of hell" (p. 180).

This ravening beast was not without a mind, for he remembered that Draugluin had been reported slain. Therefore he stopped Beren, clad in the hide of his ancestor. All would have ended in disaster there, had not Lúthien summoned up the power of her Vala birth through Melian, which enabled her to order Carcharoth to sleep. The words she uttered to Carcharoth showed not only her power but her compassion for what Morgoth had made of him: "O woe-begotten spirit, fall now into dark oblivion, and forget for a while the dreadful doom of life." Lúthien never wished harm to anyone, even Curufin, and had a matchless beauty of spirit as well as of body.

So the lovers descended where none had gone before them but the slaves of Morgoth, to Angband's lowest depths. There Morgoth himself held court, sitting upon his throne and wearing his iron crown in which were set the three Silmarils, blazing. There Beren hid himself like a wolf under the throne. But Morgoth's will stripped Lúthien of the bat's fell she wore, exposing her beauty to his lustful eyes.

While he stared at her he left her unbound so that she had time to slip into the shadows and to sing a spell of such power that he was blinded and could not see her. It put all Morgoth's court to sleep, and himself it weakened until his head bowed low under the weight of his crown and of the Silmarils now brilliantly radiant on it. And Lúthien, donning her vampire wings and soaring upward, threw her coat of darkness over his eyes and sent him a dark dream, under which he slid from his seat and lay prostrate "upon the floors of hell," while his crown rolled away (p. 181).

Even Beren lay asleep with all the rest, but Lúthien wakened him. Then with the knife Angrist, taken from Curufin, he pried a single Silmaril from the setting which bound it to the crown. Thinking, then, to take all three of the Silmarils while he had the chance, he started to pry out another, but since that was not their destiny the knife snapped in his hand and the broken piece cut Morgoth's face, almost waking him and all his court.

Beren and Lúthien fled up the endless stairs with their one Silmaril, only to find Carcharoth roused and waiting for them at the gate. Lúthien was too weary to devise another spell against him. So Beren, holding up the Silmaril, bade him be gone lest its fire consume him as it consumed all evil creatures. But the huge werewolf was too hungry to be afraid of the "holy jewel," and he bit off and swallowed both it and the right hand of Beren that held it.

Beren not being evil, the Silmaril had never burned him. But as he had warned, no sooner had Carcharoth swallowed it than it seared all his inner organs with incessant pangs and sent him howling in anguished madness, killing every living thing he met as he burst into Beleriand.

Still at the Gate of Angband, Beren lay near death from his severed wrist, envenomed by the werewolf's teeth, and Lúthien had only enough strength left to suck out the poison and staunch his wound's bleeding. From the depths below them came the vengeful noises of Morgoth and his host awakening and starting the pursuit. Just in time, alerted by Huan, the King of Eagles, Thorondor, with two of his vassals flew up from the south and bore them high above the clouds, above the lightning bolts hurled after them by Morgoth. Nor did the Eagles set them down until they reached the very dell in the Forest of Neldoreth from which Beren had stolen away from Lúthien to consummate his mission.

There Huan came to Lúthien. Together they nursed Beren as they had done before, when he was wounded in the chest by the arrow of Curufin. But the present wound was far worse, being more grievous in itself and complicated by dire poison. Long did Beren's spirit wander on the very borders of death, but Lúthien's love drew him back to life at last.

Spring came again, to the woods and to their hearts. Again the lovers roved among the trees, and Lúthien would gladly have stayed there without ever returning to her father's court. However, Beren considered it his duty to take her back to Menegroth, where she might live a life more fit for her. Upon his persuasion they returned together.

They found there a grieving king and a saddened kingdom. Daeron, greatest of minstrels, had long loved Lúthien and had written the music for her dancing and singing. After her disappearance he had wandered somewhere to the east and had never come home. And Thingol had been sending streams of messengers to Nargothrond and Himring and everywhere else he could think of, seeking word of her, in vain.

Then miraculously, as it seemed, Lúthien the lost, the loved, came home with Beren to Menegroth, followed by rejoicing crowds of Thingol's people, and presented themselves before his throne. Kneeling there, Beren claimed Lúthien. Asked by Thingol about his vow not to return without having taken a Silmaril from Morgoth, Beren declared he had fulfilled it. And, asked again to show the Jewel, Beren opened his left hand, which was empty, and held up his right arm, which had on it no hand at all. Thingol understood his meaning.

Seated one on each side of his throne, Lúthien and Beren told aloud to all the events of their quest. Hearing them the King looked at Beren with new eyes and saw how worthy he was, though a mere mortal. And the love between Beren and Lúthien he recognized as a marvel the like of which had never happened before, and which no power on Middle-earth could undo. So he smiled on their marriage.

Even as he did so, news came of the depredations of Carcharoth within Thingol's realm, all the more to be feared because of the Silmaril he had swallowed, which caused the Wolf anguish but increased his strength until he was well-nigh invincible. Accordingly, the King led against the beast a small but select band consisting of Huan and Beren and his two chief captains, Mablung and Beleg. They cornered their prey in a dark valley where Carcharoth was quenching his insatiable thirst at a waterfall of the River Esgalduin.

The Wolf went to ground among the brakes. His hunters waited for him to emerge. Impatiently Huan went in after him, at last, whereupon Carcharoth suddenly sprang out upon Thingol. Beren stepped in front of the King with his spear ready. But the Wolf, sweeping aside the puny weapon, cast Beren down and tore at his breast with fierce poisonous fangs.

Beren was rescued in turn by Huan, who leaped on Carcharoth's back. Thereupon ensued a battle so deadly and clamorous that the very rocks split and fell into the river from the heights above it. They killed each other, those two, one armed with the wrath of the Valar, the other with the hate of Morgoth. But Thingol paid them no heed, for he was trying to staunch the wound Beren had incurred for his sake.

Mablung and Beleg, running up, wept to see Beren lying there so still. And Mablung, ripping apart the Wolf's stomach with his knife, found the Silmaril still clutched in Beren's hand, which was as incorrupt as that of a saint, although long severed. Mablung gave the Silmaril to Beren, who gave it to Thingol as he had promised from the first, saying that now was his own doom "full-wrought" (p. 186). After that, he never spoke again, but he lived long enough to see and hear Lúthien when she kissed him, "bidding him await her beyond the Western Sea" (in the halls of Mandos in Valinor), for she had already determined within herself that they must be together after death.

As she requested, Beren's spirit remained in Mandos' halls, waiting for her to come to say goodbye. And come she soon did, because she could not live long without him. Normally Beren's spirit, like that of all Mortal Men, should have set out from "the dim shores of the Outer Sea" (that is, the Sea encircling all of Eä) to some destination unknown, perhaps directly to Ilúvatar. But had it done so Lúthien's spirit could never have accompanied it and would probably have had to remain in Mandos' halls with the spirits of all Elves until the end of the World, awaiting some kind of ultimate reckoning, perhaps a judgment by Ilúvatar.

"But her beauty was more than their beauty, and her sorrow deeper than their sorrows," writes Tolkien, which is his way of saying that as the daughter of a union between a Maia and an Elf she was not all Elf. She was in fact unique, for there was no record of any other such union in all the annals of Eä. So she sang on her knees before Mandos the most lovely and most sorrowful song he had ever heard. Bemoaning the separate lots which befell Elves and Men after death, she begged that hers be not different from Beren's. Both kindreds were made by Ilúvatar to dwell together in life, and they should dwell together in death also, she said.

Mandos, a pure Justice who had never before been moved to pity, was moved then, and he summoned Beren's spirit to meet Lúthien's, not in the halls reserved for the brief sojourns of Mortal Men but in those reserved for the Age-long sojourn of Elves. But he had no power to hold the spirits of Men permanently in any of his halls. These were all "within the confines of the world," and retaining Men there would have amounted to withholding from them Death, which was the gift of Ilúvatar to the second race of his Children. Mandos therefore took Lúthien's appeal to Manwë, to whom Ilúvatar revealed his Will in this sad case.

This Will offered Lúthien a choice between two courses. She could go to live with the Valar in the holy city of Valmar until the World's end, untouched by past griefs. But there Beren could not come with her lest he be deprived of the Gift of Death. Or, alternatively, she might choose to return with Beren to Beleriand. There they would both live a second life and die a second death, for she would become as mortal as he, enduring briefly all the pangs and uncertainties inherent in Men's lives.[3]

This latter choice Lúthien eagerly accepted. It gave her all that she wanted, a future which would be the same as Beren's both in life and in death. By this choice she sealed together the two kindreds. And the Eldar saw in her the forerunner of many who would choose as she did in ages to come.

Returning to Middle-earth as mortal man and woman, Beren and Lúthien came first to Doriath, where Lúthien healed Thingol's weariness with a touch of her hand. And there Melian, looking into her daughter's eyes, grieved to discern there her humanity, for it meant that they would soon be parted by Lúthien's death, a parting which would endure even after the end of the World.

These farewells said, Beren and Lúthien went to settle in Ossiriand on the island of Tol Galen in the midst of the River Adurant. There Lúthien bore Beren a son named Dior Aranel, heir of Thingol (p. 306). Later on, Dior's son, Eärendil the mariner, guided by the Silmaril delivered to Thingol by Beren, was to cross the Great Sea to Valinor and to succeed in persuading the armies of the Valar to overthrow Morgoth at last.

So ends the tale of Beren and Lúthien, replete with deep personal meanings for Tolkien and related by him with a grandeur of eloquence which he never surpassed.

IX

The Battle of Unnumbered Tears:
Nirnaeth Arnoediad

BESIDES A NUMBER of lesser skirmishes and probes, the Noldor and Sindar Elves in Beleriand fought against Morgoth five major battles over a period of some five and a half centuries. Upon the outcome of these great encounters depended not only the safety of individual lives but also their hopes as a race, their outlook upon the future, and the pursuits they were able to carry on between battles. For with Morgoth, as the Noldor discovered in the first peace conference, attended by Maedhros, there could be neither compromise nor lasting peace but only total victory or utter defeat. This series of battles, therefore, was like a spine on which hung everything else that was precious to them. So the military element must be seen as a paramount factor at work in the whole of *Quenta Silmarillion*.

The Noldor vanguard under Fëanor arrived at Lake Mithrim to find themselves in the midst of a war already launched by Morgoth against King Thingol of Doriath. The Black Enemy had sent two Orc armies against him, one to his east, the other to his west. With the help of the Green-elves of Ossiriand, Thingol had beaten off the eastern thrust, but meanwhile the western army had vanquished the foes of his ally, Círdan, and driven them back south to the Falas on the seacoast.

Having long expected a landing of foes from Valinor in

Hithlum where Lake Mithrim lay, Morgoth immediately dispatched a third Orc army against the Noldor there. But this onslaught was repelled by Fëanor and his vanguard, who pursued its survivors to the plains of Ard-galen, where Fëanor met his death. Hastening northward to the help of these survivors, the Orc victors over Círdan became the victims of a Noldor ambush captained by Celegorm, third son of Fëanor, and were wiped out. The battle of Thingol against the Orcs to his east was actually the First Battle but it received no Elvish name. The Second Battle, however, consisting of the victories of Fëanor and Celegorm, came to be called Dagor-nuin-Giliath, the Battle-under-Stars, because it occurred just before the Moon and the Sun were sent up into the sky by the Valar to illumine Beleriand.

About fifty years later came the Third Battle, Dagor Agloreb, the Glorious Battle, in which Fingolfin from the west and Maedhros from the east converged upon a host of Orcs on the slopes of Dorthonion and annihilated them. This victory enabled the Noldor to establish a partial siege of Angband on its south and west.

A long peace of some four centuries lasted while Morgoth prepared new armies and new methods. Then came suddenly his Fourth Battle, Dagor Bragollach, the Battle of Sudden Flame, so named because Morgoth's use of streams of swift-running lava, and Balrogs, and the newly matured dragon, Glaurung, struck terror into the Noldor besiegers. So irresistible an onslaught overran their strongholds, breaking the siege of Angband. The Men of the Houses of Bëor, Hador, and Haladin, who had lately entered Beleriand, fought bravely as allies of the Noldor, but in vain.

Some forty years later (about the year 495), Morgoth won his decisive victory in the Fifth Battle, Nirnaeth Arnoediad, Tears Unnumbered, as foretold in the Curse of Mandos: "Tears unnumbered ye shall shed"[1] (p. 88). Through the treachery of the Easterlings was this overwhelming defeat engendered, as will be seen. The passes of the north

were laid open to Morgoth's hosts, and they harried southward as they pleased, seeking out one by one the fortress
cities of Nargothrond, Doriath, Tol Sirion, and Gondolin,
and sacking them.

*   *   *

The heroic duel of Fingolfin with Morgoth, followed by
the recovery of a Silmaril from him by Beren and Lúthien
in the very depths of Angband, made Morgoth seem less
formidable than before, though the seeming was false.
There were no more such heroes at hand to hurt him again.
But Maedhros in particular was badly shaken by the return
of the Silmaril to the scene, because ever since coming to
Beleriand he had been doing his utmost to live down the
dire deeds of Fëanor and restore friendship with the other
Noldor leaders, both for himself and for his brothers.

Now the sudden appearance of the Silmaril in Thingol's
hands awakened the hateful, sleeping Oath which all seven
of them had sworn with their father. In despair Maedhros
feared that the actions which this Oath might require them
to take would alienate them all again from their Noldor
kin. His mind ranged round and round in a turmoil. He
could not break the solemn Oath he had sworn with his
father.[2] Yet if he could persuade Thingol to give up the one
Silmaril in his possession and if, by defeating Morgoth
once for all, he could take the other two Silmarils from him,
all occasions of conflict with the other Noldor would be
removed. He failed to see that the selfish Oath could never
bring about an unselfish peace.

He therefore joined with his brothers in writing to Thingol a demand that the King surrender his Silmaril to them
as its rightful owners. Melian urged Thingol to comply but
he refused, remembering the cost of its acquisition, and
thirsting more and more in his greed to keep it ever for
himself. Always the flaw of possessiveness lay deep in his
nature, as many of his previous actions have shown. Also,

possession of a Silmaril seems always to have laid this temptation upon its possessor.

Leaving this refusal unanswered, Maedhros pressed on with the military side of his plan by forming the Union of Maedhros (p. 188), designed to bring together in one alliance all the foes of Morgoth. To potential members of the Union he pointed out what was all too true, that without it Morgoth would pick them off one by one. In this he had the support of his friend Fingon, eldest son of Fingolfin, who, since his father's death, had become High King of the Noldor and ruler of Hithlum. The strategy they adopted called for each to muster all the allies he had and, on an appointed day, simultaneously to descend upon Angband from east and west, when Maedhros lighted a signal beacon on a peak in Dorthonion.

In his recruitments, however, Maedhros found himself badly handicapped by the misdoings and proud words of Celegorm and Curufin at Nargothrond. King Orodreth there had too vivid memories of their treasons to trust any son of Fëanor. Yet, against the King's will, Gwindor, one of the princes of that city, took northward with him a small force of Elves to serve under Fingon. From Doriath came only Mablung and Beleg, and they too, at Thingol's orders, joined not Maedhros but Fingon.

In addition to these trickles Fingon had with him the Men of Hador from Dor-lómin and ax-men from among the Haladin in the Forest of Brethil. Also the Elves of the Falas had come to him. And, most wonderful of all, after the Fifth Battle had been under way for several days, he could hear the trumpets of King Turgon of Gondolin sounding as, from his hidden city in the south, he marched up to Fingon's aid with ten thousand Elves.

On the eastern flank, Maedhros had from his brothers only remnants of the murderous Fourth Battle, but happily he received from the Naugrim of Nogrod and Belegost much substantial aid in weapons and warriors. Also Mae-

dhros trained for war the Easterlings led by Bór and Ulfang the Black, and they called into Beleriand others of
their race from beyond the Ered Luin.

As a preliminary, before the day agreed upon with Fingon, Maedhros saw the need of cleaning out all the Orc
bands still in East Beleriand and Dorthonion lest they
strike at his back. In this he succeeded, though the fighting
warned Morgoth of more to come and so lost Maedhros the
crucial advantage of surprise.

When the appointed day arrived, the armies of both Fingon and Maedhros stood poised for the attack. Maedhros
was to advance first, and Fingon was to wait until the
lighted beacon signaled that Maedhros had launched his
prong of the joint assault. But Maedhros, trusting Uldor
the Easterling, had been using him as a scout to report
Morgoth's movements, and Uldor now came crying that a
great host of Orcs was almost upon them. This was a lie,
for Uldor was a servant of Morgoth. But Maedhros believed it and decided to await their attack on the Hill of
Himring, where he could most surely hold off the foe. But
none came against him all that day or the next and, too late,
he knew himself deceived.

Depending on Uldor to delay Maedhros, Morgoth sent
a huge army of Orcs (yet only a fraction of all that he had
readied) to Hithlum, under strict orders to lure Fingon at
all costs from the bulwarks of the Ered Wethrin range and
out upon the open plain. So the Orc Captain marched his
Orcs up and down before Fingon's troops, taunting them
as cowards and challenging them to come out and fight.
This device failing, he sent heralds to them with a request
for parley. These took with them Gelmir of Nargothrond,
whom Orcs had captured in the Fourth Battle and had
afterward blinded. In plain sight they proceeded to cut off
Gelmir's hands and feet and, finally, his head.

Unluckily his brother Gwindor, just come from Nargothrond, was stationed nearby and saw the foul deed. Furi-

ously he leaped on his horse and, accompanied by those around him, slew the murderers and charged deep into their lines. Then Fingon and all his army charged also, sweeping aside all opposition until they came to Angband itself, where they broke through its great gate and fought the guards on the stairs leading down to the throne room of Morgoth. It seemed to Fingon then that he was close to final success. But through many secret doors Morgoth's main host swarmed out behind Fingon and encircled him. He was obliged to retreat homeward, cutting his way through them with dreadful losses. And next day the Orcs pressed his people together more and more tightly, slaying many.

To their rescue then hastened Turgon with a phalanx of his personal guard, which cut its way through to Fingon. Also, at last the trumpets of Maedhros could be heard nearing from the east. Arriving, he assailed the encircling Orcs from their rear. But Angband likewise had new strength to pour out—its last, consisting of Wolves and wolfriders, Balrogs, and Dragons led by Glaurung their progenitor. With all their terror these fresh reinforcements rushed between the armies of Fingon and Maedhros and drove them far apart.

Even then, the Fifth Battle might have been won had it not been for the Easterlings. Some indeed remained loyal, as did the sons of Bór, who fought to the death. But many others fled. And the final blow came when Uldor and his brothers defected to Morgoth. Turning suddenly against Maedhros' force, they struck at it from the back, even penetrating to the standard of Maedhros, where Maglor killed Uldor the Accursed. Before he died, however, Uldor called in new battalions of Easterlings he had kept hidden hitherto in the hills.

Beset on three sides, Maedhros' army melted away. "Yet fate saved the sons of Fëanor" for a future unforeseen, although all bore wounds. With a remnant of the Noldor and with their Naugrim allies, they cut their way out and escaped to Mount Dolmed, a peak in the Ered Luin (p. 193).

Last of all the followers of Maedhros to leave that stricken field were the main body of the Naugrim of Belegost. Accustomed to their smithies, they could endure the heat of fire better than any Elf or Man. Besides, they wore in battle huge masks which protected them against the flames breathed out by Morgoth's Dragons. These enabled them to stand close and hew away at the plates of Glaurung's armor. That monster did manage to strike down Azaghâl, Lord of Belegost, but not before the Dwarf leader contrived to pierce the soft underbelly with his blade. Glaurung and his brood fled in fear. Only then did the Dwarves, carrying the corpse of their Lord, return to their homes in the Blue Mountains.

While these desperate events were afoot on the battle's eastern front, things in the west went no better. Fingon, standing alone amid the corpses of his guard, fought with Gothmog, Lord of Balrogs, as Fëanor had once fought, until another of this evil race striking from behind with a whip of fire tied Fingon's arms and left him helpless against the blows of Gothmog's ax. So died Fingon, High King of the Noldor.

But Turgon fought on, as did the survivors of the House of Hador, led by Húrin and Huor. Then these two urged Turgon to leave them and return with his army to hidden Gondolin. Húrin argued that Gondolin by its very existence would continue to put fear into Morgoth's heart; and Huor foresaw that from himself and Turgon "a new star shall arise"—an almost literal vision of Eärendil's ship riding the sky (p. 194).

Shielded by what was left of the Hador of Dor-lómin, Turgon consented to escape with his army to Gondolin. Slowly the Hador withdrew behind the Fen of Serech and, thereafter, gave ground no more. In that famous last stand each died where he stood, all save Húrin, who was taken alive at Morgoth's express command and brought back to Angband, there to suffer a special torment devised for him.

Thus ended the Fifth (and last) Battle of Beleriand: Nirnaeth Arnoediad, the Battle of Unnumbered Tears, which had been foretold in the Doom of Mandos.

And indeed after that disaster many were the dead to be wept for by the survivors. Fingon lay slain and, with him, all of his Noldor except those whom Morgoth had captured and sent to work as slaves in his mines north of Angband. Slain too were all the fighting men of the House of Hador, leaving in Hithlum only old men, women, and children. Morgoth repeopled that province with the Easterlings who had aided him, but such was his ingratitude that he shut them in there as in a prison, not to depart without his leave.

The roster of the dead went on and on. Included were many Elves of the Falas commissioned by Círdan to help Fingon, as well as most of the Haladin from Brethil. And in the east had fallen almost the entire host of Maedhros— Elves, the loyal Easterlings, and many of the stubborn Naugrim. Maedhros and his brothers were reduced to a wandering life in the foothills of the Ered Lindon and among the Green-elves in Ossiriand (p. 195).

In short, the whole organized defense of Beleriand's borders against Morgoth existed no longer. Through the unguarded passes of Sirion, Aglon, and the March of Maedhros, Orcs and wolves came at will, and as far south as they willed, even to the willows of Nan-tathren, not far above the Mouths of Sirion. True, Doriath and Nargothrond and Gondolin were as yet unconquered, but Morgoth only postponed their time of tears.

He still had a score to settle with Círdan's Elves of the Falas. Consequently, in the year after the Fifth Battle, he sent an immense legion of Orcs through Hithlum and Nevrast southward along the coast of the Great Sea. One by one they besieged and leveled the strongholds which the Noldor had helped Círdan build in years past: first Brithombar, then Eglarest, and finally the watchtower of Barad Nimras. The lands between they ravaged, killing or enslaving virtually all the Elves who dwelt there. Only a few escaped by boarding ships and sailing with Círdan to the Isle of Balar. Among them went Ereinion Gil-galad, son of Fingon, who remained on Middle-earth after the First Age and, in the Second Age, captained with Elendil the Last Alliance of Men and Elves against Sauron.[3]

Morgoth's Orcs, who hated and feared the Sea and Ulmo, its Lord, never even tried to overrun the Isle of Balar, or the Mouths of Sirion either, where Círdan kept ships of shallow draft hidden among the reeds. King Turgon in Gondolin, hearing of these happenings, persuaded Círdan to build seven seaworthy ships which, sailing westward, tried to reach Valinor to beg for help. But through the storms and enchantments with which the Valar safeguarded their land none of these ships could go, and none ever returned except one, which foundered within sight of the coast. From that wreck only one passenger was cast ashore, Voronwë, whom Turgon had sent forth from Gondolin.

But no matter how numberless the tears to be shed for others or how bleak their own future, Morgoth's opponents in the Fifth Battle never gave up hope. When Fingon heard the trumpets of his brother Turgon coming up from the south to aid him, he shouted, "*Utúlie'n aurë! Aiya Eldalië ar Atanatári, utúlie'n aurë!* The day has come! Behold, people of the Eldar and Fathers of Men, the day has come!" And all who heard him cried, "*Auta i lómë!* The night is passing!" (p. 190). It cannot be an accident that Húrin, standing alone among the trolls and killing seventy of them with seventy blows of his smoking ax, carried on the affirmation, shouting "*Aurë entuluva!* Day shall come again!" (p. 195). In the deepest sense the conquered remained unconquered, even though Orcs took Húrin alive at Morgoth's command and dragged him mockingly to Angband.

But Morgoth could not rest while Turgon, who on the death of his brother Fingon had become High King of the Noldor, still lived to threaten him. Moreover, whenever their paths had crossed in Valinor long ago, Morgoth had felt a foreboding that one day ruin would come to him from this foe. And he feared the threat.

Knowing that Húrin could tell him where Gondolin lay, Morgoth questioned him, but met only with rebuff and mockery. Therefore he cursed Húrin and his wife and children and "set a doom of darkness and sorrow" upon them (p. 197). And setting Húrin in a seat high on Thangorodrim, Morgoth cursed him again and told him to watch the working out of the curse in the events below.[4] There, as long years passed, Húrin saw without flinching every step of the tragedy to come.

X

Túrin Turambar, Master of Doom

TOLKIEN began work on the story of Túrin as early as 1917 and at first called it "The Children of Húrin." Originally it was written in "an alliterative measure, a modern version of the Anglo-Saxon verse form," according to Carpenter, who gives several lines as a sample (p. 167). In style, then, it resembled *The Homecoming of Beorhtnoth*,[1] a playlet by Tolkien also couched in a loose alliterative form. Carpenter remarks (p. 73) that Tolkien himself said that he adapted the tale of Túrin from the story of Kullervo in the Finnish *Kalevala*.

The adaptation is close enough. The tale of Kullervo in Runos XXXI–XXXVII of *Kalevala* contains no hypnotic dragon like Glaurung but brings about the unknowing incest by more natural means. After a war in which Untamo defeats Kalervo, the latter's little son, Kullervo, is reared by the victor as a slave until he grows up, slays his master, and escapes. Finding that his family is still alive, although his eldest sister (whom he has never seen) has been lost in the forest while picking berries, he returns home. He is sent to pay his family's taxes and, during the journey, meets a succession of maidens who refuse his lewd invitations to come into his sledge. Finally he drags one in by force and dazzles her with gifts until she succumbs to his embraces. They compare family backgrounds. Both realize that she is his lost sister. On the way home she throws herself into a river and drowns.

Returning later to that same spot, Kullervo asks his sword (as Túrin does) whether it will kill him. It promises to do so because he is evil. He falls upon it and dies. Old Väinämöinen, speaking through the minstrel who sings the story, moralizes on the bad upbringing which caused Kullervo to grow into the wayward Man he has become.

As usual, Tolkien starts the Tale of Túrin not in its middle, like a Greek tragedy, but at its very beginning with the births of Túrin and his first sister Lalaith, Laughter, in Dor-lómin a few years before the Battle of Unnumbered Tears. From that their father Húrin did not return. We know why. Lalaith died of a plague at the age of three, but Túrin lived on in Dor-lómin long enough to suffer the oppressions of the perjured Easterlings whom Morgoth brought in to populate and rule the land. Fearing that they would enslave Túrin, his mother Morwen sent him at the age of eight to be fostered at the court of King Thingol in Doriath. And after he left, she bore to Húrin yet another daughter named Nienor, Mourning, whom Túrin had never seen.

Thingol sent messengers to Morwen inviting her and Nienor to live in Doriath under his protection but, unwilling to leave the house where she and Húrin had lived so long together, she refused. She did, however, entrust to his messengers the Dragon-helm[2] of the House of Hador to be delivered to Túrin as the most ancient of heirlooms. Until Túrin became seventeen years old, messengers from Dor-lómin continued to bring him encouraging news from home, but after that none whatever. Grim with grief, Túrin armed himself, donned his Dragon-helm, and joined Beleg Strongbow, chief of the marchwardens, in the fighting always going on along the borders of Doriath. For the times grew more and more evil after the defeats of the Fifth Battle, and Orcs came and went freely in places where they had never come before.

After three years of this service Túrin returned briefly

to Menegroth for a rest, his clothes ragged, his hair and beard uncut. There at table a Nandor Elf named Saeros, a counselor of the King but jealous of Túrin's honor as his foster son, made insulting remarks about his appearance and asked sarcastically whether the women of Dor-lómin went about naked save for their hair.

Túrin in anger threw a cup at him, inflicting a wound that bled. Next day, when Saeros ambushed him on his way back to the front, Túrin got the better of him, stripped off his clothes in revenge, and sent him fleeing naked through the woods. Falling into a river chasm, he broke his back and died. Thereupon Mablung, chief Captain of Thingol, urged Túrin to state his case before the King and sue for pardon. But Túrin, assuming prematurely for no good reason that the sentence would go against him, joined a band of desperate outlaws who preyed on anyone they met, be he Elf, Man, or Orc.[3]

Although Túrin did not return for trial, King Thingol himself looked into all the facts surrounding the death of Saeros, found Túrin innocent of any crime, and lovingly pardoned him. Bearing these tidings from the King, Beleg searched long and far for Túrin, who had meantime become captain of the outlaw band and, with the prideful self-pity which flawed his character, had named himself Neithan, the Wronged. He happened to be away from camp on the night when Beleg found it at last and received from the outlaws a cruel welcome. Thinking him a spy, they bound and mistreated him. On his return Túrin saw the sad state Beleg was in, rescued him, and renounced his enmity toward all except those who belonged to Angband.

Beleg not only told Túrin of the King's pardon but also buttressed his plea for Túrin's return by describing how the Orcs were on the move everywhere, building a road down the Pass of Anach and taking over Dimbar. But, writes Tolkien, "In the pride of his heart Túrin refused the pardon of the King," nor was he moved by Beleg's plea for help (p. 201).

Calling him "hard" and "stubborn," Beleg made ready to depart. If Túrin should ever need him, he said, let him look for him in Dimbar. But Túrin, always more adamant than he, retorted that, if Beleg wanted to see him again, let him come to the hill of Amon Rûdh, westward on the Guarded Plain of Nargothrond. Otherwise this would be their last farewell. So they parted, still friends but at a sad impasse.

Going back to Menegroth, Beleg told the King all that had befallen him. Whereupon Thingol asked Beleg wistfully what more Túrin expected him to do, beyond the pardon.

Beleg begged leave to find the King's foster son again, this time to stay with him always, guarding and guiding him. Gratefully the King consented and, as a parting gift, bestowed on him the sword Anglachel, forged by Eöl the Dark Elf from the iron of a fallen meteor. This Beleg had asked for as a weapon suited to infighting against Orcs, who were now pressing on him too many and too close for his bow to cope with them.

Although Melian warned him that Eöl had infused his own malice into the blade, rendering it perilous to wield, Beleg took it gladly and, along with it, a loaf of *lembas*,[4] waybread eaten by Elves on long journeys, to be given to Túrin when he should be found again. For a short while Beleg went into Dimbar to help the other marchwardens drive the Orcs out. Then he turned to search for Túrin on Amon Rûdh, as Túrin had directed at their parting.

Túrin had led his band to a safe lair on that steep hill. On the way they had met three undersized Dwarves and captured their leader, Mîm. The other two they shot at with arrows which, however, did not prevent them from escaping in the doubtful light of dusk. Mîm begged not to be killed; he promised, as his ransom from captivity, to show them his "hidden halls" on Amon Rûdh. Túrin spared him.

Next day he and his band followed Mîm as he led them upward on a secret path to his cave near the summit. There the vine *seregon* bloomed so red that one of the band saw it as a portent of "blood on the hill-top" (p. 203).

Túrin's dealings with the three Dwarves taught him pity. Mîm he had spared out of compassion. And when Túrin found him in one of the inner caves mourning for Khîm, his son, slain by that arrow shot after him at dusk, he would have given much to call back its fatal flight, for again he pitied Mîm. All he could do, however, was to promise to pay him gold as *wergeld* and as a mark of his sorrow, although mere gold could not ease his grief.

As Túrin talked often with Mîm in the passing days, he learned that the three Petty-Dwarves, as the Sindarin named them, were the last pitiful survivors of an ancient race who, banished from the Dwarf cities of the east, came first into Beleriand. Being unknown to the Elves there, they had been hunted like beasts and had gone into hiding. In that predicament they had dwindled in size and forgotten most of their skills as smiths. Yet they had been the first to dig the caves of Nargothrond (as well as Amon Rûdh) long before Finrod Felagund founded his city there. Hating the Grey-elves who had hunted them, and the Noldor who had stolen their homes, they had none to love but themselves. Now everywhere their smithies were cold, their axes rusted, and their very names known only to legend.

For many days Túrin listened with sympathy to this tale of long decay, but when Beleg unexpectedly returned one snowy winter night, his attention turned to his friend. Beleg won the favor of the outlaw band by healing them with gifts of *lembas* and impressing them with his strength of body and mind. But Mîm and his remaining son, Ibun, hated him because he was an Elf and had stolen Túrin's affection away from them.

To the band now captained by Túrin and Beleg came

many masterless Men and Elves, until the two leaders had under their command a formidable troop of warriors who resumed possession of the Guarded Plain. Morgoth, meanwhile, had been sending his thoughts southward to learn the plans of his enemies, but whenever he tried to read the thoughts of Melian he was blocked. Though he despatched Orc armies to find her, they always failed.

What they did find was that the once guarded Plain of Nargothrond between that kingdom and the forests of Doriath was again guarded, this time not by Nargothrond's Elves but by the mixed forces of Men and Elves secretly ensconced on Amon Rûdh. And the region they ruled had come to be known as the Land of Bow and Helm because there Strongbow's arrows flew and Túrin wore his Dragon-helm against the Orcs.

For Túrin had put on the Dragon-helm of Hador and had again renamed himself, this time as "Gorthol, the Dread Helm." Gone was his earlier self-appellation, "Neithian, the Wronged," and yet to come in his last days was "Turambar, Master of Doom." This restless changing of his name reveals something deep within his nature. Few indeed were the other Men who altered their names like this. It is as if he had no one continuing conception of himself but, rather, a series of temporary conceptions governed by the circumstances of the changing moment. This instability was to contribute to his tragic end. And it was not a trait imposed upon Túrin by Morgoth from outside but an inner need born within himself.

As soon as Túrin resumed the Dragon-helm and called himself Gorthol, he disclosed himself to Morgoth as the son of Húrin. By Morgoth's orders the Orcs encircled Amon Rûdh and, without attacking it frontally, waited until they captured Mîm and Ibun, whom they forced to show them the secret path to the summit. Out of a residual loyalty Mîm tried to stipulate that Túrin himself must not be slain, to which the Orc captain, laughing, assented readily; for his promise did not bind him not to take Túrin prisoner to Angband.

And that is precisely what happened. The Orcs, guided by Mîm, slew or wounded all the warriors on Amon Rûdh except Túrin, whom they entangled in a net which they threw over him before starting off on the return journey back to Morgoth. Though sorely wounded Beleg was not dead, and Mîm coming upon him tried to finish him off with Beleg's own sword, Anglachel. Beleg had just enough strength left to take back his sword from Mîm and thrust it through the traitor. Nor did Beleg die. Being a master of healing, he healed himself. He then looked for Túrin's body among the slain and, not finding it, knew that he must have been taken alive to Angband.

Beleg lost no time in following the tracks of the Orcs even into the haunted woods of Dorthonion, where among the roots of a huge dead tree he found Gwindor sleeping. He was that Noldor Lord of Nargothrond who had fought beside Fingon in the Fifth Battle, too rashly pursuing Orcs even to the downward stairs of Angband. But there, said Gwindor, he had been surrounded and taken. Morgoth had sent him, as he did with most of his Noldor captives, to labor in the northern mines digging for metals and gems. He had just escaped, emaciated and spent. Revived by Beleg's *lembas,* he told of seeing a company of Orcs pass that way a short time ago, whipping a tall man along the road to Angband, evidently Túrin.

Together Gwindor and Beleg stole upon the Orc camp nearby during a lucky storm of lightning and thunder, which the Orcs feared. After Beleg had killed the Wolf sentinels with his arrows, they were able to cut Túrin free from the tree to which he was fettered. And having carried Túrin away some distance, still bound, Beleg set about the work of cutting through, with the sword Anglachel, the fetters that still held him. But that malicious blade slipped and cut Túrin's foot instead.

Springing awake in the darkness, Túrin thought Beleg an Orc and, seizing the hateful steel, killed his friend with it. During a lightning flash Túrin saw what he had done. Despite a stirring in the Orc camp, he stood in the rain by Beleg's body, crazed, dumb, and weeping unshed tears.

After they had buried Beleg with his huge black bow, Gwindor took Anglachel and Melian's *lembas* and led Túrin, still dumb, to the Springs of Ivrin, where Fingolfin had held his feast of Reunion many years ago. There he urged Túrin to drink the water, kept pure by Ulmo. Túrin drank. And at last he was able to shed tears so that his madness passed away.

With Túrin sane again, Gwindor gave him back Anglachel, that fatal sword now black and blunt, a spoilage which Gwindor took to mean that it mourned for Beleg. And Túrin learned from Gwindor that, during his slavery in Angband's mines, Húrin was still there, still defying Morgoth, and that consequently Morgoth had laid a curse upon him and all his kin (p. 197). Túrin was all too ready to believe in the efficacy of this curse, for it was one of his weaknesses to lay blame for all the errors and misfortunes of his life upon some power or other which ruled his days, and which could not be escaped. In this he was unlike his father Húrin, whose stronger will refused to concede that Morgoth's will or that of any other could control him.

Gwindor took Túrin south to Nargothrond for further healing, but his sufferings had so aged Gwindor that only Finduilas, daughter of Orodreth the King, who had loved him before he left to fight in the Fifth Battle, still recognized him.

Túrin refused to allow Gwindor to introduce him in Nargothrond by any of his former names but gave himself another, newer name, "Agarwaen the son of Úmarth," the Bloodstained, son of Ill-fate, referring to his killing of Beleg. Yet Túrin was so impressive in speech and bearing that he won many hearts in the City, not least that of King

Orodreth. He looked like one of the great Noldor. Consequently many called him Adanedhel, the Elf-Man (p. 210).

The sword Anglachel, reforged but still black, flickered
with fire along its cutting edge. Túrin therefore renamed
it Gurthang, Iron of Death. So purposefully did he strike
with it on the Guarded Plain that he was referred to as
Mormegil, the Black Sword. The Elves gave him a Dwarf-
made coat of mail, and he found for himself in the armory
a gilded Dwarf-mask which he wore in battle, terrifying
those he fought against.

By these names and disguises Túrin buried himself so
deep under pseudonyms that virtually nobody in Nargothrond or outside it knew who he truly was. Against his
wishes, however, Finduilas began to give him her new love,
abandoning her old one for Gwindor. The latter then took
it upon himself to warn Finduilas against the dangers of
loving Túrin, who was merely a mortal soon to grow old,
whereas she was an Elf-maiden, immortal. The two races
should not mix. Moreover, said Gwindor, a dark doom lay
upon the Man, in which she must not entangle herself. For
although he called himself the Bloodstained, son of Ill-fate,
his true name was Túrin, son of Húrin, both of them pow-
erfully cursed by Morgoth.

Finduilas replied to Gwindor's advice only by saying
that Túrin did not return her love. But Túrin was furious
that Gwindor should "betray my right name, and call my
doom upon me, from which I would lie hid" (p. 211).

Evidently, whatever the reasons or impulses which
caused Túrin's frequent name-changing in the past, the
reason upon which he now fixed was the need to hide
himself from Morgoth's curse, of which he had just heard
for the first time. Gwindor no doubt had ulterior motives
in revealing Túrin's identity, but his reply to Túrin's accu-
sation was true: "The doom lies in yourself, not in your
name."

In other words, an armory of names could not turn aside

Morgoth's curse. Gwindor had spent years under Morgoth's fist and had come to believe that whatever Morgoth willed could not be avoided. As Húrin's continued defiance of Morgoth showed, Gwindor's fatalistic view was wrong, and his own escape from the mines likewise proved its wrongness. Yet Túrin's efforts to escape the curse by the expedient of name-changing were superficial. He would have done better to follow the example set by his father Húrin and resolutely will that, at whatever cost, he would not fear Morgoth's curse.

It happened, however, that Gwindor's revelation of the Mormegil as Túrin reached the ears of King Orodreth, who honored him highly for his father's sake. By means of these honors Túrin was enabled to change the military strategy of Nargothrond. Until then it had consisted of harrying its foes by stealth and ambush. Upon Túrin's advice, large open battle on the plains supplanted these small secret nibblings, and a stone bridge was built over the River Narog leading to the City's doors in order to permit swifter egress for its armies. Gwindor protested this policy in vain.

At first it was highly successful. Under Túrin's generalship broad areas were cleared of Orcs, to the east between the Rivers Narog and Sirion, and to the west as far as the River Nenning and the Falas. But through these temporary victories Morgoth discovered the whereabouts of Nargothrond, unknown to him before.

All this while Túrin, at his own request, remained known only as Mormegil, the Black Sword of Nargothrond, even in the rumors which reached Doriath. And this secrecy was to have unforeseen consequences. For when his mother Morwen and his sister Nienor at last came to live in Doriath they found Túrin gone long since, and no report afoot of whether he lived or died.

At this time two Elves of the people of Angrod, third son of Finarfin, came to Nargothrond with the news that they had seen great hosts of Orcs assembling near the Pass of

Sirion. Also the messengers brought with them a warning from Ulmo to prepare for the defense of the City by breaking down the new bridge across the Narog, closing its gates, and remaining on watch behind them. But Túrin prevailed in opposing these measures, especially the smashing of his bridge across the Narog, "for he was become proud and stern, and would order all things as he wished" (p. 212).

The Orc army, after first defeating the Men of Brethil, duly pressed on south against Nargothrond, preceded by the Dragon Glaurung, who with his fiery breath burned the Guarded Plain around him as he came. Then, disregarding the counsel of Ulmo, Túrin led out the host of the City onto the open plains. But the Orcs far exceeded in numbers what the scouts had reported, and Glaurung the Urulóki was there besides. Only Túrin wearing his Dwarf-mask could stand before him.

Trapped between the Rivers Narog and Ginglith, the strength of Nargothrond melted away. King Orodreth was slain and with him many more in the rout that followed. Gwindor, mortally wounded, Túrin carried from the fray and laid on the grass among the trees near at hand.

Gwindor, speaking with the verity of the dying, lamented Túrin's "prowess and pride" which had ruined Nargothrond. But with his last breath he urged Túrin to hurry back to the City and save Finduilas because "she alone stands between thee and thy doom." Túrin had no inkling of what he meant, but with the aid of hindsight we can understand him. Had Túrin loved and married Finduilas, he would not have married unwittingly his sister Nienor.

With a handful of survivors Túrin rode back in all haste to the City, only to find it already being sacked by Orcs, its women herded together outside the gates, waiting to be carried off to Angband as slaves. Among them stood Finduilas. Túrin was slashing his way through the

Orcs to free her when he was accosted by Glaurung, whose eyes cast upon him such a spell as left him paralyzed in every limb.

The "evil spirit" in Glaurung[5] then proceeded to demolish Túrin's self-esteem by reciting, one after another, all his faults and crimes, naming him an unthankful fosterling to Thingol, an outlaw, the slayer of his friend Beleg, the usurper of Nargothrond by winning popular favor away from King Orodreth, a foolhardy captain who disobeyed the counsels of Ulmo for a defense of the city, and a deserter of his mother and sister in Dor-lómin. Most of these accusations were lies either in whole or in part, especially the reference to Túrin's kindred, inasmuch as Morwen and Nienor had long since left their home and gone to Doriath at the repeated invitation of the King, who cherished them. But Túrin did not know this, and Glaurung's catalogue of his sins and follies aroused in him, as intended, the self-loathing to which he was all too prone in the devious pathways of his heart.

While Túrin stood bound under the spell of Glaurung's eyes, he had to watch the Orcs start driving the women of Nargothrond northward to Angband. With them went Finduilas, who cried out to him for the help which he was powerless to give, until her wailing died away in the distance. Then released, as he thought, from Glaurung's spell, Túrin attacked the loathsome beast with his sword. But in fact he was not free, and he supinely accepted Glaurung's mocking reminders that he owed a greater duty to his family than to Finduilas and must first go to Dor-lómin to rescue them.

Having sent Túrin off on this false trail, Glaurung despoiled the Orcs of their rich plunder in Nargothrond and, after the manner of Dragons, heaped it all together in one hoard and lay down upon it, like Smaug in *The Hobbit*. And through a fell Winter Túrin hastened on to Dor-lómin, fed full with the lies of Glaurung, and imagining how the Orcs might even now be burning his father's house or putting Morwen and Nienor to the torture.

But of course, when Túrin at last struggled into Dor-lómin through the snows, he found his father's house empty, his mother and sister gone. Seeking news of them he went to the house of Aerin, a kinswoman of his family, who had married an Easterling named Brodda. Seizing Brodda by the throat as he sat at table and drawing his sword, Túrin demanded to be told where Morwen had gone. Aerin anxiously informed him that she had long since left for Doriath to look for Túrin. Putting this news together with the report of an old family servant that she had "fled with Nienor out of Dor-lómin," Túrin drew the conclusions that the oppressions of the Easterlings had driven her out. These oppressions Túrin well remembered and hated from his own boyhood. Enraged beyond all reason by their supposed mistreatment of Morwen, coupled with the realization that Glaurung had tricked him into abandoning his pursuit of Finduilas, Túrin killed not only Brodda but all the other Easterlings at his table.

Now a hunted man, Túrin stayed briefly in one of the outlaw lairs which had sprung up among the Hador in their servitude to the Men from the East. Then he wandered on to the Vale of Sirion, tormented by the self-accusation that he had only increased the woes of his people and that they were actually glad to see him leave. As for his mother and sister in Doriath he decided not to go to them there, for he had reached such a state of despair that he believed he brought only harm wherever he went—"for a shadow I cast wheresoever I come . . . I will leave them unshadowed for a while" (p. 216).

Luckily for Túrin he still faced the labor of looking for Finduilas. But he was too late. The melting snows had wiped out the track of the Orcs who had taken her from Nargothrond. It happened however that, chancing upon some of the Men of Brethil encircled by Orcs, he put their

enemies to flight, since the Orcs feared his sword Gurthang.

From these woodsmen he hid himself under the name
Wild Man of the Woods, and when they invited him to live
with them he said that first he must find Finduilas. But
sadly they revealed that his quest was in vain. The Orcs had
murdered her and all their captives from Nargothrond
when the Men of Brethil had tried to rescue them at the
Crossings of Teiglin. And as she lay dying she asked them
to "tell the Mormegil that Finduilas is here."

They took Túrin to her grave mound, where he sank
down in a grief that was like death. Then their leader,
Dorlas, putting all things together, knew that the Wild
Man was in truth the Mormegil of Nargothrond and took
him to Brandir, their chief who ruled them, for healing.
Notwithstanding his forebodings, Brandir accepted him
and healed him.

Now Brandir was a mild, lame Man who abhorred
fighting even with Orcs. And when Túrin had won back
his health he resolved to emulate the chief by laying aside
the black sword and abstaining from battle except with
those Orcs who trespassed too near the mound of Finduilas. Against these he wielded only bow and spear. To
signify his change of mood he took the name Turambar,
meaning Master of Doom. By adopting it he apparently
intended to show his acceptance of whatever ills the future
might bring. But in view of the horrors which overcame
him in the end the name carried no small charge of irony.

These horrors began innocently enough with the arrival
at Thingol's court of refugees from Nargothrond who
spread the news that their leader known as the Mormegil
was in fact Túrin, son of Húrin. This they had learned
from Gwindor, who reported it to King Orodreth before
the City's fall. Morwen then set out from Doriath to seek
for her son, accompanied by a strong guard of Elves led by
Mablung, whom Thingol dispatched with orders to keep

her safe. Among them by ill fate came Nienor who, refusing to be left behind, had disguised herself as one of their numbers.

On Amon Ethir, a hill built up by Finrod to give a vantage point to his scouts a league outside Nargothrond, Mablung left the two women well guarded, he thought, while he and the rest of his guards went down to the River Narog to explore the terrain. But Glaurung, still inside the city, came flaming out into the waters of the river, raising foul vapors which blinded, confused, and finally routed not only Mablung but also his companions, including those he had left on Amon Ethir.

Morwen, carried off on her frightened horse, was never heard of by her children again. Nienor, thrown but unhurt, lay on the hilltop. Up to her crawled Glaurung until she could look direct into his baleful eyes. Straightway her mind became as blank of all memories of events, of all names of persons, places, things, and even of the simplest sights and sounds, as a baby's fresh from the womb.

When Mablung returned with three of his Elves he had to lead Nienor by the hand slowly toward Doriath, for all the horses had bolted. As they neared its bounds and slept, worn out by the long journey afoot, a roving Orc band fell upon them. Nienor's fright restored her sight and hearing, if not her memory. Tearing off her clothes and running naked through the woods, she outdistanced Mablung's Elves and was lost to sight.

Nienor ran until, wearied, she lay down to sleep. When she woke in the bright morning she took pleasure in the sunlight and in all the forest lives around her as if seeing them for the first time. But like an untutored child she could not remember their names, and always she sensed behind them a darkness without form, which she could not resolve into its parts. Next day a thunder storm terrified her and, running on, she huddled at last, drenched and naked, on the grave mound of Finduilas.

Coming to safeguard the grave as was his custom, Turambar found and pitied her. Wrapping her in his cloak he took her to a shelter where the woodsmen could warm and feed her. Vaguely she recognized in him some link with her shadowed past and clung to him. But when he asked her name and her family, she could only weep, not knowing the answers. He comforted her then and gave her the name Níniel, Tear-maiden, so near and yet so far from her true name, Nienor, which signified Mourning.

Because of her long exposure to the elements she contracted a fever and had to be carried to Amon Obel, where the women of Brethil, tending her, also taught her to speak. The Chief, Brandir, healed her fever and, in so doing, came to love her, but she loved only Turambar. He returned her love and asked her to marry him. But Chief Brandir, foreboding some evil, persuaded her to wait, telling her meanwhile that Turambar was really Túrin, son of Húrin. She had no memory of that name, but it shook her, she knew not why.

Three years later, however, Níniel and Turambar were wed at a great midsummer feast. And by the next spring Níniel was with child. At that time Glaurung, having learned that Turambar was in Brethil, emerged from his lair in Nargothrond to do such further mischief as he might. He moved to the western shore of the River Teiglin, ready to make an incursion into Brethil, which lay on the other bank. As formerly in the defense of Nargothrond, Turambar had now taken over Brandir's functions as chief and "ordered things as he would" (p. 220). So when he was asked how best to slay the Great Worm, he advised against any mass onslaught, for he knew that only cunning and luck would serve. Accordingly, with two companions, Dorlas and Hunthor, Brandir's kinsmen, Turambar went to Nen Girith (the falls of the River Celebros into the Teiglin), where the huge Beast lay.

At that point the waters of the Teiglin ran along the

bottom of a narrow gorge between high cliffs separated by
no more than a few yards, an easy place for crossing from
one bank to the other. Turambar therefore boldly planned
to climb down the eastern cliff, swim the river, and then
scale the western cliff so as to come up underneath Glaurung where he had no armor. Near midnight the Worm
flung the forepart of his body over the gorge and began to
pull his hinder parts across. Turambar and Hunthor were
then swimming the river, but Hunthor was killed by the
fall of a rock when the Dragon moved. So Turambar hur-
ried to climb the western cliff alone, and, drawing Gurthang, he buried the blade in the Worm's vitals. Glaurung's
death scream pierced through the woods round about.[6]

In order to recover his sword, which was still fixed in the
Dragon's underbelly, Turambar crossed over again to the
eastern bank and, setting his foot on his prey, pulled Gurthang out, saying, "Thus is Túrin son of Húrin avenged!"
But Dragons do not die quickly, however mortal their
wounds. As Turambar freed his blade and the black poisonous blood spurted on his hand, Glaurung opened his eyes
and gave him a look of such hatred that he swooned as if
dead, and the sword Gurthang lay under him. And Níniel,
who had followed Turambar to be with him in his peril,
upon hearing Glaurung's scream fell into her former darkness again and was powerless to leave the spot where she
waited, at Cabed-en-Aras near the falls of Celebros.

All the people at Brethil who had come to watch the
fight, from a distance, and had witnessed the devastation
wrought by the Dragon's death throes, concluded wrongly
that Glaurung had triumphed and slain Turambar. Brandir was of that opinion too and, loving Níniel, came to her
and led her gently away from where she sat. But when she
saw that he was not taking her to Turambar, she ran back
to where her husband lay unconscious. Weeping, she
bound up his burns and called his name. But Glaurung was
not yet quite lifeless. Having received death from Túrin, he

used his last strength to deal death to Nienor in words, congratulating her for having found her brother Túrin at long last and having become his wife.

As soon as Glaurung fully perished, the spell of the oblivion he had so long cast over her dissolved on the instant, and a clear memory of her past days, with their deadly significance, burst upon her. Looking down on Túrin's body, and thinking him slain, she immediately decided to kill herself, as shown by her first words, "Farewell, O twice beloved!" and by her last, "O happy to be dead!" (p. 223). Túrin twice loved indeed, as brother and husband. Moreover, the terrible irony of Túrin's calling himself Turambar, Master of Doom, flashed upon her as she addressed him, "master of doom, by doom mastered!" Overcome by the horror of her incest and by the pain of her double loss, she cast herself down from Cabed-en-Aras into the wild water below, seeking release on the other side of life from a doom which she did not deserve. The scene of her suicide was shunned thereafter by all—Man, bird, beast, and tree.

Brandir, having seen and heard all that passed, told his people of it, and of the deaths of Níniel and Turambar, and all wept. But he erred about Turambar, who returned to the people even as Brandir ended his tale. Having lain unconscious throughout Níniel's farewell to him, he knew nothing of it and of her subsequent suicide at Cabed-en-Aras. Brandir therefore retold the story.

But Turambar, dazed by wrath, thought that everything Brandir had spoken or done came from his jealousy of the love between Túrin and Níniel. For he knew that Brandir loved her, too. Whereupon Brandir, also enraged, repeated Glaurung's words that the two were brother and sister, and that Turambar brought a curse upon his kin and on all those who helped him.

All the more angry because he half believed that Brandir had spoken truly of the incest, Turambar cursed Brandir and killed him. Then he fled away to the grave mound of

Finduilas, where he sat reviewing his life and begging her for counsel. Should he go to Doriath to find out the truth about his mother and sister once for all, or should he seek death in battle? No voice rose from the earth to answer his plea, but Mablung of Doriath came. Upon being questioned, he confirmed the loss of Morwen and the spell of oblivion that had fallen upon Nienor. Then Túrin could no longer postpone the certainty that Brandir had told the truth and that Níniel was Nienor his sister, whom he had married and who had lately killed herself.

Laughing wildly "as one fey" he saw the whole course of his life as "a bitter jest indeed" and sent Mablung back to Menegroth with a curse. Then he ran with speed to Cabed-en-Aras, where Nienor had drowned herself. There he saw that even the trees were dying. And drawing his sword Gurthang, in which Eöl's malice still dwelt, he asked the blade whether it would kill him quickly. Its cold voice replied that it would gladly drink his blood so as to taste no longer the blood of Beleg and of Brandir, both of whom Túrin had slain unjustly. Setting its hilt firmly in the earth, Túrin threw himself upon its point and so died, at last.

Mablung and his Elves, as well as the Men of Brethil who followed him to Cabed Naeramarth, saw there the dead bodies of Glaurung and Túrin. And all grieved for him, especially Mablung, who bitterly blamed himself for confirming Túrin's fears. All present lit a great fire on which they burned the Dragon to ashes. But over Túrin they heaped a grave mound, laying beside him the fragments of Gurthang, which had shattered when Túrin cast himself upon it. Then the Elves sang a lament for Túrin and Nienor and set up a stone on which they carved in runes of Doriath the inscription TÚRIN TURAMBAR DAG-NIR GLAURUNGA (Túrin Turambar Bane of Glaurung),[7] and below it the two names of his sister and wife: NIENOR NÍNIEL.

In reflecting upon this grim tragedy of incest and suicide

the reader is likely to ask sooner or later whether it is consistent with the doctrine underlying the whole of *The Silmarillion*, that Elves and Men have been created with wills free to choose between right and wrong. This is to ask whether Morgoth's curse upon Húrin and his children succeeded, and this in turn is to ask whether Morgoth or Ilúvatar by his Providence governed the course of their lives.

We know the answers in general. Tolkien has been repeating them again and again from the Music of the Ainur on. In the foregoing tale, however, Ilúvatar has permitted Glaurung to deceive and paralyze the will of Túrin from the time midway through the story, when the Dragon first encounters him at the sack of Nargothrond, until Túrin kills him just before the final catastrophe. And in his sister Nienor the paralysis goes so deep as to reduce her mentally to a little child, without memory, intelligence, or will. Clearly during these hypnotic trances neither brother nor sister is responsible for what is done.

Before and after the trances, however, free choices are made by Túrin which develop his situation in a direction leading toward his suicide. His mistaken wrath and pride in the Saeros episode make him an outlaw and cut him off from Thingol of Doriath, the chief friend and source of information not only for Túrin himself but also for Nienor and for Morwen, their mother.

Similarly, in his arrogance at Nargothrond he overbears the wisdom of both Ulmo and King Orodreth, bringing irretrievable ruin and death to that land—its king, its army, and its people, specifically Finduilas whose love might have saved him. Moreover, had not Túrin made the mistakes which brought Nargothrond down, Glaurung would not have been able to occupy it as a place from which to undo both him and his sister.

But Túrin, one of the most complex characters in *The Silmarillion*, has virtues too: loyalty to a friend like Beleg, pity for the hapless such as the Petty-dwarves, and the childlike Nienor, and great personal courage in battle. However, even his pity, a major virtue, traps him and Nienor into an incestuous union, for which neither is to blame since neither knows it to be incestuous. What are they to do when they recognize it for what it is? And who is to forgive them for it?

Unable to forgive themselves for what they abhor, and not thinking of the possibility of appealing to Ilúvatar, they can only put an end to it by death, which they hope will wipe out the guilt and shame they feel. Tolkien leaves us to join in what Mablung's Elves did, lament for the unhappy pair and celebrate on Túrin's gravestone his final, indubitable feat of arms, the killing of Glaurung—alone, unassisted by any other, Elf or Man.

And perhaps this one mighty deed redeemed all his past errors and follies. For never again would Glaurung, Father of Dragons, freeze with his glance any victims and toy with them body and soul. Nor is it recorded that any of his brood ever inherited or acquired that deadly power.

XI

The Ruin of Doriath

THE TALE OF TÚRIN, Master of Doom, is full of ironies, from its title on down to many of the individual events which compose it. That Túrin, doomed from the first by the curse of Morgoth, by the flaws of his own nature shown at Nargothrond, no less than by his virtues, such as his loving pity for Nienor, should choose to call himself Master of Doom is crammed with ironies enough to curdle the most steadfast temper. And Túrin's was not steadfast.

The present chapter, which follows hard upon his death, similarly tells how so innocent an act as Húrin's gift of Nauglamir caused the King's death and the ruin of Doriath. True, Thingol's lust for the Silmaril brought him by Beren combines with his arrogance to the Dwarves to help bring on the tragedy, but the consequences are out of all proportion to their cause. And therein lies irony of a different kind, but irony nonetheless. Readers who judge *The Silmarillion* too somber should not miss Tolkien's adeptness in displaying this mood.

During the many years of Túrin's life, and for a year after his death, Húrin sat in the stone seat on Thangorodrim where Morgoth put him to view the sufferings and the death of his children. And view them he did, but through the lying eyes of Morgoth, which multiplied their evil and scanted their good. Then Morgoth set Húrin free, yet not altogether free, for he purposed to use Húrin as an instrument to do more mischief, especially in Doriath, which the Black Enemy hated and feared because Melian withstood his will.

Being thus unchained, Húrin, white with age yet still indomitable, went first to his former home in Dor-lómin, only to find that the remnants of his own House of Hador avoided him. They knew that he had just been released from Angband and suspected that he still served the aims of Morgoth. Already embittered, Húrin grew more bitter still, and thought to beg refuge in Gondolin, where King Turgon had once welcomed him in his youth, long ago.

From a peak in Ered Wethrin he could see the heights of the Crissaegrim that hedged the Vale of Tumladen round about. But when he went there, the one entrance to it was blocked by fallen rock, and the Eagles were not in sight, either, to fly him over the mountains as they had done once before. Not that they had failed to discern him or to report his presence to King Turgon, but he too believed that Húrin had allied himself with Morgoth, and denied him entrance. Even so, by shouting aloud his plea for Turgon to let him in, Húrin unknowingly betrayed to Morgoth the whereabouts of the secret city which he had long sought.

Wearied, Húrin fell into a sleep in which he dreamed that he heard the voice of his wife Morwen calling to him from the Forest of Brethil. In the days that ensued, he traced the voice back, over the Crossings of Teiglin, where the march-wardens feared him as a revenant[1] from some grave-mound, and onward to the stone erected by Mablung's Elves over the corpse of Túrin. At its foot lay Morwen, dying now, old and grieving. She did not understand the inscriptions on the stones, not having witnessed the events that led up to their writing. But she did know that she and Húrin had come too late to save their children.

"They are lost," she informed him, meaning that she had searched in vain for Túrin and Nienor. And she asked Húrin to tell her, if he knew, how Nienor found Túrin. Húrin, having watched the whole story unfold, could have answered her question, but he knew that to do so would require him to relate the tragedy of their incestuous union. So he gave no answer but let her die in peace. It was some comfort to him to be able to say as he looked down on her face, calm and untroubled in death, "She was not conquered." That is, one supposes, she was not driven to suicide as her children were by the deceits of Morgoth perpetrated through Glaurung.

The death of his beloved Morwen roused Húrin to "anger . . . mastering reason" and begot in him a resolve to exact vengeance for his own wrongs, and those of his wife and children, from everyone with whom they had ever had dealings at any time. Before he left for Nargothrond he dug for Morwen a grave near Túrin's and added her name to those already on the headstone (p. 229).

Húrin's business at Nargothrond was with Mîm, the Petty-dwarf, who had betrayed Túrin to the Orcs and whom he had watched come to take possession of the heaped treasures of the city after Glaurung left. Mîm defiantly identified himself as the last of his race and therefore their rightful owner. Then Húrin declared himself the father of Túrin, the victim of Mîm's treachery. Terrified, Mîm offered Húrin the treasure if he would spare his life, but in keeping with his intention of vengeance Húrin slew Mîm. From the piled hoard of treasure Húrin selected and took with him only Nauglamir, best of necklaces ever made by the hands of Dwarves.

His next stop was Doriath. Standing before King Thingol Húrin threw down Nauglamir on the floor, crying out caustically that it was a guerdon for the King's safekeeping of his wife and his two children. Out of pity Thingol subdued his anger, and Melian reminded Húrin that whatever he had seen was through the eyes of Morgoth and therefore subtly twisted. The truth, she told him, was that Túrin, as well as Morwen and Nienor, had been honored in Doriath and urged not to depart. Húrin could not disbelieve her.

Understanding the guile of Morgoth he rid himself of it at last. With honest gratitude he proffered the rich necklace to the King "as a gift from one who has nothing." The sadness of these words suggests that Húrin no longer had any motive to go on living. And indeed he threw himself into the Great Sea—he who was "the mightiest of the warriors of mortal Men," as Tolkien writes for his epitaph (p. 232).

Nauglamir now belonged to Thingol, and so did the Silmaril which Beren had won for him. Always prone to the vice of possessiveness, the King became so enamored of that Great Jewel that he wished to have it on his own person day and night. The idea came to him to have it set in Nauglamir. Then he could wear it around his neck at all times. This task he entrusted to the Dwarves of Nogrod, who came to work in Menegroth's caves in large armed companies, the times being perilous. As they worked on the setting, these Naugrim secretly lusted to carry the necklace back with them to Nogrod, so beautifully did its many jewels reflect the changing hues of the Silmaril.

When the work had been completed, the King went alone to receive it from the Dwarves, but they refused to give it up. Nauglamir, they said, was the labor of their ancestors, stolen by Húrin from Nargothrond, and rightly belonged to them. Thingol sensed under these words their lust to keep the Silmaril for themselves and, his anger blinding him to his peril, he scorned them aloud as a stunted people and dismissed them from Doriath without recompense. The Dwarves murdered him then and fled homeward with the new Nauglamir through the Forest of Region. But only two lived long enough even to cross the River Aros, Doriath's eastern border, for all the rest were slain by its Elves, who took back the necklace. These two contrived to reach Nogrod but told their tale awry. By feigning that their companions had been slain in Menegroth by Thingol's command in his jealous greed for the necklace and the Silmaril, they roused the inhabitants of Nogrod to send a great host westward against Doriath.

Luckily for them, that realm lay unprotected now by the Girdle of Melian. Although a Maia of great power, Melian, by taking the form of an Elf in order to unite herself with Thingol and bear him a daughter, had rendered herself subject to the laws of the flesh on Middle-earth. But she had also gained power over its substance, and by this power she had been enabled to surround Doriath with a protective Girdle. Now that Thingol had died and gone to Mandos, a change came over Melian also, by which she lost the power to project the Girdle. Staying only to bid Mablung send a message to Beren and Lúthien on the island of Tol Galen in Ossiriand that the Silmaril was endangered, she left Middle-earth. Being Vala-born, she easily passed through the spells and hazards of the Great Sea and returned to Valinor, where she sought comfort for her sorrows in Lórien, her original abode.

Unresisted, the Dwarf host of Nogrod passed through the woods of Doriath until they reached Menegroth of the Thousand Caves. There indeed they met stiff resistance from the Sindarin Elves loyal to Thingol. The two races fought bloody battles in the Caves, begetting a hatred and distrust between them which lasted long and was healed only in the War of the Rings in the Third Age. But the Dwarves were victorious and sacked the Caves, killed Mablung, and carried off Nauglamir in which the Silmaril was still set.

Beren and Lúthien in their mortal lives on Tol Galen had a son Dior, who married Nimloth, a kinswoman of Celeborn, Prince of Doriath, husband of Galadriel. Dior and Nimloth had two sons and a daughter called Elwing, who was later to wed the great mariner Eärendil. But that was for the future.

Rumors of the passing of a great host of Dwarves circulated among the Green-elves of Ossiriand, and soon afterward came a messenger from Doriath telling Beren of the disaster there. Beren and Dior rallied these Elves and led them north to the River Ascar, along which ran the Dwarf road to the Ered Luin. There they waylaid the returning Dwarves as they were climbing the steep banks of the River Gelion and killed many with their arrows. Those of the Naugrim who survived to reach the foothills were set upon by huge Ents, the Shepherds of the Trees, who hated all Dwarves for using their axes to fell the forests. The Ents' lethal powers are narrated at greater length in *The Lord of the Rings*. Suffice it to say that not one Dwarf, out of all that great host, ever came back to Nogrod.

In the ambush by the River Gelion Beren killed the Lord of Nogrod and took from his body Nauglamir. Set in it he found the Silmaril which he himself had loosed from Morgoth's Iron Crown. After throwing into the River Ascar all the rest of the treasure plundered from Doriath, for the Dwarf King had cursed it, he carried the necklace back to Tol Galen. There Lúthien, wearing it, shone with a beauty never before seen on Middle-earth and worthy of Valinor. Indeed it may well be that the Silmaril hastened her death and Beren's, heightening her loveliness until she became too bright for Earth.

But now that Thingol was dead and Doriath needed a king, the title descended to his grandson Dior, through Lúthien. Therefore Dior, with his wife and children, went to Menegroth to claim his throne. There he was received with acclamation by the leaderless Elves, and he worked to reclaim the glory and power which had vanished from Doriath. Then on an autumn night a lord of the Green-elves came to Dior without words and put into his hands Nauglamir with its inset Silmaril. He understood this to be a sign that Beren and Lúthien had died and gone like other mortals to "a fate beyond the world" (p. 236).

Rumors of the Silmaril's presence in Doriath sped abroad and came to the ears of Fëanor's seven sons, still

bound by the hateful Oath they had sworn to their father
for all the days of their lives. While Lúthien wore the Great
Jewel no Elf dared try to take it from her. But when it
passed to Dior the seven sent him a claim of ownership. He
did not vouchsafe them any answer.

Thereupon Celegorm, not Maedhros or Maglor, led his
younger brothers in a sudden swoop upon Menegroth.
Then again blood flowed in the Thousand Caves and, as in
another Kinslaying, Elf slew Elf. Three of the brothers,
Celegorm, Curufin, and Caranthir died there, as did Dior
and his wife Nimloth also. Their two young sons were
seized by Celegorm's servants and left to starve in the
woods. Maedhros disowned this foul deed and for a long
time searched for the children to succor them, but in vain.
They were never heard of again. However, Dior's daughter
Elwing, followed by some few Elves, escaped with the Silmaril to the Mouths of Sirion where the River flowed into
the Great Sea.

So ended Doriath. One by one all the realms of Beleriand
were falling like leaves from a dying tree: Hithlum, Dorthonion, Himring, and Himlad along its northern frontier;
Thargelion also; the Falas and mighty Nargothrond; and
now Doriath, most ancient of them all. Only Turgon's
Gondolin still stood untouched and that, too, was soon to
be brought down. The Noldor and their allies were being
driven into the Sea by Morgoth and those who did his
bidding. Nowhere on Middle-earth did there seem to be
any untapped strength which could withstand him. And
the Valar were allowing no cry for help to come to them
across the Great Sea.

XII

Tuor and the Fall of Gondolin

As the close of the foregoing chapter suggests, the fall of Doriath was another of the cumulative disasters which were bringing both the Noldor and the Sindar to the verge of extinction on Middle-earth. And their pitiful remnants could see no hope of rescue by anyone anywhere in Beleriand. Only across the Great Sea still dwelled the Valar in the plenitude of their power, but so hidden that none from the mainland could reach them. Nevertheless they were the only possible source of help, and the eyes of the fugitives turned toward them in growing desperation. All who had tried to cross the Great Sea westward had perished. What was needed was a savior who could somehow manage to penetrate through storm and enchantment, carrying a plea for aid.

Though none knew it save Ulmo, the man Tuor, who was to become the father of that savior, had already been born in Mithrim, where he was fighting the Easterlings sent in by Morgoth. Therefore Ulmo called him to the seacoast in Nevrast and guided him at all points along the course which eventually took him into Gondolin, to marriage with King Turgon's daughter Idril Celebrindal, and so to the fathering of Eärendil, their son, the savior so long desired. Ulmo's foreknowledge of the high destiny assigned to Tuor by Ilúvatar stands out when Ulmo's one vain attempt to preserve Túrin by preserving Nargothrond is compared with his constant watch over Tuor in reaching the hidden realm of Gondolin, where Idril awaited him.

Now it may be asked why Ulmo did not guide Túrin into Gondolin, rather than Tuor. Their origins and early experiences were quite similar. Túrin's father, Húrin, fought side by side with Tuor's father, Huor, in the Battle of Unnumbered Tears, for they were brothers in the House of Hador, as genealogical tables show (pp. 307–08). Consequently Tuor and Túrin were first cousins, both born in Hithlum at a time when that province was restocked by Morgoth with repressive Easterlings. To escape them, Túrin's mother sent him to be fostered by King Thingol. But Tuor, both his parents being dead, was reared by Greyelves in the Caves of Androth in the wilds of Hithlum. After mishap to these Elves, Tuor served the Easterlings for three years as a slave before escaping back to the caves, whence he harried the oppressors.

The primary answer to the question why Ulmo chose Tuor rather than Túrin for Gondolin must lie in the Providential will of Ilúvatar. But even without that divine choice, it is clear that even on a worldly level Túrin suffered from a pride and instability which made him unsuitable, as against Tuor's steadfastness and his faith in Ulmo, which fitted him for the great role that was his to play.

As for literary backgrounds, Carpenter's biography (pp. 92, 95–96) informs us that "The Fall of Gondolin," written early in 1917, was the first tale of *The Silmarillion* to be set down on paper. In that year Tolkien's wife Edith made a fair copy of it for him. No source for the story is known.

*   *   *

Summoned by Ulmo and traveling by hidden ways, Tuor reached the coast of Nevrast where the Great Sea called to him. He tarried there until the sight of seven swans flying southward in formation seemed to him a sign that he should follow them. Thus he came to the deserted city of

Vinyamar, where King Turgon had ruled long ago before building Gondolin. At Ulmo's command he had left there sword and shield, helmet and body armor to identify the messenger Ulmo would send to warn the King when Gondolin lay in peril (pp. 125–26).

All these trappings of war Tuor put on and stood upon the shore while Ulmo spoke to him out of a tempest, bidding him go in search of Gondolin. To aid in this quest Ulmo gave him a cloak of invisibility, like Lúthien's. And next morning Tuor found on the beach Voronwë, a mariner of Gondolin vainly commissioned by King Turgon to sail to Valinor for help, and saved by Ulmo when his ship foundered offshore in the storm. Told by Tuor of the command laid upon him by Ulmo, Voronwë gladly agreed to show him the way into Gondolin. During the journey there they chanced to see Túrin with his black sword hurrying north,[1] but they exchanged no greetings, for neither knew the other.

At the one entrance to Gondolin, Tuor and his guide were seized by guards and taken through seven gates to the last and strongest of them all, whose warden was Ecthelion of the Fountain. When Tuor threw open his concealing cloak, Ecthelion, recognizing by the arms he wore that he was the prearranged messenger from Ulmo, had trumpets blown to announce him. Tuor was led speedily to Turgon, now High King of the Noldor. On the right of his throne sat Maeglin, son of Eöl the Dark Elf and of Aredhel, Turgon's sister. But on the King's left sat Idril Celebrindal, his daughter. Before them all Tuor repeated the words of Ulmo warning Turgon that the Curse of Mandos, whereby all the works of the Noldor should come to naught, was soon to be fulfilled. Therefore he bade the King to abandon Gondolin, however much he loved it, and to go down Sirion to the Great Sea.

Then Turgon remembered the counsel of Ulmo not to trust too well the work of his own hands, for the only true hope of the Noldor lay with the Valar. But Turgon had grown overproud of his city's impregnable strength and of its secrecy, never yet breached. So he refused to heed the warning of Ulmo. Yet he did blench at the memory of the Curse of Mandos, which foretold the ruin of all the works of the Noldor by treason from within (p. 88). Consequently, the secrecy of Gondolin he made more secret still, blocking the sole entrance with an avalanche of rock. And he would not hearken, or act, when the Eagles reported to him the fall of Nargothrond and, later, the ruin of Doriath. Only, distrusting the sons of Fëanor, who had helped to cause that ruin, he vowed never to help any of them again. And he forbade his subjects ever to climb the mountains standing watch around the city.

Tuor was happy to remain in Gondolin, whose beauty entranced him. Moreover, he and Idril came to love each other. Seven years later, they were married with the consent of the King, who believed that the fate of the Noldor was somehow wrapped up with Tuor's. Well he remembered the words of Huor, Tuor's father, spoken to him during the Battle of Unnumbered Tears, that out of Turgon's House "shall come the hope of Elves and Men . . . from you and me a new star shall arise" (p. 194). Huor meant, of course, Eärendil, son of Tuor and Idril.

At the marriage feast only Maeglin did not rejoice, for in his ambition he had long coveted Idril as a consort who would make him Turgon's heir.[2] And when she bore Eärendil to supplant him yet further, Maeglin was filled with a speechless fury. Not the less so when the boy grew to be as beautiful and wise as his Elfin mother and as hardy as Tuor, his human father. Besides, he was drawn to the Sea as Tuor was.

None in peaceful Gondolin (save the King) knew that Morgoth had heard the cries of Húrin outside its mountains beseeching admission and was, therefore, aware of the general region in which it stood. Or that Morgoth's spies were diligently seeking its precise location. But Idril had heard her husband deliver the warning of Ulmo. Foreboding evil, she had a long tunnel dug under the northern wall of the city, debouching far out upon the plain, so secretly that only the diggers knew of it, certainly not Maeglin, whom she distrusted.

Being half Noldor through his mother Aredhel, Maeglin had the Noldor gift for finding and mining metals in the mountains surrounding Tumladen. And if he and his faithful crews often climbed down their outer sides, who was to know of this violation of the laws of King Turgon? On one such occasion, by accident or design, he fell into the hands of Orcs, who haled him off to Angband. Threatened with torment there, and driven no less by his hatred of the married pair, he struck a bargain with the Dark Lord. Maeglin, in payment for revealing paths over the mountains into Gondolin known only to himself, and giving help from within the city to the invading armies, was to rule the hidden realm under Morgoth and to have the full possession of Idril. Then Morgoth set him free to go back to Gondolin and await the time agreed upon.

The assault mounted against Gondolin by the Dark Lord was no weak one. He sent not only his usual masses of Orcs but also Balrogs rarely used, and Werewolves, and many fearsome Dragons spawned by Glaurung. Moreover they came by night over the highest part of the northern mountains where the watchmen were few and, as a final touch, when everybody was feasting to celebrate the advent of Summer. The heroic deeds nevertheless performed by the defenders of the city are told in full in the lay entitled "The Fall of Gondolin," declares Tolkien, referring presumably to an earlier, verse version from which he derived the prose we now have (p. 242).

But the prose narrative selects as samples only some of these deeds. One such is the fight between Ecthelion, warden of the main gate, and Gothmog Lord of Balrogs, who slew Fëanor in the First Battle and Fingon in the Fifth. From these past victories may be judged the might of Ecthelion in killing him, though Ecthelion was killed also. Again, King Turgon and his guard fought to the death to defend his royal tower, until it was overthrown and they with it. And Tuor strove against Maeglin on the city walls, casting him far out to be broken on the rocky slopes below. Thus was fulfilled the curse which Eöl, his father, had directed against Maeglin long ago when Eöl himself was thrown to his death from the walls, while Maeglin stood wordless and heedless: "Ill-gotten son! Here shall you fail of all your hopes, and here may you yet die the same death as I!" (p. 138).

In the wild confusion around them as Gondolin was being stormed, Tuor and Idril gathered such remnants of its people as they could and led them out through the secret tunnel. Emerging, they were concealed in part by the clouds of steam which arose when the fiery breath of Morgoth's Dragons met the water of Gondolin's many fountains.

Safely they reached the foothills and climbed on up toward the high, cold passes, although hindered with wounded men and with many women and children. The pass they were aiming for was Cirith Thoronath, the Eagles' Cleft, but the approach to it was a narrow path with a cliff on one side and a precipice on the other, where they were set upon by Orcs led by a Balrog. From the Orcs they were saved by Thorondor and his brood of Eagles, who struck at the Orcs and confused them so that the able-bodied warriors of Gondolin could drive them over the precipice. But from the Balrog they got free only by the valor of Glorfindel, Chief of the House of the Golden Flower.[3] He it was who dueled with the Balrog on a pinnacle of rock whence both fell to their deaths, as Gandalf and the Balrog were to do on the bridge of Khazad-dûm in *The Lord of the Rings*. Thorondor bore Glorfindel's body up from the depths and they buried it under a mound of stones, on which flowers bloomed ever afterward.

Thus Tuor and the survivors from Gondolin lived to march south down the Vale of Sirion to Nan-tathren, the Land of Willows. Through it flowed the River Sirion, in which Ulmo's power still reigned, protecting them. There they rested and were healed. But, sorrowing, they composed and sang many songs about Glorfindel. And Tuor made one for his son Eärendil about Ulmo's speaking to Tuor in a storm. Then grew in the hearts of both a longing for the Sea. For that reason they and their people traveled on to the Mouths of Sirion, where they joined the refugees from Doriath, led by Elwing, Dior's daughter. And to them came also the mariners of Círdan.

All busied themselves in building ships along the coast of Arvernien, where Ulmo still held sway. There, Turgon having died in the fall of Gondolin, Fingon's son Ereinion Gil-galad became High King of the Noldor on Middle-earth. Late in the Second Age he was to become a leader of the Last Alliance between Elves and Men and to perish on the slopes of Baradûr in an attempt to storm Sauron's stronghold, as told in *The Lord of the Rings.* [4]

Ulmo, however, taking pity on the desperate plight of the Noldor on Middle-earth, went to Valinor to beg the other Valar to forgive and rescue them, and to recover from Morgoth the Silmarils in which still shone the light of the Two Trees, preserved nowhere else in Eä. Clearly these ends could be achieved only by a full-scale war against the Black Enemy.

But Manwë refused, as of that time, for he was awaiting the coming of some messenger born of both Elves and Men who would beg pardon and pity for both races. As for the Oath of Fëanor's sons to their father, even Manwë perhaps had no power to unbind it until they themselves surrendered their sole claim to the Silmarils, which was false, inasmuch as the light of these Jewels had been made by the

Valar, whereas Fëanor had devised only the shell to contain it.

Tuor, as he aged, heard more and more the call of the Sea. Therefore he built a kingly ship, Eärrámë, meaning Seawing, and with his wife Idril sailed away into the West, whence they never returned. It is said that Tuor was the only mortal Man who was allowed to share the fate of an Elf after his death, for his spirit went with that of Idril his beloved, to wait with hers in the Halls of Mandos. Contrariwise, Lúthien so loved Beren that, being herself an Elf, she nevertheless persuaded the Valar to let her share with him the fate of mortals after death. So much did love accomplish.

XIII

Eärendil and the War of Wrath

WHEN TUOR AND IDRIL did not return, their son
Eärendil took over the rule of the remnants from Gondolin. And he married Elwing, the daughter of Dior, now
queen of the Elves from Doriath. In this way they united
the two peoples and Eärendil became their lord. But, being
restless on land, he resolved to sail as far as need be into the
West, partly to search for his parents and partly in the hope
of reaching the Valar to plead with them to amend the
sorrows of Middle-earth.

For these purposes Círdan, the master shipwright, built
for Eärendil a vessel called Vingilot, the Foam-flower,
loveliest of ships. Tolkien tells that Eärendil's first, unsuc-
cessful attempts to reach Valinor are sung in "The Lay of
Eärendil," evidently the original verse narrative from
which the present prose version was derived (p. 246). The
cause for these early failures was that Eärendil left Elwing
grieving on shore, cherishing in his absence the Silmaril
which she brought with her from the ruin of Doriath.
From one such defeated voyage Eärendil hastened toward
home, warned by dreams that she was in danger.

And in fact she was. For when Maedhros learned that
Elwing yet lived and possessed the Silmaril of Doriath, he
was torn by conflicting thoughts. On the one hand, sick-
ened by the evil deeds done by his brothers at Doriath,
especially the death of Dior's two young children, he was
minded to leave Elwing alone. But on the other hand he felt

tormented by the old obligation to carry out his Oath to his father Fëanor to retake the Silmarils at all costs, no matter who held them.

So Maedhros and his remaining three brothers, Maglor, Amrod, and Amras, came together from their wanderings at his summons. They sent letters to Elwing and her people, as friendly as possible yet nonetheless stern, demanding the return of the Silmaril. This demand Elwing and her folk rejected, remembering the dangers Beren and Lúthien had faced to steal it from Morgoth, also Dior's death in its defense, and their belief that its holy presence was blessing their works and lives at the Havens.

Then occurred the last and worst of the Kinslayings of Elf by Elf, another of the great wrongs which stemmed from "the accursed oath" (p. 247). The four remaining sons of Fëanor, with their liegemen, descended suddenly upon the unprotected dwellings along the coast. So dire was the deed that some of the sons' followers refused to take part in it, and some actually fought on Elwing's side. Nevertheless Maedhros and Maglor triumphed, if triumph it can be called. Amrod and Amras, youngest of the sons, were slain, together with many of their victims. Elwing's sons Elrond and Elros were captured, but Elwing threw herself into the Sea still wearing the Silmaril, so that the victors could not seize their prize after all.

Elrond and Elros were kept safe by Maglor, who came to love the boys, and they him. For he wearied of his dreadful Oath. Nor did Elwing die. Ulmo shape-changed her into a white seabird on whose breast shone the Silmaril, lighting the waters ahead as she flew. Seeking Eärendil's ship, she fell swooning down upon it one night, exhausted almost unto death. Eärendil lay close to the bird to warm it and, in the morning when he awoke, found his wife sleeping in his arms.

When she told him of the latest horrors perpetrated by the sons of Fëanor at the Havens, Eärendil lost all hope of peace on Middle-earth and, resolving not to go back there, turned again toward Valinor for help. With the Silmaril on his forehead he stood at the prow of Vingilot, directing his course by its holy light. Through its aid his ship escaped the Enchanted Isles and crossed the shadows of the Shadowy Seas which the Valar had interposed between Aman and Middle-earth, until at last Eärendil anchored her in the Bay of Eldamar. Neither he nor anyone else could have made that dreadful voyage without the Silmaril.

When Eärendil, the son of a union between Elf and mortal Man, and therefore able to speak for both races, stepped ashore on the land of the Valar, he feared their anger for having pierced their defenses without their leave. So he told Elwing to stay aboard the ship. But she, rather than lose him by the sundering of his fate from hers, came ashore through the foaming breakers, yet remained on the beach while he went alone to deliver to the Valar the message which only he could properly speak.

At first Eärendil could find nobody either in Valmar or in Tirion and was turning sadly back to the shore when Eönwë, herald of Manwë, greeted him aloud from the crest of a wayside hill, saying, "Hail Eärendil . . . the longed for! . . . Hail Eärendil, bearer of light before the Sun and Moon! . . . jewel in the sunset, radiant in the morning!" (pp. 248–49).

In these words Eönwë was echoing, and expanding upon, two lines from Cynewulf's Anglo-Saxon poem *Crist* (Christ), which, as Carpenter tells, stirred Tolkien deeply as early as 1913 and inspired in him the idea of Eärendil's voyage and its outcome: "Eala Earendel engla beorhtast / ofer middangeard monnum sended." Carpenter has translated these words as "Hail Earendel, brightest of angels / above the middle-earth sent unto men."[1] Here are suggestions for the blaze of the Silmaril which he was to wear through the skies, and for his function as a beacon of hope to the afflicted who looked up to him from Middle-earth.

According to Carpenter, by a year or two later Tolkien had written a poem entitled "The Voyage of Earendel the Evening Star,"[2] probably a part of "The Lay of Eärendil," mentioned at the start of the present chapter. In it Tolkien referred to Eärendil's "bark" and portrayed its comings and goings as those of the Evening Star (which is also the Morning Star), in other words, the planet Venus. The same conception appears in Eönwë's greeting quoted above.

After being thus welcomed, Eärendil was taken before a Council of the Valar, to whom he declared his errand on behalf of both Elves and Men. He asked pardon and pity for the Noldor, and mercy and help for the Two Kindreds, Men and Elves. This prayer the Valar granted.

After Eärendil had left the Council to return to Elwing on the shore, Mandos cited to it the law of Ilúvatar forbidding Mortal Men to set foot on Valinor. Should then Eärendil, a Man, be allowed to live after breaking this divine law? he asked. Looking ahead into the Second Age, we shall see that the law under discussion was to bring about Ilúvatar's destruction of Númenor when her rulers sent fleets against Valinor to seize immortality for themselves. In their pride they did not realize that their human bodies as designed by Ilúvatar were not capable of deathlessness. Hence Mandos' invoking of the law against Eärendil.

Without denying the law, Ulmo raised the question whether it applied to Eärendil at all. Was he to be treated as the son of Tuor, his human father, or of Idril his immortal Elven mother? Mandos countered by reminding Ulmo that Idril's father was Turgon, a prince of the Noldor, who chose to go into exile from Valinor despite the decree of perpetual banishment imposed by Manwë upon them when they left the Undying Lands (p. 88). The pardon just granted to the Noldor, he affirmed, did not include a permission to re-admit them to Valinor.

Then Manwë asserted his power and his right to judge

the complex, far-reaching issues of the case. No penalty, he said, should fall on Eärendil, since his voyage to Valinor was motivated by his love of the Two Kindreds, or on Elwing, who came with him because she loved him. In so decreeing, Manwë placed, as Tolkien always did, a high premium upon faithful love. He then continued with a momentous edict, covering all the half-elven ever afterward, that although Eärendil and Elwing must never return to Middle-earth, they and their sons Elrond and Elros must choose whether to belong to the race of Elves or to the race of Men, and thus "under which kindred they shall be judged" (p. 249).

Here Tolkien makes it plain, once for all, that both Elves and Men faced a final judgment, but that the types of judgment differed for the two races. Elrond, as will be seen, chose Elfhood and became in the Third Age the chief organizer of the forces arrayed against Sauron. But his brother Elros chose Manhood, became the first King of Númenor in the Second Age, and died after a life of 500 years.

When Eärendil and Elwing in Valinor were informed of Manwë's judgments, Eärendil asked his wife to choose first. She decided to be numbered among the Elves, and Eärendil chose the same for her sake, although he would have preferred to remain among Men, his father's people (p. 249). Then the Valinor "hallowed" his ship Vingilot and carried it across Valinor to the encircling Sea and, lifting it up, set it to sailing through the seas of the sky. After ascertaining that Eärendil was "weary of the world," that is, of the whole surface of Eä, and would gladly leave it, they set him at the ship's helm with the brilliant Silmaril upon his brow. At times he steered invisibly far above the stars, but at sunrise and sunset he came down near Valinor where he could be seen and where Elwing could soar up to meet him in the form of a white bird.

At the first rising of Vingilot the people of Middle-earth

took it as a sign of hope for deliverance from Morgoth. And Maedhros and Maglor recognized the Silmaril which they had deemed lost forever when Elwing, wearing it, had thrown herself into the Sea. Maglor rejoiced that its glory should delight all beholders yet be safe beyond Morgoth's reach. But Maedhros expressed no joy and was silent.

Morgoth at first doubted the meaning of the new star, his pride convincing him that it had none. The fear of a war with the Valar had long ago left him, for he was sure that he had succeeded in alienating the Noldor from them. That the Valar might still act out of pity he never dreamed, knowing no pity himself. But already their host was assembling, strengthened with their Maiar, with the whole body of Vanyar Elves, and with those of the Noldor under Finarfin who had not followed Fëanor into exile. The Teleri had never quite forgiven the Noldor for seizing and burning their ships. However, at the behest of Elwing their kinswoman, they provided the ships and seamen needed to transport the Valar host to the northern coast of Beleriand.

Beautiful and terrible as were the Valar and their allies, they were far outnumbered by the hosts of Morgoth, which were so huge that even the broad plain of Anfauglith could not hold them all. But numbers could not save him. In the ensuing War of Wrath all the Balrogs died, except a few that fled deep underground; and all the Orcs, though a small handful lived on to breed future evils; and all the Easterlings who had turned against the Men of the West to enslave them.

Only when Morgoth loosed as a last resort whole squadrons of winged Dragons, bred in secret and never before seen, were the Valar taken aback for a time. But then Eärendil in Vingilot, escorted by fierce birds of prey captained by Thorondor, swept down close to Middle-earth and met the Dragons in aerial combat. All day and all night they fought, until at dawn Eärendil slew their leader, Ancalagon the Black, whose body tumbling down smashed into the towers of Thangorodrim and scattered them in fragments. With him fell also nearly all the Dragons. Angband being thus opened up, the Valar descended its stairways to the depths, where they found Morgoth begging for pardon, as was his wont when cornered. But they bound him in chains and beat his iron crown into a slave-collar round his neck. The two Silmarils he had worn they gave in trust to Eönwë, Manwë's herald, to guard them.

The countless slaves freed from Morgoth's dungeons in the north saw a world in which Beleriand was no more. For the fury of the contending armies had torn the land apart in chasms, into which the Sea poured until it covered that whole region of Middle-earth right up to the Ered Luin mountains. Hills, forests, rivers—all were drowned.

Then Eönwë called upon all the Elves from Beleriand, including the few Noldor yet alive, to come to Valinor. But Maedhros and Maglor would not, holding themselves, though now "with weariness and loathing," still bound by their Oath to take back from the herald the two Silmarils entrusted to him, even if they had to fight the whole host of the Valar and stand alone, they two, against the world. And to that effect they wrote a message to Eönwë, demanding that he surrender the Silmarils which their father Fëanor had made long ago (p. 252).

But Eönwë answered that their right to inherit Fëanor's work had been canceled by their many cruelties, especially their killing of Dior and their massacre of the helpless at the Havens. Let them return to Valinor and stand trial before the Valar. Unless they did so, he had no authority to give them the Great Jewels.

Maglor longed to obey, in the hope that if he and Maedhros went, the Valar would at some future time forgive them and restore the Jewels uncompelled. But Maedhros, more realistically and more in keeping with the Oath's provisions, argued that the Valar were far more likely to deny them possession of the Silmarils for all time, in which case the brothers would be faced with the hopeless alternative of doing battle with them in their own holy realm.

So round and round went the thoughts of the two brothers in their last pitiable attempt to find some honorable way out of their fearful Oath. To Maedhros, Eönwë's view that their crimes extinguished their title to the Silmarils did not seem germane at all. The Oath did not forbid any measure they might take, however criminal, in carrying it out. But it did require what Maedhros feared, a vain war even with the Valar on their own ground.

Next Maglor suggested that if Manwë and Varda, who were named by the Oath as witnesses, made its fulfillment impossible, that alone would void it. And he was right as far as he went. But he had forgotten that the Oath was sworn to "by the name of Ilúvatar" (p. 83).

Maedhros reminded him of the fact by asking how their voices begging for release could "reach to Ilúvatar beyond the Circles of the World? And by Ilúvatar we swore in our madness, and called the Everlasting Darkness upon us . . ." For Maedhros wrongly thought of Ilúvatar as having left Eä and as being inaccessible to prayer.

Then Maglor showed his concern for others, not merely for himself and his brother, saying that although Darkness was to be their lot no matter whether they kept the Oath or broke it, "less evil shall we do in the breaking." It was this wish to save others which saved Maglor in the end and the lack of it, in the same degree, which condemned Maedhros to a fiery death.

But Maedhros could always dominate his younger brother. So here, too, Maglor yielded to his will. Disguising themselves, the two crept by night into Eönwë's camp, where the two Silmarils were kept under watch, and they slew the guards. But they could not escape because the clamor of the slaying waked the camp against them. Though Maedhros and Maglor prepared to fight until they died, Eönwë mercifully restrained his troop, thereby allowing the raiders to escape with the Jewels and without a fight. Then each brother took one Silmaril, thinking it evident that "fate" wanted such a division.

Yet when Maedhros felt the Silmaril burn his hand, as it had burned Morgoth's brow, he knew that Eönwë had spoken truly and that his right to it had been forfeited and his Oath had expired. And knowing all these things he knew also that his murders to possess the Jewel had been needless. Deeply afflicted, he despaired. And not wishing to prolong a life misspent, he threw himself into a fiery chasm, taking with him into Earth's embrace the Silmaril he held.

Maglor, too, could not long endure the pain of his Silmaril and hurled it far out into the great Sea, for he understood, like Maedhros, that the Jewel was no longer his to keep. Yet he did not kill himself either by fire or by water. He was sublime in his music and that comforted him, as music can. Therefore he wandered always alone on the shores of the ocean, voicing in sad songs his remorse for the misdeeds of his past. So of the three Silmarils one found its home in the heavens where Vingilot sailed, one in the depths of the Sea, and one in the fires far under the Earth.

*   *   *

After the victory in the War of Wrath many of the Elves on Middle-earth built ships in which they sailed to Valinor. Among these the Vanyar returned in triumph to their abodes on the slopes of Taniquetil near Manwë. The migrant Sindarin of Beleriand made their homes on Tol Eressëa, the Lonely Isle, but often visited Valinor, where the Valar pardoned them for helping the rebellious Noldor, and Manwë loved them. For it was his nature to love and be merciful wherever possible. The Teleri forgave the Noldor for the Kinslaying and the loss of their ships. And most of the Noldor, whom Mandos had cursed when they persisted in going into exile, were now dead after defeats and sorrows. So he revoked his curse for those who survived. But this revocation did not constitute a welcome to them to return to Valinor. So they lived with the Sindar in Eressëa.

Some of the Sindar and, of course, all the surviving Noldor leaders remained on Middle-earth during the Second and Third Ages. Among the Sindar who stayed to the end was Círdan the Shipwright at the Havens, for he knew that his task of building ships able to sail to the Undying Lands would not be over until the last Elf on Middle-earth had either sailed for Valinor or had chosen to "wane and become as shadows of regret" in a world ruled by Men, as Mandos had prophesied (p. 88).

Also bound to Middle-earth was Prince Celeborn of Doriath by reason of the love of his wife Galadriel for the beauty and peace of Lothlórien which they had planned together. Here it was that the Fellowship of the Ring came for rest after the loss of Gandalf on the bridge at Khazad-dûm. Here, too, Galadriel refused Frodo's offer of the One Ring which would have corrupted her with its power. And she gave to Sam a phial full of water from her "mirror" suffused with the light of Eärendil's passing, to help him traverse the dark places that lay ahead.

Gil-galad, son of Fingon, stayed on as High King of the Noldor, to whose standard rallied nearly all the Elves of his race, except the Noldor smiths in Eregion under Celebrimbor, son of Curufin. These were the smiths lured by Sauron into the forging of the Rings of Power for Elves, Dwarves, and Men. But the One Ring he forged for himself, by which to rule all the others. And having won from the smiths all the knowledge they had, he invaded Eregion with his Orcs and slew as many of the Noldor smiths as he could find, including Celebrimbor. The remainder were taken by Elrond to a refuge at Imladris (Rivendell).

Then, angered, Gil-galad made with Elendil the Last Alliance of Elves and Men, which stormed Barad-dûr and killed Sauron, at the cost of the lives of the two captains. Isildur cut from Sauron's dead finger the One Ring he wore, but lost it soon. All this happened in the Second Age. The Ring did not appear again until Bilbo won it from Gollum late in the Third Age, precipitating the War of the Rings.

But to return to the First Age. After the Valar captured Morgoth in Angband they pushed him out into the Void through the Door of Night, the only Door in the Walls of the World (p. 254). But the fact that ever afterward this exit had to be guarded by sentinels suggests that Morgoth did not die, and might perhaps try at some future date to force his way back through it. So also does Eärendil's perpetual watch upon the ramparts of the sky. Tolkien mentions no such attempt by Morgoth. But the Black Enemy left behind him a legacy of lies in the hearts of Elves and Men, a seed that cannot be rooted out but renews itself and bears evil fruit until the World ends.

As the Envoi remarks (p. 255), it is the implanting of this seed by Morgoth and his servants, and the reaping of its fruits in the destruction of Elves and Men, that constitutes the theme of *The Silmarillion*. This Envoi sounds much like a minstrel's envoi of explanation and apology to his audience for the tragic songs he has been singing to them.

Compare, for instance, Tolkien's ending to a Breton lay, "The Lay of Aotrou and Itroun," which he published in *The Welsh Review* in December, 1945, a dark tale ending with the deaths of both Aotrou and Itroun. The minstrel comments in the final stanza:

> Of lord and lady all is said:
> God rest their souls, who now are dead!
> Sad is the note and sad the lay
> but mirth we meet not every day.
> God keep us all in hope and prayer
> from evil rede and from despair,

> by waters blest of Christendom
> to dwell, until at last we come
> to joy of Heaven where is queen
> the maiden Mary pure and clean.

Tolkien can end the "Lay" like this because it is explicitly Christian throughout. But, whatever his personal preferences, he cannot end *The Silmarillion* in this way. It is set far back in a pre-Christian age, and its theme is Morgoth's implanting of the seeds of evil in the hearts of Elves and Men, which will bear evil fruit until the last days. The work is therefore a tragedy, moving from the high and beautiful to fatal endings, with the connivance of wills free to choose but too often preferring what is bad or unwise to what is true and good. Whether these choices can be changed for the better, Manwë, Varda, and Mandos may know, but they have not revealed it yet. So the future is not without hope.

*   *   *

Here, then, closes *The Silmarillion* proper, and with it the First Age of the World. Having thought about it and written first drafts of some of the tales since his youth, and having revised them again and again until the end of his life, Tolkien regarded it as his major work. It became for him a seedbed for his histories of the Second Age *(Akallabêth)* and the Third Age *(The Lord of the Rings)*.

Consequently, much that appears in embryo in *The Silmarillion* can be found in full flower in these other works. For instance, the Ents, who were barely mentioned in it (pp. 45–46, 235) as Shepherds of the Trees became important actors in *The Lord of the Rings.* And the same is true of the *palantíri*, which were merely "seeing stones" in *The Silmarillion* (p. 64) but became precious and powerful instruments to be fought over in the Third Age.

Similarly, although *The Silmarillion* told how Death,

originally intended by Ilúvatar as a gift to Men, was corrupted by Morgoth into a thing of fear and horror, it did not make much of this corruption. The Edain, the three tribes of Men who fought side by side with the Noldor against the common Enemy, were brave warriors unafraid of death. But Tolkien made such fear the central theme of *Akallabêth*. There it brought on an invasion of the Deathless Lands by a Númenórean armada bent on seizing immortality by force. But Ilúvatar, having decreed that mortals cannot live on the Undying Lands, could not permit this open rebellion against him to win even the appearance of success. Therefore he overwhelmed both the armada and Númenor itself with a great wave that sank them all into the Sea.

As for Sauron, he acted in *The Silmarillion* as Morgoth's vilest and most trusted lieutenant, following him deep into the frauds of evil. These arts he practiced upon Ar-Pharazôn in Númenor in the Second Age, encouraging him step by step into rebellion. And of course in *The Lord of the Rings* he seduced the Noldor smiths of Eregion into making for him Rings of Power for Elves, Men, and Dwarves, expecting to control all these by his own One Ring and so to become King of the World, as his teacher Morgoth always claimed to be. Sauron's evil presence therefore does much to link together the histories of the first three Ages of Eä.

XIV

Akallabêth: The Downfall of Númenor

IN THE FOREGOING thirteen chapters *The Silmarillion* proper has been considered in detail. But as its editor, Christopher Tolkien, tells us in the Foreword (p. 8), it was his father's "explicit intention" that *Akallabêth* and *Of the Rings of Power,* although "separate and independent," should be included in the same volume with *The Silmarillion.* In this way "the entire history is set forth from the Music of the Ainur in which the world began to the passing of the Ringbearers from the Havens of Mithlond at the end of the Third Age."

That is to say, Tolkien wished his readers to have a panoramic view of the whole sequence of Middle-earth's history from its inception on through the three ensuing Ages. And for this wish of his we can be grateful. For although we already know much about the Third Age through *The Lord of the Rings,* we know very little about the Second Age, which is the epoch covered by *Akallabêth.* The latter work is indeed the essential link between *The Silmarillion* on the one hand and *The Lord of the Rings* on the other, without which we would lack an appreciation of the many significant connections between Tolkien's two major histories.

Akallabêth is only a score of pages long. And since it is focused rather steadily on Númenor as the title indicates, it gives small attention to events occurring on Middle-earth contemporaneously throughout the Second Age. Yet the

Númenóreans as great seamen constantly sailed back and
forth between their island and the mainland on errands of
trade and colonization. It seems desirable, therefore, to
flesh out the account of events on Númenor with Tolkien's
own summary of the history of the Second Age on both
Middle-earth and Númenor.[1] And this I have done here.

The history of Númenor was composed about 1930, according to Carpenter (pp. 170–71). One of its origins was a
nightmare, probably derived from the legend of a lost Atlantis buried under the sea, which had bothered Tolkien
since childhood—a dream of a huge wave towering up over
green islands. "The Númenórean story," says Carpenter,
"combines the Platonic legend of Atlantis with the imagi-
native qualities of *The Silmarillion.* "

*   *   *

After the War of Wrath "most of the Noldor returned into
the Far West and dwelt in Tol Eressëa, the Lonely Isle,
within sight of Valinor."[2] This allusion, however, is to the
common folk of the tribe, not to its leaders. With the returning Noldor went also many of the Sindarin of Beleriand. But others of the Sindarin remained on Middle-
earth, traveling eastward through the forests and becoming
Silvan Elves. Those of the Noldor who stayed on did not
wander off but dwelt together in Lindon north of the River
Lhûn under their High King, Gil-galad, son of Fingon.
Galadriel lived for a time with her husband Celeborn south
of the Lhûn before they traveled eastward looking for a site
on which to found Lothlórien. She had not yet been pardoned by the Valar for her share in supporting the rebellion of Fëanor, nor did she ever ask it of them.

Likewise a band of Noldor smiths under Celebrimbor,
son of Curufin, went to live in Eregion, attracted by the
news that the Dwarves of Moria had found a vein of precious *mithril* there. A close friendship grew up between the
two peoples, springing from their mutual interest in smith-

work. For Celebrimbor was a grandson of Fëanor, supreme among smiths.

After Morgoth's overthrow by the Valar in the War of Wrath, the Easterlings who had fought on his side fled swiftly back to those eastern regions of Middle-earth whence they had come at his summons. There they made themselves rulers over the members of their own race who had never gone to Beleriand. And evil rulers they proved to be, for they had learned only too well the lessons taught them by Morgoth. Through them his will still worked its mischief on Eä even after the Valar had exiled him forever. Accordingly, the Easterling armies returned from time to time, to harass the Elf-friends, those three Houses of the Edain who had fought for the Valar—the Houses of Bëor, of Hador, and of Haleth.

Taking counsel together the Valar, who recognized the malice of Morgoth behind this implacable harrying, decided to make for the Edain a separate land where enemies could not reach them. At their command Ossë, the Maia of Ulmo, lifted up from the sea bottom a large hospitable island. Númenor was its name. It was made firm by Aulë, not to be moved, and graced by Yavanna with greenery of every sort, from grass to lordly trees. Meanwhile Eönwë, herald of Manwë, came among the Edain who were to inhabit Númenor and bestowed on them not only much wisdom and power but also a life-span far longer than that of other mortal Men. And the Elves of Tol Eressëa came too, contributing fragrant flowers and refreshing fountains from their own land (p. 260).

When Númenor was ready for occupancy the Edain set sail toward it, guided by Eärendil's star. And as they neared the island it shimmered before their eyes like a mist gilded by the sun. Unmarred it was, and beautiful, and new, fresh from the hands of the Valar. Its settlers came to be called the Dúnedain, the Edain of the West. In *The Lord of the Rings* Aragorn always traced his ancestry back to them through

Elendil's son, Isildur. Well might he be proud of it. For the Men of that island at first were tall, wise, keen of eye, and unafflicted by any illness of body. Moreover they had unusually long lives.

Led by Elros, son of Eärendil, whom the Valar had appointed to be Númenor's first King, the Edain landed at the island's westernmost part, named Andúnië because it faced the sunset. Upon exploring inland they found towering in its midst a tall mountain, Meneltarma, Pillar of Heaven, on which stood an unroofed temple sacred to Eru-Ilúvatar, the only temple of any kind on Númenor, and indeed anywhere else on Middle-earth or even in Valinor. Unroofed it was in order that people who came to worship there might behold the stars of Varda, and the glory of them, set there by their Maker to bear witness to his creation. Also, in order that from time to time they might glimpse the passing of Eärendil in Vingilot and thereby take hope for the days and years to come.

At the mountain's base were to lie the tombs of the Kings. Close by, on a hill, the Dúnedain built the city of Armenelos, none fairer, within which Elros raised a tower and a citadel. In plan this city was reminiscent of Gondor, which in turn seems to have been modeled upon Gondolin, and that upon the Elfin city of Tirion on the mount called Túna in Valinor.

One command only the Valar laid upon the Dúnedain in exchange for the gift of Númenor: that no ship of theirs should ever sail westward far enough to lose sight of the coasts of Númenor. Northward, southward, and eastward to the shores of Middle-earth they might freely go, but not far westward lest, tempted by the lure of immortality, they should search for Eressëa and Valinor where no death came.

This law was known to Númenóreans as the Ban of the Valar, which they never violated during the days of their obedience. Yet the desire to reach the Undying Lands lay dormant in their hearts even then. On clear days from the crest of Meneltarma, or from some ship lying off the western coast of Númenor as far as the Ban allowed, they could, in fascination, gaze westward at a harbor and a tower, and behind these a city shining white. Most Númenóreans thought they were seeing Valinor, the Blessed Realm, but the wisest of them knew that what they beheld was Avallónë, the harbor of the Elves on Eressëa.

From these Eldar the Dúnedain received birds, flowers, and healing herbs. But most precious of all was a seedling of Celeborn, the White Tree, then flourishing in Eressëa. Celeborn in turn had been a seedling of Galathilion planted on Túna in Valinor. And Galathilion was "the image of Telperion" which Yavanna made for the Valar after Morgoth and Ungoliant poisoned the original Tree and killed it. The seedling brought to them from Eressëa the Dúnedain named Nimloth and planted in the King's courts in Armenelos, where it prospered and bloomed (p. 263).

So civilization throve in Númenor. Loremasters preserved in their books the memory of the past and the wisdom of the present. Shipbuilding and other practical crafts its citizens practiced, too, but only those of peace, for the Dúnedain avoided war and whatever was warlike. As mariners unsurpassed, they explored the wide oceans to the north and south, and even adventured upon the Sea encircling Middle-earth.

Discovering in the course of their long journeys that the light of knowledge and wisdom was failing on the mainland, they considered themselves bound in duty and compassion to help the human settlements there. Not that they ever stayed on the mainland long enough, at first, to found any permanent settlements of their own. But they brought to Middle-earth not only wine, with vineyards to produce it, but also corn. They taught the people how to sow and reap it, and to grind it into grain for bread; also how to cut lumber and carve stone for the betterment of their brief lives. Thus busily employed, the Men along the coastal lands of Middle-earth freed themselves from the Easterlings and learned not to fear the darkness of the night. But more and more as the years went by, the Dúnedain themselves hungered to sail to Avallonë, there to escape death by winning life everlasting, like the Elves who dwelt there. Old age they feared and the weakness it brought, as compared with the never-fading immortality of the Eldar. This discontent Morgoth had taught them from the first, and they remembered it. Therefore the Men of Númenor, first silently, then openly, began to complain against the doom of death put upon them, and specifically against the Ban of the Valar, which they had come to think of as robbing them of their chance for immortality. And since they were masterful mariners who could brave all seas, they asked aloud why they might not sail to Eressëa, and even to Valinor, to taste there the happiness of the Powers who ruled the world.

Hearing these grievances, Manwë sorrowed at the cloud of Morgoth's evil gathering over Númenor, even though Morgoth himself had been exiled forever and was not there. Consequently he sent messengers to its King and his subjects with a major pronouncement about the natures of mortality and immortality, and about the question why Ilúvatar in creating Eä had apportioned them as he had (pp. 264–65). Now this King was not Elros Tar-Minyatur, who had died in the year 442 leaving his land content, but one of his line ruling many centuries later, who did not know how to command obedience to the Valar but, in fact, partly shared the unrest voiced by those he ruled. This was Tar-Atanamir, who became King in the year 2251 and ruled for several centuries thereafter.

Manwë's messengers told this King, first, that Ilúvatar's decrees allotting length of life could be changed only by him who created life. Moreover, they said, it was not Valinor nor Eressëa that rendered its inhabitants immortal but rather their own preordained natures. So if the King and his subjects were to sail to those deathless lands they would only die the sooner because their nature could not endure the strength of the light that shone there. Tar-Atanamir objected that his forefather Eärendil had landed in Valinor and was still alive. To this the messengers replied that, being of mixed Elfin and mortal blood, Eärendil had chosen to be numbered among the Elves, a choice that prevented him from ever returning to mortal lands. The Númenóreans, being mortal Men, could not live both on Valinor and on Númenor. Immutably the law of Ilúvatar was, "That cannot be." Not even the Valar had the power to take away the gifts of Ilúvatar, which he bestowed on his Children when they were in the making, long before what they did or did not do in the War of Wrath. To the Elves he gave immortality, but its penalty was that they could never escape from the world so long as it lasted. Mortality he gave Men, but not as a punishment. It was, rather, a gift which allowed them to escape from the world with all its weariness and pain. Neither mortals nor immortals had any reason to envy each other.

But the Númenóreans insistently asked why they should not envy the Deathless. The Dúnedain alone, they said, were required to rely blindly on belief and hope in a future beyond the world, of which they knew nothing. Yet they, too, loved the Earth and their life on it.

Then the messengers conceded that Ilúvatar had not told the Valar exactly what was to happen to the souls of Men beyond the world. But the Valar were sure that Eä was never meant to be Men's true home. Ilúvatar intended human death and departure from Eä as a gift to be accepted gratefully, without fear and repining. If the idea of dying now troubled Men with gloom and grief, the fault was Morgoth's, who had had free access to the human race at the time of its awakening, and had implanted in Men ideas dark and false about the manner and meaning of death.

King Elros Tar-Minyatur and his contemporaries had welcomed their lot with calm and content. If the Dúnedain now, 1800 years later, had begun to look darkly at death again it was a sign that Morgoth's lies had sprung up once more to lead them into error. Let them beware of disobeying Eru-Ilúvatar! He expected the Dúnedain to trust him, not Morgoth, lest they become enslaved again by the Dark Enemy. Let them rather cherish the hope that beyond death all their desires would be fulfilled. Ilúvatar had given them a love of Arda, and he never acted without a purpose. What his purpose was for Men after death would be revealed to them in Ilúvatar's own good time.

To this grave warning Tar-Atanamir, thirteenth of Elros' line, gave no answer and no heed, nor did most of his subjects. Being a proud and greedy Man, he sent his ships to Middle-earth not to teach, as of old, but to collect tribute, enriching himself and his people while they lived. This King, indeed, clung to his sceptre even after he had grown far too old to wield it. In this he violated the custom of Númenor, according to which the King surrendered his kingship as soon as his heir became full grown in body and in mind. This custom Aragorn observed at the beginning of the Fourth Age, as is told in *The Lord of the Rings*.[3]

Tar-Ancalimon, who succeeded his father Atanamir finally, resembled him in pride and disdain for both Elves and Valar. In his reign this enmity divided the people of Númenor for the first time. The majority, who accepted the King's views and were known as the King's Men, estranged themselves willfully from the Eldar and the Valar. But the minority, although still loyal to the King, favored friendship with the Eldar and obedience to the Valar. Known to the other party as the Elendili, or Elf-friends, they called themselves the Faithful, but even they were slightly infected by the fear of death (p. 266).

The King and his Men feared to break the Ban of the Valar. But their dread of death turned their energies in-

ward into searches for the means of prolonging life, or even
bringing it back again after their death. All they discovered, however, were ways of embalming and keeping
corpses unrotted. And they covered the island with stately
tombs. In *The Lord of the Rings* Faramir described in almost
identical terms the death-grief of the Númenóreans who
founded Gondor.[4] Both there and on Númenor itself many
sought oblivion of the future in revelry and feasting, and
in the piling up of riches. Either way, fewer and fewer of
the Dúnedain offered their first fruits to Eru or went to
worship him on Meneltarma. Thus they abandoned belief
in Eru just when they most needed his consolation and
guidance.

Many, too, built strong towers on the coasts of Middle-
earth and lived there in order to be free of Númenor, which
seemed to them to reek with death and with thoughts of
death. But even on Middle-earth the Númenóreans no
longer helped its folk by teaching them rightly the arts of
life. Instead, they lorded it over that people, giving little
and taking much in order to enrich themselves.

The Elendili kept themselves apart from these unhealthy
and oppressive practices. Their ships went northward to
King Gil-galad and his Noldor Elves in Lindon, north of
the River Lhûn. Desiring friendship with the Noldor, they
gave them all the help possible against the depredations of
Sauron who, having fled away secretly from the War of
Wrath against Morgoth, had hidden himself for a while
until he began to look about him for new dominions east
of the Ered Luin some 500 years later. Soon Sauron discovered a new source of danger and opportunity in the growing power of Númenor. And about the year 1000 of the
Second Age he began to build a new stronghold of Barad-
dûr in Mordor, which he completed some 600 years later.

Sauron, however, had not spent all these centuries in
erecting a mere place of safety in which to defend himself.
Being an apt pupil of Morgoth he had acquired from him

an appetite to rule all of Middle-earth and its peoples as their King. But he had his own notions of how to accomplish this aim. Morgoth as a Vala could command Balrogs, turn Elves into Orcs, and breed Dragons and Werewolves with which to conquer his foes through force. Sauron as a mere Maia of Aulë had no such powers. But he conceived the scheme of controlling the minds of Earth's principal races—Elves, Dwarves, and Men (Ents and Hobbits did not count with him)—by persuading them to wear Rings which he, Sauron, would control by one overpowering Ring which he himself was to wear. These, and later the *palantíri,* were his chief weapons.

But how to forge Rings of such potency? With the aid of the Noldor smiths in Eregion, of course. By their aid, without disclosing his aims, he forged them, almost all. Only when Sauron slipped the One Ring on his finger in the year 1600, and boasted of its power, did Celebrimbor realize how he and his Elves had been betrayed.[5] A century later, Sauron invaded Eregion with his Orcs, laid waste the country, and slew Celebrimbor. Sent by King Gil-galad, Elrond retreated with the survivors of the Noldor smiths to Imladris (Rivendell), where he established a refuge for them. It was to this struggle for Eregion that Tar-Minastir in the year 1700 sent a large navy crowded with armed men who helped Gil-galad's forces to rout Sauron and to drive him out of that land.

For many centuries after this reverse, Sauron, afraid that the Númenóreans might march inland against Barad-dûr if he fought against them prematurely, waited until division and disruption from within weakened them enough to permit his safely wiping out their strongholds on the coasts of Middle-earth. A watershed in the fortunes of Númenor was reached in the year 2899 when Adûnakhor, nineteenth of his line, ascended to the throne, calling himself Lord of the West. To the Faithful his use of this title seemed presumptuous, since it belonged to the Valar. Also this King forbade the use of Elven-tongues by his subjects, among themselves or in his presence.

Yet Ar-Gimilzôr, twenty-second of his line, turned out to be a still greater enemy to the Faithful. He not only banished the Elven tongues but also punished those who welcomed the ships from Eressëa which sometimes came secretly to Númenor's western shores. Moreover, the White Tree growing near his throne he left, symbolically, untended and declining in luster. Besides, he ordered the Elendili shifted from the island's western regions to its eastern, where he set a watch upon them. But from their harbor of Rómenna they still sailed northward to maintain contact with the Eldar on Middle-earth under King Gil-galad. This the Kings of Númenor allowed, so long as those who sailed away never returned. But voyages to or from Eressëa they did not permit lest their rebellious doings should come to the ears of the Valar. Of course Manwë knew them all. So the Valar withdrew their favor from the Kings of Númenor, and no more ships from Eressëa came to them out of the West.

Next in honor to the Kings, all of whom were direct descendants of Elros in the male line, stood the Lords of Andúnië, descendants of Elros in the female line through Silmarien, born in the year 548, daughter of Tar-Elendil, fourth King of Númenor. These Lords were always loyal to the Kings; nevertheless they also loved the Eldar and revered the Valar. They therefore helped the Faithful whenever they could, but covertly, trying all the while to heal the widening breach between them and the Kings.

When Ar-Gimilzôr came to the throne he reluctantly married Lady Inzilbêth, niece of the Lord of Andunië at that time—reluctantly because, despite her great beauty, he knew her to have been taught by her mother to agree with the Faithful (p. 268). Of this union were born two sons: Inziladûn, the elder, who resembled his mother in mind and body; and Gimilkhâd, the younger, who favored his father.

In the year 3175 Inziladûn became King and reverted to the old ways, in the hope of halting the long decay of the realm. Tar-Palantir he named himself, after the Elven fashion.[6] Peace he declared for the Faithful, and he himself resumed the worship of Eru on Meneltarma. Also he tended the White Tree, prophesying that if it should ever die, the line of Kings would die with it. But his repentance did not appease the long-accumulated wrath of the Valar, especially since most of his people did not repent with him. His brother Gimilkhâd, leading the King's Men, opposed him at every turn, openly and secretly, until he felt himself alone and spent his days looking longingly into the West for ships which never came. And his brother's son, Pharazôn, warred often with the Men on the coast of Middle-earth in order to enlarge his rule over them. He won dominion and riches there and, on Númenor, renown which endeared him to the hearts of the people.

When Pharazôn came back to Númenor after his father's death, and when Tar-Palantir soon died of grieving and left no son but only a daughter, Míriel, who should by law have inherited the scepter, Pharazôn forced her to marry him. Thus he breached not only the laws of succession but also those which forbade the union of first cousins. By these means he usurped the crown, naming himself Ar-Pharazôn the Golden as his wealth and power increased.

Compared with the twenty-three rulers of Númenor who had preceded him over the years, he was by all odds the most tyrannical and the proudest, traits hardly to be admired. And as he sat enthroned in Armenelos, his capital city, his thoughts were all of war, for while on Middle-earth he had learned of Sauron's power and ambition. Now he heard that the Enemy was pressing down upon the coastal cities, thinking to drive their Númenórean inhabitants into the sea and then dubbing himself King of Men, a title which Ar-Pharazôn also desired.

Therefore, thirsting for power unfettered by any opposing will, and determined to make himself indeed King over all, Pharazôn gathered the vastest of armies and built ships for transporting them. Without consulting the Valar or anybody else, he set sail for Umbar, the great haven carved by the sea into the land far to the south of the Mouths of Anduin. And after marching inland for seven days he encamped upon a hill surrounded by all his host. Thence he sent heralds to Sauron, commanding him to come and swear fealty to Ar-Pharazôn as King over the whole of Middle-earth.

Calculating that his armies were too weak to oppose so vast a gathering of strength, Sauron obeyed without a struggle, for he schemed to gain by subtlety what he could not gain by force. So he humbled himself before the King and spoke only what sounded meek and wise. But Ar-Pharazôn, undeceived, haled him back to Númenor as a surety for his oaths of allegiance, just as Sauron had hoped, since the move multiplied his chances for mischief. And when he saw the glories of Armenelos his resolution was fortified by envy and hate.

Within the space of only three years Sauron, by cunning flattery and by dealing out bits of his hoarded knowledge as yet unknown to Men, had wormed his way deep into the King's counsels and become the target of fawning attentions by others close to the throne. Amandil, lord of Andúnië, and some of the Faithful resisted Sauron's blandishments, but many gave in, and those who did not came to be branded as traitors. This falling away was caused by Sauron's campaign of lies against the Valar, who were the chief bulwark of those holding fast to the old truths.

Far in the West, Sauron assured the people of Númenor, lay not Valinor but many rich lands ripe for the taking, and beyond them not Eru's Light but a holy Darkness in which lived a Lord who, out of Darkness, had created worlds for them to seize. When Ar-Pharazôn asked Sauron who this Lord was, he affirmed that Eru-Ilúvatar was only an invention of the Valar to keep Men in servitude to them as his oracles. In truth, however, said Sauron, the Lord was Melkor, who would free them from their bondage to the Valar and would make them stronger than ever before. Thus Sauron cynically preached the great blasphemy of the First Age when Morgoth had been his master. And he laughed to himself at the success of his hidden jesting.

Believing these lies, Ar-Pharazôn took to worshiping the Darkness and Melkor its Lord, and in this folly most of his people imitated him. Yet a remnant of the Faithful gathered on the island's east coast around Amandil and his son Elendil. These were famed seamen, descendants of Elros Tar-Minyatur though not members of the ruling House to which the crown belonged. Amandil and Pharazôn had been friends in their youth, but when Sauron came to Numénor Amandil was dismissed as a councilor of the King, for Sauron hated him more than any other Man in the kingdom. Yet he was so noble and so great a captain that he was still honored by many. Consequently neither the King nor Sauron dared do worse to him yet.

Foreseeing that Evil would soon extend so far as to endanger every one of the Elf-friends, Amandil drew to himself at Rómenna on the east coast all those he deemed still Faithful. And indeed what he feared soon befell. Though none yet ventured to defile the Temple of Eru-Ilúvatar on Meneltarma, the King ordained that no Man might worship there. But when Sauron urged him to cut down Nimloth, the White Tree growing in his court, reminding all beholders that it was a gift of the Eldar and the Valar, the King at first refused. For he remembered the prophecy of Tar-Palantir that the death of that Tree would end the reign of the Kings in Númenor.

Knowing that Ar-Pharazôn would yield to Sauron's urging sooner or later, Amandil sadly related to Elendil and his two sons the whole history of the Two Trees of Valinor. Whereupon Isildur, the older son, disguised himself and, in spite of the guards set over Nimloth by Sauron, stole one fruit from it and escaped, with many wounds. But these were healed as soon as the fruit, when planted, sent up a slender shoot green with leaves.

Then the King had Nimloth hewn down, as Sauron advised, and burned the wood on the altar of a magnificent new temple erected by Sauron at Armenelos in mockery of Eru's shrine at Meneltarma. Hard upon this first offering followed human sacrifice to Melkor in order that he might take away Death. Often the victims were chosen from among the Faithful, on the pretext that they were rebels against the King, or plotters against those of their own kin who did not believe as they did.

Yet this new manner of worship did not banish death but rather hastened it. The lives of the Númenóreans were not long and untroubled as of old but became briefer and were often cut off by sickness, madness, and the very fear of dying which they sought to exorcise. Moreover Sauron went about a program of setting the poorer folk in envy against those who had power and riches, and turning the rich and powerful in revenge against the poor, until the land stood poised on the brink of civil war. Yet individually many Númenóreans prospered, for with Sauron's aid they built bigger and bigger ships and engines of war wherewith they seized the goods of Men on Middle-earth, and sacrificed the Men themselves on their altars to Melkor.

By such means Ar-Pharazôn made himself the grimmest tyrant since Morgoth, save that his crimes all came from the whisperings of Sauron. But even the most exalted of mortals grow old, and the King watched death's approach with terror and anger. Then Sauron, who had long planned for these last days, told the King that now he was strong enough to seize immortality, regardless of the Ban of the Valar against sailing westward from Númenor.

Evading the warning of the Valar to Tar-Atanamir a thousand years earlier that immortality could not be conferred by any land whatever but must reside in the nature of those who came to it, Sauron persuaded Ar-Pharazôn that by conquering Valinor he would acquire endless life and the power to rule the whole world in place of the Valar. Even so, said Sauron, he need not allow all of his subjects to become immortal but only those who, in his personal judgment, were worthy. So, as quietly as possible, the King began preparations greater than ever seen before for war upon the Valar.

Amandil heard of these armaments with dread, knowing well that Men could not hope to overcome the Valar. And, remembering the voyage of Eärendil, he formed the desperate resolve to violate the Ban by sailing to Valinor alone, not to give warning to the Valar, for they needed none, but to beg them for mercy to Men and deliverance from Sauron. This resolve he confided to Elendil, who foresaw bloody retribution by the King and his minions upon the Faithful as soon as Amandil's voyage became known.

But Amandil assured him that he would sail in a small bark by such roundabout routes that none would know of his going. And he advised Elendil that during his absence he should gather together all the Faithful, with their families and their most cherished goods, into a few ships which might lie unnoticed off the island's eastern shore. There let them wait, not joining the King's armada or aiding in his mad purposes, but ready to flee into exile from Númenor, which was too polluted by evil to endure much longer. So Amandil set forth. He was never heard of again.

As his father had instructed, Elendil assembled a fleet of ships, nine in all, and put aboard them the Faithful, their families, and the possessions they treasured most. Among these were many objects of beauty, and jewels, and scrolls preserving the wisdom of Númenor. Important among them were the Seven Stones, the *palantíri* made long ago by Fëanor in Valinor, apparently given in some fashion to the Eldar and by them to the Faithful, foreseeing a future need. And in his own ship, Isildur stored the sapling sprung from the fruit he had stolen so daringly from Nimloth the Fair.

As Gandalf was later to describe the coming of Elendil and his fleet to Middle-earth,

> Tall ships and tall kings
> Three times three,
> What brought they from the foundered land
> Over the flowing sea?
> Seven stars and seven stones
> And one white tree.[7]

Before Númenor was drowned, however, Ar-Pharazôn and his warriors did not lack ominous signs of disaster to come. Manwë sent clouds shaped like eagles, from which lightnings struck down on Men everywhere, and on the dome of Sauron's temple, shattering it. But Sauron stood unharmed, so that the people obeyed him like a god. Besotted, they did not heed the earthquake that shook the ground under them. Nor the volcanic eruption of Meneltarma. Nor Manwë's Eagles flying upon them in battle array out of a burning West and covering the sky (p. 277).

Ar-Pharazôn hardened his heart and sailed into the forbidden seas. First enclosing Tol Eressëa, he sailed on to Aman the Blessed. There, awed, he almost turned back; but driven by pride, he himself first set foot upon it, claiming the land as his own. And that night he and his host camped in Tirion on the hill of Túna, mysteriously emptied now of Elves.

Unwilling to destroy so many thousands of the Children of Ilúvatar, Manwë called upon their Maker. Then Ilúvatar opened a deep chasm in the sea between Númenor and the Deathless Lands. Into it the ocean poured in cataracts from every side, sweeping down with them the proud ships of Ar-Pharazôn, every one. Upon the King himself and all his hosts in Túna the hills fell, burying them "until the Last Battle and the Day of Doom" (p. 279). This is one of Tolkien's references to a final Battle at the end of the world of Middle-earth, but between whom and with what results he never tells.

So perished utterly Ar-Pharazôn and his navies. But the island of Númenor was not to escape either. Being close to the deep chasm carved into the bottom of the Sea, it was sucked down into it with all its people, gardens, palaces, tombs, arts, and wisdom. And as Númenor sank, one last giant wave, curling high, swept over and buried it forever, although many of the Faithful believed that the shrine to Eru on Meneltarma still stood high above the Sea.

Perhaps Amandil did reach Valinor after all and Manwë did listen to some part of his plea for mercy upon Men. Whatever the reason, Elendil and his nine ships were spared, for they lay at some distance off the eastern shores of Númenor and were sheltered from the pull of the chasm and from the full rage of the storm which came out of the west. Yet they were driven helplessly eastward until, many days later, they were cast upon the coasts of Middle-earth.

As for Sauron, he had made sure that he did not go aboard any of the ships of Ar-Pharazôn, for shall a god leave his temple untended? With his usual hideous jocularity he sat on his black seat there laughing when he heard the trumpets sound for Ar-Pharazôn's ships and also when the storm thundered over the Sea. To him these were signals of his revenge upon the Númenóreans and proud Ar-Pharazôn for the past indignities they had heaped upon him on Middle-earth. But he did not laugh when, with his seat and his whole temple, he himself sank with Númenor under the Sea.

Fear filled him when he saw how unexpectedly terrible was the anger which Ilúvatar had unleashed on the once favored island and on the seas around it, and even upon him, Sauron Gorthaur. Not that, being of no mortal flesh, he failed to survive the wreckage he had helped to make. His spirit rose out of the depths and returned to Mordor, but he could never again wear a body that looked winsome to human eyes. Therefore he put on again the One Ring and made for himself a new and terrible shape, malice incarnate, especially in his Eye.

Even so, Sauron soon found that he still had to deal with Men from Númenor, the Faithful led by Elendil and his two sons, Isildur and Anarion. About the year 3320 of the Second Age these survivors established on Middle-earth the North and South Kingdoms and taught the wild Men who lived there a degree of civilization they had never met with or imagined before.[8] But the hearts of the Faithful still yearned westward to Númenor that was no more, and to the Deathless Lands of Eressëa and Valinor. Their mariners made voyages farther and farther west until they circumnavigated the whole world and proved it round, not flat as it had been before the drowning of Númenor.

By this the Faithful knew that the Valar had lifted these Lands "into the realm of hidden things." But they saw that the Elves who remained in decreasing numbers on the mainland could still, if they wished, sail to the Deathless Lands. So loremasters became aware that for these Elves there must still be a "Straight Road" running there as by a lofty bridge, invisible to Men and impassable to all of mortal flesh. For Men all roads across the Sea were "bent," and returned to where they began. But rumors arose that on occasion seamen, and others who were about to die, might win from the Valar the grace or favor to enter upon the Straight Road, whence they could watch the world's surface "sink below them." And so they would come at last within sight of Avallónë, city of the Eldar on Eressëa, or perchance see the beaches of holy Valinor itself and white Taniquetil soaring up, before they died (p. 282).

Elendil and his sons were not to live in peace for long, as length of years was counted among the Faithful. Some hundred years after they had founded the North and the South Kingdoms, Sauron attacked the South Kingdom. He opened his campaign by assaulting and capturing Isildur's city of Minas Ithil, Tower of the Moon, set on a high place of the Ephel Dúath mountains to keep watch over Mordor.[9] This capture he made by the power of his nine Ringwraiths and the terror they inspired. He changed its name to Minas Morgul, Tower of Sorcery, and garrisoned it with many Orcs.

Then he burned the White Tree which Isildur had planted there; and he took back with him to Barad-dûr for his own use the *palantír* belonging to Isildur. Isildur himself escaped to his father in the North, while his brother Anárion held fast to the capital city of Osgiliath, Fortress of the Stars, built on both banks of the River Anduin. Thereby he blocked Sauron's access also to Anárion's own city of Minas Anor, Tower of the Sun (afterwards known as Minas Tirith), across Anduin at the foot of Mount Mindolluin.

When Elendil learned from Isildur what Sauron had begun, he formed with Gil-galad, High King of the Noldor on Middle-earth, a league to carry the war to Sauron in his stronghold of Barad-dûr inside Mordor, there to end him totally once for all. Therefore, in the year 3430, the two rulers gathered a vast expeditionary force, to which Elendil contributed Men from both Kingdoms and Gil-galad all his Noldor and Sindar Elves. This came to be known as the Last Alliance between Elves and Men because never again were the Elves left on Middle-earth numerous enough to attack the Enemy with arms.

The army of the Alliance met Sauron's troops of Orcs, Trolls, and Ringwraiths on the Dagorlad, Battle Plain, just north of Mordor, and defeated them. So great was the carnage on both sides that the place had become known as the Dead Marshes when Frodo and Sam traversed them in the Third Age. Thereupon the victors stormed the gates of Mordor, in which storming Anárion met his end, and went on to lay siege to Barad-dûr itself. In the perilous encounters that ensued, Elendil and King Gil-galad killed Sauron but were themselves both slain.

Isildur, unhurt, saw the One Ring on the hand of Sauron's corpse and, greatly desiring it for himself, cut it off the finger it adorned and put it on his own. The Ring made itself precious to him, as was ever its way. Yet it betrayed him in the end, for on his journey northward he found himself trapped by Orcs at the Gladden Fields beside the Anduin. Donning the Ring to make himself invisible to them (such was its power), he dived into the river to swim away. But as if it had a will of its own the Ring slipped itself off his finger so that he became visible, and the Orcs shot him from the bank with their arrows. The Ring sank to the bottom, to be found and worn by Gollum many years later in the Third Age.

* * *

The Silmarillion deals almost wholly with Elves, whereas *Akallabêth* tells a tale almost exclusively about Men. This vital difference changes the nature of the struggle between Good and Evil in these two histories. For one thing, of course, Men are mortal, Elves are not. For another, Morgoth has had Men to himself, unguarded, for a long time after their first awakening and has implanted in them seeds of discontent and fear which can never be wholly expunged. One of the most potent of these seeds is an entirely warped view of death. Ilúvatar has given death to Men as a gift which releases them from the travails of life and of old age. But Morgoth has surrounded death with fears and sorrows which make it a lifelong dread.

What *Akallabêth* does is to show how in most Númenóreans Morgoth's lie gradually prevails over Ilúvatar's truth. To be sure, they are put to a severe, unending test, for Tol Eressëa, where immortal Elves dwell, can be seen from Mount Meneltarma on a clear day, and Elves sail thence to Númenor periodically with useful gifts. Besides, the Valar have imposed a Ban against the Númenóreans' ever going there in return, which tends to irk humans impatient against constraint.

Historically, the first Númenóreans, under the wise kingship of Elros, brother to Elrond, have been grateful for their new land and have put aside, by the use of will and common sense, all temptation to complain. But by the year 2251, when Tar-Atanamir is King, the poison of discontent has spread so deeply that Manwë sends messengers to him and his people to remind and rebuke. Their basic error, as the messengers find, is a belief that living in Eressëa and Valinor will of itself confer immortality upon them, whereas in truth it will be lethal to all mortals and will surely kill them. Although thus warned, the Númenóreans let their fears and longings continue to control them more and more.

Sauron, be it noted, does not come to the island until the year 3262, some 57 years before Númenor is drowned by Ilúvatar. His chief function is to justify to the Númenóreans their hunger for immortality by destroying all the old truths about Ilúvatar and the Valar and the Elves, and substituting the old, discredited lies of Melkor, in claiming to be mightier than Ilúvatar and Lord of the whole Earth, as if these are newfound truths. Bolstered by this veneer of

false religion and philosophy, Ar-Pharazôn and his followers give full rein to their appetites and to the evil deeds
which these appetites demand.

Yet in the main the Númenóreans, except the Faithful,
were self-corrupted and succumbed to their own self-
aroused terror of dying. In all probability the same tragic,
total disaster to Pharazôn's fleet and to the island itself
would have happened even without Sauron.

XV

Of the Rings of Power and the Third Age

THE PREVIOUS CHAPTER has dealt primarily with the
island of Númenor, and only incidentally with the regions
of Middle-earth which lay east of it on the mainland across
the sundering Sea. But the present chapter reverses that
emphasis and focuses chiefly on those mainland regions, for
there Sauron, having escaped the War of Wrath, was slowly
beginning to build his power again early in the Second
Age. Lacking the forthright power of Morgoth the Vala, he
resorted to lies and cunning to achieve his aim, which was
to rule the whole Earth. But he needed an instrument.

How Sauron found it in the Rings of Power being forged
by the Noldor smiths in Eregion about the middle of the
Second Age, and how the Faithful escaping from Númenor
under Elendil and his two sons, Isildur and Anárion, established at the end of that Age two Kingdoms stretching from
Annúminas in the north to Gondor in the south are events
known generally to readers of *The Lord of the Rings*. But
Tolkien's account of these developments and others like
them in the Third Age, as outlined in the present chapter,
supplies a number of new details, new insights, not hereto-
fore known, which should engage the attention even of
those who know *The Lord of the Rings* well.

For whereas in *The Lord of the Rings* the events of the
Third Age are shown moving widely among many lands
and peoples, the present narrative stays rather close to Sauron and his agents, to Saruman and his Council of the Wise.

Aragorn, Arwen, and the Hobbits, for instance, do not appear at all until the very end of Tolkien's history *Of the Rings of Power.* These large omissions, however, give Tolkien space to bring to the people and subjects he does treat details of event and character not found in *The Lord of the Rings.*

* * *

Sauron, a Maia seduced by Melkor in the earliest epoch of Earth's making, became his chief lieutenant, most perilous by reason of his power to put on many deceptive shapes, some so fair to look upon as to win trust even among those who hated evil. When Morgoth had been overthrown by the Valar at the end of the First Age, Sauron went in an honest guise to Eönwë, herald of Manwë, and begged for pardon of his past, some say with true repentance, some say not. But when Eönwë ordered him back to Valinor to be judged by Manwë, he was ashamed to abase himself so low. So his pride overcame the relics of his better nature and he lost his chance for redemption. And hiding himself on Middle-earth, he allowed the bonds of memory, wherewith Morgoth still chained him, to draw him back into the old familiar patterns of thought. Yet he did nothing harmful during the first five centuries or so of the Second Age.

During these years many of the Eldar who had lived through the geographical cataclysms wrought in Beleriand by the Valar in the War of Wrath were allowed by their mercy to return to Eressëa and Valinor. Others from Doriath and Ossiriand chose not to follow their example, but wandered in the forests eaŝt of the Ered Luin Range before settling down as Silvan Elves. Of these was born Legolas, who became one of the Fellowship of the Ring, as told in *The Lord of the Rings.*[1]

Although numbers of the common folk of the Noldor returned to the Undying Lands, many preferred to dwell in Lindon near the Gulf of Lhûn under Gil-galad, son of

Fingon, with whom stayed also Elrond Half-elven, son of Eärendil and brother of Elros Tar-Minyatur. And farther to the southeast in Eregion, near the Dwarves of Khazad-dûm, Noldor smiths established a flourishing city, Ost-in-Edhil, friendly to the Dwarves, about the year 750 of the Second Age.[2] In the making of jewels they surpassed all others save Fëanor himself, for their ruler was Celebrimbor, son of Curufin, fifth son of Fëanor. Nor was it strange that King Gil-galad and Celebrimbor dwelt apart, Fëanor's descendants having been estranged from their Noldor kin all during the First Age. At about this time when Eregion was being occupied by the Noldor smiths, Galadriel (herself a Noldor princess) and her husband Celeborn of Doriath also passed through it on their way eastward to seek out and to found Lothlórien.

As Sauron looked about him, in these first centuries of the Second Age, at the scattered tribes of Men, and the random groupings of the Elves, and the Númenóreans who came and went in a world left desolate by the War of Wrath, he concluded that the Valar had forgotten Middle-earth. And, his pride once more on the rise, he determined to master them all.

The evil left latent in Men by Morgoth rendered them easy prey for Sauron. Not so the Elves. Although he donned his most open face, the Noldor Elves under Gil-galad and Elrond wanted none of this plausible stranger, whoever he might be. Even this rejection, however, he turned to his advantage when he went to the Elven-smiths of Eregion. To them he hinted that the rejection was motivated by a selfish resolve not to let him brighten and civilize other lands such as Eregion, lest he make it as wise and powerful as their own realm in Lindon.

The smiths of Eregion took the bait gladly, partly because their love of Middle-earth warred in their hearts with their longing for Valinor, unsettling them, and partly because they were eager to be taught Sauron's promised knowledge. As Tolkien puts it, "they took thought, and they made Rings of Power. But Sauron guided their labours . . . for his desire was to set a bond upon the Elves . . ." (p. 287).

Now Sauron did not know how to make a Ring of Power any more than Morgoth knew how to make a Silmaril. Evil is negative and lacks the ability to create anything new. But the Elven-smiths did know the secret by inheritance from their ancestor Fëanor. Therefore Sauron cunningly proposed that he and they should share equally all that they knew. By this unequal bargain, said Elrond at his Council in *The Lord of the Rings*, the Elves "grew mightily in *craft*, whereas he learned all their *secrets*, and betrayed them, and forged secretly in the Mountain of Fire the One Ring to be their master."[3]

In other words, all that the Elves received was instruction in the techniques of forging. What they gave in return was knowledge of the theory and methods of enclosing vital energies within Rings—in this case, the racial energies of the Elves, Dwarves, and Men who wore them. The knowledge which Sauron had tricked from Celebrimbor and his smiths he used covertly in forging the One Ring in the fires of Mount Doom, although in order to make it strong enough to control all the other Rings he was obliged to pour into it "much of his strength and will." While he wore the Master Ring he could not only observe all that was done through the lesser Rings, but also he could see and govern the very thoughts of their wearers.

Celebrimbor alone seems to have had some inkling of Sauron's treachery. On that fatal day in the year 1600 when Sauron finished forging his One Ring and slipped it on his finger in Mordor the Elf leader in Eregion somehow "became aware of him." Across the leagues he heard the harsh clangor of Sauron's voice reciting the words inscribed on his Ring in the Black Speech ending "One Ring to rule them all . . ." Then the Noldor smiths knew they had been betrayed.

The nine Rings of Men had already been distributed to produce the nine dreadful Nazgûl, the Ringwraiths, three of them being great lords of Númenórean race. Likewise the seven Rings for Dwarves had been delivered to their appointed recipients but, since Dwarves were a hardy people with strong wills of their own, their Rings did not reduce them to becoming Sauron's slaves, though they deepened their wearers' greed for gold (p. 288).

The three Elf Rings the Noldor smiths of Eregion still had in their possession. In each Ring was set a great jewel. One was Nenya, the Ring of Water, also called the Ring of Adamant. Another was Narya, the Ring of Fire, or the Red Ring. And the third was Vilya, the Ring of Air, known too as the Ring of Sapphire. Individually each of the three gave to the one who wore it power over its own element, but all the rings likewise guarded their wearers against "the weariness of the world."

Celebrimbor hid these three rings by giving them to the three Elf leaders then most prominent on Middle-earth, with a warning not to wear them so long as Sauron wore the Ruling Ring. To Galadriel he gave Nenya, by whose power she was enabled to bring Lothlórien into being and to maintain it against Dol Guldur, Sauron's fortress right opposite her golden realm where the *mellyrn* grew. To King Gil-galad went Vilya, but he left it with Elrond at Imladris before going with the Elves and Men of the Last Alliance to meet his death in the storming of Barad-dûr. And Círdan received Narya, though he entrusted it later to Mithrandir (Gandalf) as needing it more than he himself did.

These three Rings had been made by Celebrimbor alone and were unsullied by the touch of Sauron. Nor could Sauron ever discover their whereabouts, since their owners obeyed the warning not to wear them until he lost the One

Ring. This happened at the siege of Barad-dûr, when he was slain by the Last Alliance and Isildur cut it from his dead finger at the end of the Second Age. Later reincarnated, he sought it throughout the Third Age in vain, for Frodo destroyed it in the fires of Mount Doom, as narrated fully in *The Lord of the Rings*.

But to return to the forging of the Rings of Power in the Second Age. The Noldor smiths discovered that the affable Sauron whom they had welcomed and trusted could be an implacable foe. Some hundred years after the making of the One Ring, he invaded Eregion with an army of Orcs, demanding the surrender of the three Elven Rings, which he claimed for himself, falsely, on the ground that they could not have been made without his skills. Not getting what he sought, he laid waste the land and its city of Ost-in-Edhil, and slew Celebrimbor. But Elrond, sent by King Gil-galad, retreated with the surviving Noldor to Imladris (Rivendell), where he established a refuge for them.

It was at this time that King Tar-Minastir dispatched a large navy bearing a large army to Lindon in aid of Gil-galad who, adding these forces to his own, routed Sauron out of the whole province of Eriador.

Nevertheless, Sauron's lust for dominion swelled until he aped Morgoth's desire to make himself Lord of the Earth. To that end he schemed to destroy not only all the Elves still on Middle-earth but also the Númenóreans. He wore a mask which made him seem wise and fair in the eyes of all beholders. But chiefly he resorted to force and fear in achieving his ambition, and he gathered together all of Morgoth's evil creatures which yet lived—Orcs, wargs, huge spiders, and the like. With these he frightened many of the Elves back to the Undying Lands, and killed others. Gil-galad in Lindon and Círdan at the Havens he did not yet dare to assail. However, the Easterlings and Southrons, numerous and well armed, he ruled as he pleased, for they worshiped Sauron as both god and king after he ringed Mordor with fire from Mount Doom.

Some hundreds of years before the Second Age ended, Sauron was forced to turn his attention away from Middle-earth and toward Númenor for a while, because King Ar-Pharazôn seized him and took him back as a hostage to his island kingdom. His machinations there have been told in *Akallabêth*. In the drowning of that island and all who inhabited that once wise and obedient land, Sauron's body perished with the rest.

But his dark spirit lived on to return to Middle-earth in search of another body to occupy. Once there, he discovered that in his absence King Gil-galad had enlarged his realm to cover broad lands north and west of Lindon, and now his rule stretched also eastward across the Misty Mountains and the River Anduin to the very edge of the forest called Greenwood the Great. Later, this name was changed to Mirkwood when Sauron cast his power over it from his stronghold of Dol Guldur opposite Lothlórien.

While Sauron sat in Mordor considering how to overthrow so strong a rival who threatened his lordship over Middle-earth, his foe was further strengthened by the arrival of the Faithful, whose nine ships came tempest-tossed from Númenor after the seas had drowned it. Elendil's four ships landed in Lindon and were welcomed by Gil-galad.

Pushing on up the River Lhûn, Elendil founded as his capital the city of Annúminas on the shores of Lake Nenuial (Evendim, or "Lake of Twilight"). This area came to be known as the Lost Realm of Arnor after it was depopulated and finally abandoned. But Elendil's folk found homes also in the more southerly parts of Eriador and in the hills of Rhudaur. And they built a watchtower on Amon Sûl (Weathertop), and another on Emyn Beraid (Tower Hills), looking always westward to the Sea from which they had come.

But Isildur's three ships, and his brother Anárion's two,

were blown far south to the Bay of Belfalas, where the River Anduin flowed into the Sea. Sailing up the Anduin, they founded the realm of Gondor in a region to which the Faithful had often sailed in the days of Númenor's glory. They had intermarried with the folk of that land, and thus had become kindred to many. Warm, therefore, was the reception accorded to the sons of Elendil. As the capital city of Gondor they built Osgiliath, situated on both banks of the River Anduin.

For himself Isildur erected Minas Ithil, the Tower of the Rising Moon, overlooking the Mountains of Shadow which encircled Mordor, in order to keep watch upon Sauron; whereas Anárion had as his residence Minas Anor, the Tower of the Setting Sun, as a watch and ward against the untamed tribes of the Men of the dales. Farther afield, they built defenses also at Helm's Deep and at Erech, where lay Isildur's Stone of Erech, and at Isengard the Pinnacle of Orthanc, a tower of adamantine rock, later occupied by Saruman. The role played by all these works in the War of the Rings is narrated at large in *The Lord of the Rings*. But the thrones of Isildur and Anárion stood side by side in the Great Hall of Osgiliath to signify that the realm of Gondor belonged to neither one nor the other, but to both.

The most precious treasures brought by the two brothers from Númenor were the White Tree and the seven *palantíri*. This Tree was the seedling of Nimloth the Fair which Isildur stole before Sauron wickedly persuaded Ar-Pharazôn to chop it down. Nimloth's ancestry traced back to a living image, in Tirion, of the original White Tree evoked by Yavanna in Valinor before the Count of Time began. As a memorial of these holy ancestors, Isildur planted the seedling in the garden of his tower in Minas Ithil. But the seven *palantíri*, devised by the genius of Fëanor in Valinor before Morgoth marred him, were divided among Elendil and his two sons. Elendil had three, his sons two each. Elendil placed one in Annúminas and one each in the towers of Weathertop and Tower Hills. The other four went to Osgiliath, Minas Ithil, Minas Anor, and Orthanc.

Since the War of the Rings was fought mainly in the South, Elendil's three northern *palantíri* did not play a part in it. All we know is that Elendil, while he lived, felt drawn to the friendly Elves at Eressëa and used the Stone at Tower Hills to gaze out over the Great Sea toward the Tower of Avallónë upon Eressëa "where the Master-stone abode and yet abides" (p. 292). As for the four southern *palantíri,* the one at Minas Ithil was seized by Sauron when he overran its Tower shortly before the Second Age ended. It was used by him late in the Third Age to deceive for evil ends Denethor, the Steward at Minas Anor, and Saruman in Orthanc, whose use of their *palantíri* gave Sauron access to their thoughts and, ultimately, the power to command them. The Stone at Osgiliath seems to have been shattered in the heavy fighting there; at least we never hear of it again. Readers of *The Lord of the Rings* are familiar with most of these events.

Outside *The Lord of the Rings,* however, it is only at this point in his summary of the Third Age that Tolkien informs us how the seven Seeing Stones came into the hands of Elendil and what a wide range of remarkable powers was theirs. The Stones were given secretly by the Eldar of Eressëa to Amandil, father of Elendil, "for the comfort of the Faithful of Númenor in their dark days," when all traffic with Eressëa was forbidden by the more and more tyrannical rulers set over the island. Presumably these Eldar who gave the Stones were Elves at whose side the Men of the Houses of Bëor, Hador, and Haleth, the Elf-friends, had fought in the hopeless Battles of Beleriand, and who were grateful to their descendants now on Númenor.

But what Elves were these, and how did they come to possess these wonderful Stones made by Fëanor in his best days on Aman? And if the Elves had them while the war against Morgoth still dragged on, why were they never used against him? In the calamitous Fifth Battle, "Of Unnumbered Tears," for instance, ownership of a *palantír* by Fingon in the west and another by Maedhros in the east would have prevented the mistimings and delays which led to their defeat. But neither there nor anywhere else in *The Silmarillion*, or in *Akallabêth*, do we find even a mention of the *palantíri*.

Perhaps the best answer to the questions why the *palantíri* were not used at all in the war against Morgoth in the First Age, and how they came to Eressëa in the Second Age, is that their maker, Fëanor, left Valinor so hastily that he had no time to take them with him. So they remained safe but inactive in the keeping of the Valar until the need for them by the Faithful became urgent. Thereupon the Valar gave them to the Eldar on Eressëa, who in turn bestowed them on the Faithful. Only in the hands of the Faithful did their full powers become known through constant use.

These Stones were described at the time of their making merely as Seeing Stones by which the far could be brought near (pp. 64 and 346). And so they remained until they appeared in *The Lord of the Rings* and in Tolkien's summary *Of the Rings of Power and the Third Age*. In this latter work he refers to them as bestowing the power to look into the past, "things far off, whether in place or in time" (p. 292). Usually each Stone called to each, so that eyes looking into one of them would normally see only things near another Stone. "But those who possessed great strength of will and mind might learn to direct their gaze whither they would." This Aragorn did later on in the Third Age. And thus on Númenor the Faithful often became aware of the secret counsels of their foes and were enabled to foil them.

Now it happened that in the same year of the Second Age which saw the founding of Arnor in the north and Gondor in the south, Sauron's spirit rose from his drowned body in Númenor and returned to Mordor where he made himself a new body, hideous to behold, because his "honest" looks had left him forever when he died under the waves.[4] Nevertheless he put on the One Ring and prepared for war against both the Noldor under Gil-galad and the newcomers from Númenor, who had established a continuous realm from Osgiliath in the south to Annúminas in the north. To that end he summoned together his allies the Easterlings, the Southrons, and those many renegade Númenóreans on Middle-earth whom he had subverted to his will before, notably Herumor, and Fuinor who held sway over the cruel Haradrim south of Mordor.

With their aid and that of the Ringwraiths, Sauron drove Isildur out of Minas Ithil, renamed it Minas Morgul (Tower of Sorcery), and chopped down the White Tree planted there. But Isildur and his three elder sons escaped downriver on Anduin, taking with them a seedling, and sailed northward along the coast in search of Elendil. Anárion still held Osgiliath against Sauron, but he knew that he must lose it unless help came soon from the north.

A century later, learning from Isildur of Anárion's need, Elendil and Gil-galad formed the Last Alliance between Elves and Men and assembled such a host as had not been seen since the Valar gathered for the overthrow of Morgoth. Crossing the Misty Mountains from Imladris, they came down upon Mordor from the north; and on Dagorlad, the Battle Plain outside its north gate, they fought against the hosts of Sauron and prevailed over them. None of their foes could withstand Aeglos, the spear of Gil-galad, or Narsil, Elendil's shining blade. Therefore the Alliance were able to storm the Gate of Mordor and, once inside, besieged Barad-dûr for seven long years, enduring its darts and arrows and its many sorties. There Anárion died.

When Sauron himself emerged at last to break the siege he slew both Gil-galad and Elendil but was himself slain by them. Narsil was broken in the fighting, but with its shards

Isildur cut the One Ring from Sauron's finger and put it on his own. Sauron's spirit fled far and took on no physical form for many a year, being weakened by the loss of the Ruling Ring into which he had poured so much of the strength of his body and his will. So ended the Second Age.

The Third Age began with Isildur's labors to put Gondor on a firm footing before going north to take over the rule of Elendil's realm of Arnor, leaderless now since his death. First, he razed Barad-dûr level with the ground. But he would not listen to the counsel of Elrond and Círdan, who were with him, to unmake the One Ring then and there by casting it into the fires of nearby Orodruin (Mount Doom) where Sauron had forged it. Perhaps its spell was already at work upon him, for he refused to part with an object of such beauty, claiming it rather as *wergeld*[5] for the deaths of Elendil and Anárion. Thereafter, as a memorial to his brother, he planted in Minas Anor the seedling he had preserved from the White Tree at Minas Ithil. And the kingship over the South Kingdom he left to Meneldil, Anárion's son, counseling him how best to rule.

Then Isildur with his three elder sons departed for the North Kingdom of Arnor, which he proposed to rule as his father's heir. But, as has been told before, he and his sons were waylaid by a large band of Orcs at the Gladden Fields and all were killed. Isildur had been betrayed by the One Ring, which, by the will of Sauron inherent in it, slipped off his finger and so made him a visible target for the arrows of the enemy. But his squire Ohtar, bearing the shards of Narsil, escaped with them and, after long wanderings, reached Imladris. There he gave them to Valandil, fourth son of Isildur, who was then a child too young for combat. Elrond had left him there for safety when his father went south against Sauron with the other chieftains of the Last Alliance. And Elrond, returning unharmed from the siege of Barad-dûr, prophesied that Narsil would never be re-forged until the One Ring was found again and Sauron had come back to Mordor.

Valandil as King of Arnor ruled from Annúminas, but so many of Elendil's Númenóreans had been slain in the prolonged struggle against Sauron, and in the Gladden Fields afterward, that he could not populate all the sites which Elendil had built. Consequently, after the death of Eärendur, the ninth king after Valandil, his folk, known as the Dúnedain of the North, did not stay united in one realm but broke up into small separate lordships, which their enemies conquered and absorbed one by one. Not the least of these foes was the Witch-king of Angmar, whose realm lay not far to the east. So the Dúnedain became an obscure people wandering in the wild, their origins forgotten by all others save Elrond. Yet Isildur's heirs well knew who they were, for their line remained unbroken from father to son, and they kept carefully the shards of Narsil.

The fortunes of Gondor in the south meanwhile were happier yet not happy enough. For many centuries in the Third Age it flourished and grew wellnigh as splendid as Númenor in the days of its glory, until it reached the apex of its power with the conquest of Harad far to the south.[6] After that victory Gondor slowly declined as its Númenó-rean blood became mingled with that of lesser Men, so that their life span decreased and their wisdom shrank. Six centuries later, a plague came out of the east which killed not only many of Gondor's people but also King Telemnar, twenty-third in the line of King Meneldil, with several of his children. And the White Tree died in his courts.

But not yet was Gondor broken. Telemnar's successor, King Tarondor, planted a seedling of the Tree in Minas Anor in 1640, and for centuries afterward his successors repelled Wainriders and other invaders. Eärnur even took a fleet north to defeat Angmar's King at Fornost. This Captain of the Ringwraiths, having called together the other eight of them at Mordor, launched an attack with them against Minas Ithil 25 years later, overran it, and captured its *palantír*. When Eärnur became King of Gondor, the Witch-king challenged him to single combat, which Eärnur accepted, riding alone to Minas Ithil (renamed Minas Morgul). Betrayed by the Nazgûl, he was taken and tortured until he died. Since he had no children, the line of Meneldil died with him. Thereafter the throne of Gondor was occupied by a line of Stewards, of whom Mardil became the first in 2050.

Nearly 500 years passed. The youthful Rohirrim under Eorl the Young came, bringing their herds of fine horses, together with their language and their customs, which closely resembled those later known as Anglo-Saxon. After driving out the wild inhabitants, they settled on the grassy plains of Rohan, northwest of Gondor. Like liegemen holding a fief from their overlords they fought for that City in all its wars thereafter.

To the north of Rohan lay Lothlórien, ruled by Galadriel and her husband Celeborn, once a prince of Doriath in the First Age. About that lovely land both Rohan and Gondor had heard only falsehoods, so that they feared it without cause. Yet it was modeled by Galadriel upon the gardens of Lórien in Valinor, which she had known there before she followed Fëanor into exile on Middle-earth. And not in name only, for she made it a place of healing and of rest, as was its counterpart in the land of the Valar. Gandalf, for one, came there to regain his strength at the time of his rebirth after his fatal contest with the Balrog on the bridge of Khazad-dûm. So, likewise, came the Fellowship of the Ring after the rigors of Moria. And although it was a place of peace yet guarded by its Elves, it was to be one of the staunchest allies of Gondor in the contest with Sauron which was soon to come.

For Sauron, recovering from the death inflicted on his body by Gil-galad and Elendil in their siege of Barad-dûr, was taking shape again in Dol Guldur directly opposite Lothlórien. Empowered by Nenya, the Ring of Adamant (sometimes called the Ring of Water), which she wore, Galadriel was holding Sauron at bay there and keeping her realm in being by the Ring's virtues, while at the same time she watched him and came to know him for what he was. His Nazgûl, she knew, had been sent ahead to prepare Mordor for him against the time when he could rule from there again.

Arrayed against Sauron also was Elrond, wearer of Vilya (the Ring of Sapphire), who sustained Imladris as a place of refuge and of wisdom for Elves and Men throughout the Third Age. There he dispensed counsel freely to all who sought it. And there in particular he harbored the heirs of Isildur in childhood and in old age, knowing that one member of that blood line had a great destiny to fulfill in the Third Age. Meanwhile he kept the shards of Elendil's blade, Narsil, until in due time they were forged together again.

Additionally, at the Grey Havens in Lindon still lived a handful of the Noldor Elves of Gil-galad. They worked under Círdan the Shipwright, building and tending the ships on which those Elves who had grown weary of the world set sail for the Undying Lands. Círdan, who had been a builder of ships as long ago as the First Age, stood high among the Wise. To him had been entrusted the Third Ring of the Elves, Narya the Great (the Ring of Fire), but he had given it to Gandalf when the Istari landed on Middle-earth about the year 1000 of the Third Age.

It was common knowledge among the Elves that if Sauron materialized again, either he would find the One Ring again and use it, or at best his foes would destroy it. But in either case the three Elf Rings must lose their powers, and everything done by their means would be undone. Then would end the Third Age, when the Elves must depart from Middle-earth, and the Fourth Age would bring in the Dominion of Men.

Looking back from the vantage point of the Fourth Age, Tolkien declares that all has come to pass as the Elves foresaw (p. 299). The One Ring, he says, has been destroyed in the fires of Mount Doom and, with it, Sauron's power to exist in a physical body; the Seven made for the Dwarves have been either eaten by dragons or melted in the Dwarves' smithies; and the Nine which produced the Nazgûl, failed when Sauron's failed. Likewise, the Three Rings forged to bind the Elves lost all their power, though not their beauty, when the One Ring returned to its elements. Therefore they were being openly worn by Gandalf, Galadriel, and Elrond as they embarked from Mithlond at the end of *The Lord of the Rings.* Behind them on Middle-earth the three Ring-wearers left much that was beautiful and good, but also many evil creatures—Orcs, trolls, dragons, wolves, and other beasts of prey. Yet Dwarves still forged and carved unrivaled works of metal and of stone.

From this long backward look Tolkien returns to Sauron slowly shaping a new body for the habitation of his spirit at Dol Guldur at the southwest corner of Mirkwood about the year 1100 of the Third Age. And to the seven Istari or Wizards coming from the Undying Lands at about this same time to help those valiant enough to resist the gathering Dark. Led by Saruman (Curunír) and Gandalf (Mithrandir) they traveled far and spoke with many. But they had different natures and consequently different missions. Saruman frequented the haunts of Men, being subtle in speech and skilled in smithcraft. Gandalf, on the other hand, clove chiefly to Elrond and his Elves at Rivendell. After journeying in the east, where he probably spoke with the Easterlings, Saruman returned to settle down in the abandoned tower of Orthanc. But Gandalf the tireless wandered everywhere in the north and west, without ever taking up any fixed abode.

Gandalf it was who, first suspecting the cause of the growing darkness in Mirkwood forest, found Dol Guldur and visited it, as *The Hobbit* relates. But Sauron was unready as yet and fled from him. So Gandalf watched and waited until Sauron had completed his metamorphosis and had returned to Dol Guldur in the year 2460.

Three years later, at Gandalf's suggestion, the Wizards and the Lords of the Eldar formed a Council of the Wise, or White Council, consisting mainly of Saruman and Gandalf for the Wizards, and for the Elves Elrond, Galadriel, and Círdan. Of this Council Saruman was chosen to be the head because he had most deeply studied Sauron's ways, against the vote of Galadriel, who in her wisdom had already begun to distrust his probity and championed Gandalf as the worthier choice. And her doubts proved to be all too true, for even at the Council's first meeting Saruman's pride and desire for mastery showed in his resentment against any who favored Gandalf in his stead.

This Council of the Wise corresponded, on a more potent level, to the Council of Elrond summoned in *The Lord of the Rings*, years later.[7] Both dealt with the same theme—how best to counter the growing power of Sauron. Elrond's Council resulted in the creation of the Fellowship of the Ring, whose members pledged themselves to help Frodo in his mission to destroy the Ruling Ring in the fires of Mount Doom. But when the White Council first convened, the Periannath (Hobbits) had begun to occupy the Shire only a few hundred years earlier, and the danger from Sauron was not nearly so imminent. It began to become much more so, however, when Gandalf daringly reentered Dol Guldur and found in its dungeons (resembling those in Tol Sirion in the First Age) numerous captives, including Thráin the Dwarf, from whom Sauron had wrung by torture the last of the Seven Rings of Power made to bind the Dwarves. From Thráin and the other prisoners Gandalf learned that Sauron was gathering all the Rings of Power he could lay hands on and, moreover, was searching everywhere for the Ruling Ring and for the heirs of Isildur who, as Sauron thought, must either have that Ring or know where it could be found.

This information Gandalf laid before Elrond, who broodingly remembered the scene on the slopes of Barad-dûr when Isildur cut the One Ring from Sauron's finger but refused to heed the urgings of Círdan and Elrond himself that the evil thing must be thrown then and there into Mount Doom, near at hand. Gandalf ever hopeful, however, reminded Elrond that the One was lost soon afterward and was still unfound. While it remained so, Sauron, having poured much of his power into its making, could be beaten by his foes if they acted quickly.

Thereupon the White Council met again. Gandalf urged an immediate attack on Dol Guldur, but Saruman counseled patience. He believed, said he, that the One Ring would never be found again. Lost by Isildur in the swift currents of the Anduin, it had no doubt been swept out to Sea, where it would be discovered only when Middle-earth ended. But these words did not express Saruman's true thoughts, for he expected that the Ring could indeed be found, well knowing from his studies that it had a life of its own and would reveal itself in time. When it did so, he was resolved to possess it and to wield it for his own sake, to gain dominion over the whole world.

Saruman's eloquence carried the day, and the Council took no action at all. Afterward, Elrond confided to Gandalf his foreboding that the One would turn up somehow and with it would come a war which would end the Third Age in utter darkness and defeat. Gandalf, however, expressed his belief in the power of weakness and humility to save the world where strength failed. And out of this trust was to come his approval of the choice of Frodo as Ring-bearer when a choice had to be made at Elrond's Council.

In order to seize the One Ring if any should uncover it, Saruman set a watch upon the Gladden Fields, where it had last been seen. But, perceiving that Sauron's servants were active there too, he entered the tower of Orthanc, fortified it, and studied there all he could find written in books concerning the Rings of Power and their forging. Meanwhile, as his eyes and ears in the outside world, he used birds lent him by his brother wizard Radagast, unsuspecting of Saruman's treachery. Yet so many creatures of evil came to Dol Guldur and were directed by Sauron against Elves and Númenóreans that the White Council met again, for the last time, in the year 2953.

At that meeting Gandalf again urged the Council to strike against Dol Guldur at once. He declared that, found or not found, the Ruling Ring was not needed by Sauron for his conquests to come, so long as it remained in existence somewhere. Even without its use, he already had the Nine Rings devised to enslave mortal Men, and by their power ruled the nine Nazgûl. And of the Seven Rings for Dwarves he had recovered three, by which he had brought three of the Dwarf-fathers and their tribes into his grip.

This time Saruman readily agreed to aid in the attack on Dol Guldur, but only for the private reason that its obliteration from the shores of Anduin would allow him to extend his search for the One Ring to a stretch of the River he had never been able to search before. So the Wise launched their attack at last and easily overran Dol Guldur. But they had waited too long and the stronghold was empty. Two years earlier, Sauron had left Dol Guldur secretly for Mordor, where he rebuilt Barad-dûr, leaving in Dol Guldur only three of his Ringwraiths.

Then the foreboding of Elrond that the Ruling Ring

would be recovered came true. As told in *The Lord of the Rings* I, 62, Déagol the Hobbit saw it glittering as he fished in the waters of Anduin. But Sméagol (Gollum), lusting for the Ring, killed him, and with it fled into the depths of the Misty Mountains. This happened when the line of the Kings failed in Gondor and the first Steward took the throne for a while. In a pool far within a cavern of Orcs, Gollum kept his "precious" for long centuries, until Bilbo the Hobbit won it from him in a Riddle Game and took it home with him to the Shire, "the land of the Periannath, the Little People, the Halflings, who dwelt in the west of Eriador" (p. 303).

Nobody but Gandalf had ever paid them much attention before. So it was he who first saw that the One Ring had fallen into their hands. But he knew too well its evil appetite to breed in its wearer the power and the will to become as dark a lord as Sauron himself. Therefore, with the help of Aragorn's Dúnedain of the North, he mounted a watch over the Shire and awaited developments. These came soon enough in the form of the Black Riders, the Ringwraiths, sent by Sauron to seize the Ring from the Little People.

In the few paragraphs remaining in *Of the Rings of Power* (p. 303), Tolkien has summarized the crucial events of *The Lord of the Rings* occurring in the years 3018–3019. These culminated in the siege of Gondor by Sauron's outnumbering armies; the casting of the Ring by Frodo into the flames of Orodruin; the ascension of Aragorn to the throne of Gondor, as was his right; the finding of another seedling of the White Tree, which thereupon was planted in the courts of the new King; and Aragorn's marriage to Arwen, daughter of Elrond and grand-daughter of Galadriel, the Evening Star of the Elves, her people. Yet so swift is the summary that Tolkien has found no time even to mention the Ents, or the cleansing of the Shire and the death of Saruman, or the very names of Pippin and Merry.

By decree of the Valar, all the Elves on Middle-earth

must leave it and return to the Undying Lands, else they would dwindle there until they forgot all their high knowledge and were themselves at last forgotten by Men. For Men's sole rule over Middle-earth was inaugurated by the dawning of the Fourth Age when Aragorn was crowned King of both Kingdoms, North as well as South. To be sure, Arwen stayed on Earth as his wife, but by doing so she surrendered her Elven immortality and embraced the same human death which ultimately overtook the Man she loved. Great was her sacrifice for his sake, as great as Lúthien's for Beren, and sad her everlasting parting from her father Elrond. For he, with all the other chieftains of the Elves left for Valinor aboard a ship built by Círdan at the Havens in Mithlond, never to return.

As they prepared to embark, Gandalf-Mithrandir wore openly Narya (the Red Ring of Fire), one of the three Elven Rings, which had been given to him by Círdan. The Shipwright hoped that it would help him to "rekindle hearts to the valour of old" against Sauron (p. 304). Ever since, Gandalf had done just that by going tirelessly wherever the need for him was direst, turning up always at some critical juncture of events in the war against Sauron. And although many others had done their share, he emerged in the end as the chief architect of victory.

Like the other two Elven Rings, Narya lost all its virtue at the instant when the Ruling Ring went back into the flames in which it had been forged a whole Age ago. So now it could be safely worn in the sight of all. Likewise Elrond wore a Ring of gold inset with the great Sapphire, Vilya, mightiest of the Elven Rings. And Galadriel wore Nenya, which was made of *mithril* and bore a single white stone of Adamant, as is told in *The Lord of the Rings*.[8]

Accompanied by Bilbo and Frodo, the Hobbit Ringbearers, whose fidelity deserved priceless reward, the three Elven Ringwearers stepped aboard Círdan's ship, which carried them along the Straight Road into the Ancient West. They watched the Bent World fall away under them as they rose above the mists of the world into the serene air of Valinor. They would find peace there, and rest from their labors in the gardens of Lórien, if rest they needed. And they would sing of the past and the future as Elves do. Yet no song of theirs would ever be heard on Middle-earth, for even of songs there could be no returning.

As the years of the Fourth Age multiplied, Men found more pressing subjects to sing about than the deeds of a race which had vanished from the Earth and was gone. Valinor was now farther from Middle-earth than it had been before the drowning of Númenor. Thus, for Men, the Elves passed away out of story and of song.

OVERVIEW

So now Tolkien's intention to set forth the entire history of Middle-earth from the time of its Creation to the end of the Third Age has been fulfilled. And if this history is viewed as one entire whole, there is no need to append to it the sort of apology he set at the end of *The Silmarillion* for writing a tale which goes ever downhill from the high and the beautiful to darkness and ruin.

True, *The Silmarillion* is a tragedy for the Noldor and Sindarin Elves and for the Edain, their human allies. And *Akallabêth* also narrates a downfall, both moral and physical, for these Edain when they are given Númenor to inhabit. But *The Lord of the Rings* (and its brief summary in the work entitled *Of the Rings of Power*) moves upward to a victorious ending. The One Ring carried by Frodo tempts all the chief persons, whether Hobbits, Men, or Elves, who encounter it, but few succumb: not Frodo and Sam, not Bombadil, not Aragorn, not Galadriel, not Elrond or any representative of the Free Peoples who attend his Council at Rivendell, not Faramir, and of course not Gandalf. Gollum and the Ringwraiths are its chief permanent victims, Boromir only a temporary one. Others like Denethor, Saruman and his tool, Wormtongue, are seduced by Sauron through the *palantíri*, not through the Ruling Ring.

At the end of the Third Age the South and North Kingdoms are reunited under Aragorn, a strong and just ruler, with his Elfin spouse Arwen. Sauron having been disposed of forever, there are no major enemies in sight, and Aragorn will know how to deal with the Southrons and Easterlings and Wainriders if they venture too close to his Kingdom, whether North or South.

Running through all three histories is the central theme of a contest between Good and Evil. The evil is both external (engendered by some Dark Lord like Morgoth or Sauron) and internal (in the choices made by wills left free by Ilúvatar). In *The Silmarillion* the external and the internal threats are well balanced. The external comes from Morgoth and Sauron, aided by Orcs, Balrogs, Dragons (especially Glaurung), Werewolves, some Easterlings, and much else. The internal evil resides, typically, in the divided wills of Fëanor and his sons, in Eöl and Maeglin, sometimes in King Thingol, in some of the Edain like Túrin, and in some Dwarves including Mîm, the Petty-Dwarf.

In *Akallabêth* the evil is almost exclusively internal, with the *caveat*, however, that Morgoth put it there in the first place. But in *The Lord of the Rings*, although Sauron's armies are barely defeated by the united forces of Gondor, Rohan, and Aragorn, right wills and right choices prevail in almost all his foes.

Tolkien drops here and there in *The Silmarillion* references to a Last Battle which will bring Middle-earth to an end. In view of the war between Good and Evil which goes on under differing forms throughout the first Three Ages, can we doubt that the Last Battle will be between the same two antagonists? The Fourth Age starts off favorably under the firm but tactful rule of Aragorn, but so did the Second Age in Númenor under Elros Tar-Minyatur. Yet think how it deteriorated under later monarchs.

Everything considered, therefore, we are obliged to conclude that all these wars with their varying outcomes, and indeed the whole history of Middle-earth from Age to Age, lie in the Providence of Ilúvatar. He permits the free wills of Valar, Elves, and Men alike to operate as they please in order to test his Creatures and their love for him.

Chronology of the First Age
Notes
Bibliography
Index

Chronology of the First Age

A CHRONOLOGY cannot provide specific dates until some objective means exists for measuring the passage of time. It can, however, indicate the sequence in which various events occur. That is the situation in *The Silmarillion* until the Two Trees begin their regular waxing and waning in Aman. Each complete cycle of their Lights constitutes one day twelve hours long. That manner of reckoning, though, is available only to the Valar, who dwell in sight of them, and not to the dwellers on Middle-earth, who cannot see the Lights.

Nor is there any definite way of comparing the Years of the Trees to the Years of Middle-earth, although Tolkien at one point assures us that the Years of the Sun are "swifter and briefer than the long Years of the Trees in Valinor" (p. 103). Presumably, then, the three "Ages" during which Melkor lies chained in Mandos' vaults are also longer than the Ages on Middle-earth, though we are not told how much longer.

It is not until the Sun is first made by the Valar and set in rotation round a flat Middle-earth (such was our World in those ancient days, says Tolkien) that we Earthlings acquire a familiar, objective means of numbering the Years. And until the end of the First Age these count up to only about 560.

Even among these it is not always possible to be sure of the exact date of any given event, since only too often Tolkien does not give us outright references to dates. Then we are left to derive approximations from all the indirect evidence available.

I. BEFORE THE FIRST RISING OF THE SUN

Ilúvatar creates Eä (our World) by the Music and by bestowing Being upon it.

The Ainur descend as Powers (Valar) to the island of Almaren on Middle-earth. Their Names and Functions.

They wage the first War against Melkor to prevent him from spoiling their work in shaping Eä.

Morgoth flees from Tulkas the Strong.

Yavanna plants the Seeds of all growing things.

Aulë constructs and sets in place Two Lamps, whose Light brings Middle-earth's first Spring.

Melkor digs his underground fortress of Utumno.

Now feeling safe, he destroys the Two Lamps and hides in Utumno.

In the ensuing Darkness the first Spring dies.

The Valar move to Aman the Blessed (Valinor) and fortify it.

Yavanna sings up the Two Trees, Telperion the White and Laurelin the Golden, to replace Aulë's two broken Lamps.

The Count of Time begins on Aman. After an hour of waxing, Telperion shines at its full for six hours, then wanes for an hour into darkness. Laurelin, likewise, first has an hour of waxing while Telperion wanes, then shines at its full for six hours until its hour of waning mingles with the hour of Telperion's rekindling. Taken together, the two six-hour periods of full shining are accounted a single day of twelve hours.

Aulë makes the Seven Fathers of the Dwarves.

For Yavanna's sake the Ents are born; for Manwë's, the Eagles.

Varda (Elbereth) scatters silver dews of Telperion through the skies to make new stars and constellations for the expected coming of the Elves, the Elder Children of Ilúvatar.

The Elves awaken at Cuiviénen. Melkor transforms captured Elves into Orcs.

The outraged Valar break open Utumno, capture Melkor, and chain him in the Halls of Mandos for three Ages, during which a Long Peace lasts.

In the First Age of Melkor's Bondage

The Valar summon the three Elf tribes (Vanyar, Noldor, and Teleri) to live with them in Aman. Each tribe has inherent traits of its own.

Elwë (Thingol) of the Teleri meets and marries Melian the Maia in Beleriand. They found Doriath. Lúthien, their daughter, is born.

Melian throws a protective Girdle around Doriath.

The Elves arrive in Aman.

Fëanor is born there. His mother Míriel dies of his birth.

Fëanor's father, Finwë, King of the Noldor, marries again, his second wife being Indis of the Vanyar. Their sons, Fingolfin and Finarfin, are born.

In the Second Age of Melkor's Bondage

Fëanor marries Nerdanel of the Noldor. Their seven sons are born. She deserts them.

Fingolfin and Finarfin marry. Each has several sons and daughters.

The descendants of Aulë's Dwarves come to the Ered Luin mountains and found Nogrod and Belegost.

They build Menegroth of the Thousand Caves for Thingol and Melian.

In the Third Age of Melkor's Bondage

Wolves, Orcs, and other evil creatures roam in Beleriand. Menegroth is fortified against them.

Melkor is unchained. He precipitates quarrels between Fëanor and Fingolfin by whispering lies about both.

Fëanor fashions the three Silmarils, each enclosing the Lights of the Two Trees.

He has further quarrels with Fingolfin. Mandos banishes him for twelve years from the Noldor city of Tirion.

Fëanor builds a stronghold of his own at Formenos, north of Tirion, where he is joined by his seven sons and by his father, Finwë.

Melkor (now called Morgoth, the Black Enemy) is sought by the Valar as the chief begetter of the quarrels but flees, apparently northward.

Morgoth circles back to southern Aman and makes a pact with Ungoliant. Jointly they kill the Two Trees.

On their flight back to Middle-earth Morgoth kills Finwë and steals the Silmarils at Formenos, Fëanor being absent, by command, at a feast of the Valar.

They ask Fëanor to restore to Yavanna the Light of the Two Trees by breaking open the Silmarils. He answers neither aye nor nay.

Hearing of the tragedy at Formenos, Fëanor rushes back to Tirion.

Morgoth escapes from Ungoliant on Middle-earth and rebuilds Angband, mustering Orcs and Balrogs there.

Fëanor incites the Noldor in Tirion to pursue Morgoth to Middle-earth both to avenge King Finwë and to recover the Silmarils.

Fëanor and his sons all swear the Oath "that none should take" to kill anyone who keeps a Silmaril from them.

He disregards a warning from Manwë not to leave Valinor.

He leads the Kinslaying of the Teleri at Alqualondë.

Mandos curses Fëanor and all the Noldor who follow him.

Fëanor steals the Teleri ships to transport to Middle-earth those Noldor most loyal to him; lands at the Firth of Drengist, burns the ships, abandoning Fingolfin and the main Noldor host in Araman; encamps with his followers on the shore of Lake Mithrim.

He repulses and shatters an Orc army secretly sent by Morgoth.

Pursuing its remnants to Ard-galen, Fëanor is slain by Balrogs. His body instantly crumbles to dust.

The First and Second Battles of Beleriand

First Battle: Morgoth hurls two Orc armies against Doriath, one to its east, one to its west. Thingol's Elves rout the eastern army with the help of Green-elves and Dwarves. This victory is won before any of the Noldor land in Beleriand.

Second Battle: Dagor-nuin-Giliath, Battle under the Stars, is so called because neither Moon nor Sun has yet risen, although the Valar are preparing both. The army of Círdan, ally of Thingol, has been defeated by the western Orc host and pushed far south to the seacoast. This Orc host, marching back northward to aid those Orcs defeated by the Noldor at Lake Mithrim, is ambushed and wiped out by Celegorm, third son of Fëanor.

Expecting the imminent birth of Men, the Second Children of Ilúvatar, the Valar resolve to guard them against Morgoth's darkness by lighting all of Eä with a Moon and a Sun.

The Moon (a radiant silver flower of Telperion transparently encased by Aulë) being ready first, Varda sends it up into the sky from the Pelóri mountains in Valinor. So it seems to rise first in the west, but its assigned course is to pass under Eä and make its rising in the east.

At the Moon's first appearance Fingolfin and his host, safe at last from their crossing of the Helcaraxë, set foot on Middle-earth. They greet it with silver trumpets.

II THE SOLAR YEARS

Year

Seven "days" later the Sun (one golden fruit from Laurelin) rises similarly above the Pelóri, but is designed to circle under Eä and bring morning to the east.

1–20 According to the Sun's coming and going begins the Count of Time on Middle-earth, its first rising being the first day of the first Year of the Sun. Its Years are "swifter and briefer than the long Years of the Trees in Valinor" (p. 103).

On the day of its first rising Fingolfin and his host march into Mithrim, saluting it with horns and banners.

On the same day the race of Men awake in Hildórien.

Morgoth immediately comes to corrupt them by laying upon their hearts a darkness of fear and enmity against the Elves which can never be expunged. But he is called back to Angband, having only partially completed this task.

After the First and Second Battles Morgoth lures Maedhros into a conference at which he is seized by Balrogs and nailed by one hand to a cliff in Thangorodrim.

His friend Fingon finds him and, lifted up by Thorondor, King of Eagles, frees him by cutting off his hand.

Maedhros, grateful, begs Fingolfin's pardon for the desertion in Araman. Also renounces in his favor the office of High King of the Noldor.

Thingol declares his rule not only over Doriath but also over all of Beleriand; forbids Noldor settlements anywhere except in wild, unoccupied lands; denies access to Doriath by any except members of the House of Finarfin, his kinsman.

All the Noldor are dismayed, but Caranthir, fourth son of Fëanor, angrily attacks Angrod, reporter of Thingol's claim. To ensure peace Maedhros takes all six of his brothers far eastward to the Hill of Himring. There he makes them wardens of the March of Maedhros against Morgoth's incursions from the north.

20 Fingolfin as High King holds a statesmanlike Feast of Reuniting, Mereth Aderthad, near the pools of Ivrin, to heal all breaches. All the Noldor princes attend, notably Maedhros and his brother Maglor the Minstrel, with some of their warriors. Also the Sindar leaders, save only those of Doriath. All swear oaths of friendship. To bring Noldor and Sindar closer together, the Noldor there speak Sindarin.

50 Warned by Ulmo in their dreams to build cities impregnable to Morgoth, Finrod and Turgon travel together looking for

Year

proper sites. With help from Dwarves, Finrod founds Nargothrond in caves dug into the bank of the River Narog, resembling Menegroth.

51 Under Ulmo's guidance Turgon discovers among the mountains the hidden value of Tumladen, in which stands a hill of
rock on which to erect a city modeled after Tirion upon Túna
in Aman.

c. 55 **The Third Battle of Beleriand, Dagor Agloreb, the Glorious
Battle**

A huge legion of Orcs attacking Dorthonion is crushed between the forces of Fingolfin and Maedhros, who assail it
simultaneously.

The Noldor leaders establish a tight siege of Angband which
lasts nearly 400 years.

c. 100 Turgon builds and secretly occupies the hidden city of Gondolin. Ulmo promises him that it will be the last of the Noldor
strongholds to fall, and that he will send a warning of peril
before that happens.

c. 155 Morgoth probes the defenses of Hithlum by sending a brigade
of Orcs around it to attack from its west. Fingon falls upon
them at the Firth of Drengist and drives most of them into the
Sea.

c. 255 Perceiving that unaided Orcs cannot prevail against the Noldor, Morgoth breeds Glaurung, the first Fire-drake. It emerges
from Angband prematurely and is driven back in by a cavalry
of Elves, who shoot arrows into its soft scales.

c. 256– A Long Peace ensues while Glaurung grows to maturity. The
c. 450 Noldor find leisure for the arts of mind and hand. In many
regions they merge with the Sindar. Sindarin becomes the
dominant speech for all the Elves of Beleriand. But the Noldor princes retain Noldorin, the High Speech of the West,
among themselves, and as a "language of lore."

c. 300 Through his mother Aredhel, sister of King Turgon, Maeglin
gains access to Gondolin. Unable to win the love of Idril, the
King's daughter, he seeks selfish power there.

c. 350 Three tribes of Men first enter Beleriand: the people of Bëor,
the Haladin, and the Hador. By invitation of the Noldor lords
Bëor's tribe joins Angrod and Aegnor, sons of Finarfin, in
Dorthonion. The Hador settle in Hithlum under Fingolfin.
The Haladin choose to live in the Forest of Brethil.

c. 450 Húrin and Huor of the House of Hador, being fostered in
Brethil by their uncle, Haldir, lose their way after fighting Orcs

Year

and are carried by Thorondor's Eagles into Gondolin. They persuade King Turgon to release them.

455 *The Fourth Battle, Dagor Bragollach, the Battle of Sudden Flame*

Morgoth suddenly succeeds in breaking the Siege of Angband. With swift rivers of lava he burns Ard-galen into ashes. Then with Glaurung, Balrogs, and vast battalions of Orcs, he pens Fingolfin and Fingon in Hithlum; overruns Dorthonion, killing Angrod and Aegnor; smashes open the whole March of Maedhros except the Hill of Himring, held by Maedhros and Maglor.

455 Celegorm and Curufin unwisely flee to Nargothrond.

Finrod, hurrying his army northward into the fray, is trapped in the Fens of Serech, saved only by Barahir, to whom he gives his ring and swears an oath of friendship.

Fingolfin challenges Morgoth to single combat, lames him, but is killed. Fingon becomes High King.

457 Barahir sends the women and children of Bëor's tribe to the Haladin and the Hador. He fights on in Dorthonion's highlands with twelve men, among them his son, Beren.

Sauron drives Orodreth from Tol Sirion and, as Morgoth's chief lieutenant, occupies its tower and dungeons with his Werewolves.

Easterlings enter Beleriand for the first time, many of them already corrupted by Morgoth. Maedhros allies himself with Bór and Ulfang, the former faithful, the latter not.

462 Morgoth sends a large force of Orcs against Hithlum. Húrin holds the pass of Eithel Sirion against one army. With Círdan's aid Fingon slaughters another coming down from the north.

Húrin marries Morwen and rules the Hador in Dor-lómin.

c. 465 By a trick Sauron learns the whereabouts of Barahir's band and dispatches Orcs, who slay them, all except Beren.

469–
c. 490 Beren fights on alone for four years, then goes south to the forest of Neldoreth, where he and Lúthien meet and love.

To win Lúthien, Beren is required by Thingol to bring back as a bride-price a Silmaril from Morgoth's crown.

Finrod Felagund dies while saving Beren from a Werewolf in Sauron's dungeon at Tol Sirion.

Lúthien and the hound Huan rescue Beren by driving Sauron from Tol Sirion.

Year

While Morgoth and all his court slumber under Lúthien's spell of sleep Beren pries loose a Silmaril from his iron crown.

Carcharoth swallows the Silmaril in Beren's hand and, tortured by pain, ravages Doriath. In hunting the beast Beren is mortally wounded while saving Thingol's life. Beren gives Thingol the Silmaril, cut out from Carcharoth, and perishes of his wounds. Lúthien dies of grief.

In Mandos' halls Lúthien sings so sweetly of her love for Beren that Manwë, empowered by Ilúvatar, allows the lovers to return together to Eä as mortals, there to share the fate of Men when they die again.

They settle on Tol Galen in Ossiriand and have a son, Dior, who is heir to Thingol's throne.

487   Húrin's son, Túrin, is born to Morwen.

c. 490   Maedhros tries to form a Union of all those who will fight against Morgoth, especially with Fingon, but neither Nargothrond nor Doriath joins. Fingon has the help of Círdan's Elves from the Falas and of all the Edain. Maedhros has to rely on the Easterlings and a contingent of Dwarves.

495   *The Fifth Battle, Nirnaeth Arnoediad, the Battle of Unnumbered Tears*

As in Dagor Aglareb, the Glorious Battle, Fingon and Maedhros are to attack simultaneously from west and east. But Maedhros is delayed on the Hill of Himring by the false reports of Uldor, his Easterling scout. And Fingon, leaving his defenses too soon, is surrounded by Orcs and killed. Maedhros, hastening to Fingon's aid, is betrayed by Easterlings.

The Hador of Dor-lómin, captained by Huor and Húrin, fight to the last. Húrin is captured alive and taken to Angband.

Tuor is born. His mother, Rían, dies of grief for her slain father, Huor.

All the sons of Fëanor are wounded but escape to Mount Dolmed.

Hithlum has lost all its fighting Men and most of its Elves. Morgoth repopulates it with Easterlings. He ravages the Falas, driving Círdan and his Elves to the Isle of Balar.

Seven ships built by Círdan for King Turgon, to plead for help from the Valar against Morgoth, are all wrecked.

Morgoth, unable to break Húrin's will and force him to reveal the location of Gondolin, curses him and sits him, bound, on

Year

a high peak whence he must watch evil overtake his wife and children.

Morwen sends Túrin, age eight, to Doriath to escape slavery under the Easterlings and to be nurtured by King Thingol.

Year of Lamentation for the Battle of Unnumbered Tears.

496 Morwen gives birth to Nienor, Túrin's sister, whom he does not see.

505 Now eighteen, Túrin begins to fight Orcs on the borders of Doriath.

508– Túrin returns to Menegroth to rest. Kills Saeros. Presuming
c. 515 himself an outlaw, he gathers a band of desperate men on Amon Rûdh; is betrayed by Mîm; kills his friend Beleg by mistake; and is taken by Gwindor to Nargothrond. Finduilas falls in love with him, in vain.

511 Tuor is fostered secretly by Grey-elves in the Caves of Androth in Mithrim.

514 Tuor captured and enslaved by Easterlings.

516 Ulmo warns King Orodreth to throw down the new bridge across the River Narog, to shut his city's gates, and to keep his army safe behind them. Túrin persuades the King to ignore Ulmo's counsels.

517 Tuor escapes; returns to the Caves of Andros; lives there as an outlaw, harrying the Easterlings.

Morgoth looses against Nargothrond a host of Orcs led by Glaurung. The King, by Túrin's bad advice, leads out his army; is defeated and slain at Tumhalad.

Nargothrond is sacked. The paralyzing spell of Glaurung's eyes holds Túrin immobile, then deceives him into making a vain journey to Dor-lómin to save Morwen and Nienor, who have already fled to Doriath.

Under the same spell, Nienor loses all memory of who she is. Running naked to the Forest of Brethil, she is pitied and then loved by Túrin, who has taken refuge there.

520 Túrin and Nienor are married.

521 Nienor becomes pregnant. Glaurung, about to ruin Brethil, is mortally wounded by Túrin, single-handed. Before he dies, Glaurung tells Nienor that she and Túrin are brother and sister.

522 Nienor drowns herself in the River Teiglin. When Túrin hears the full story, he kills himself by falling on the point of his sword Anglachel.

Year

The Elves of Doriath build a grave mound honoring Túrin as Glaurung's Bane.

523 Morgoth releases Húrin after 28 years. Shunned by his own people in Hithlum as a servant of Morgoth, Húrin finds Morwen dying on Túrin's grave mound but withholds from her the manner of his and his sister's death.

524 Húrin seeks vengeance on all who have injured his family; kills Mîm in Nargothrond; selects from Glaurung's treasure only Nauglamír, the Necklace of the Dwarves; caustically gives it to Thingol for "safekeeping" his family; casts himself into the Sea.

Tuor, called by Ulmo, finds in Vinyamar the armor and weapons left by King Turgon to identify the messenger warning of imminent peril.

525 Ulmo orders Tuor to seek out Gondolin and deliver his message; saves Voronwë, a mariner of Gondolin, to guide him there.

Thingol has Dwarves from Nogrod set his Silmaril in Nauglamír. Dwarves kill Thingol; are themselves killed by Doriath's Elves, all save two.

Melian, at her husband's death, withdraws her protecting Girdle and returns to Valinor.

Tuor repeats to King Turgon Ulmo's counsel to abandon Gondolin and take its people to the Mouths of Sirion. Turgon refuses to leave the city.

526 Nogrod sends an army of Dwarves to Doriath. Entering Menegroth, Dwarves win a bloody battle with the Elves there.

527 Dwarves march eastward with Nauglamír and its Silmaril; are ambushed by Green-elves of Ossiriand led by Beren, who takes the necklace home to Tol Galen for Lúthien to wear.

Ents kill all the Dwarves who survive the ambush.

c. 528 Dior, son of Beren and Lúthien, succeeds to the throne of Doriath.

Beren and Lúthien die; go together, like others of the race of Men, to a future beyond the World, having sent the Silmaril to Dior.

c. 530 The seven Sons of Fëanor attack Dior to recover the Silmaril; kill Dior and most of his people in a second Kinslaying. Celegorm, Curufin, and Caranthir are slain.

Elwing, Dior's daughter, escapes with the Silmaril to the Mouths of Sirion.

532 Tuor marries Idril Celebrindal, Turgon's daughter, after seven years in Gondolin.

Year

533 Eärendil, their son, is born.

540 Morgoth surprises and overthrows Gondolin, aided by treacherous information from Maeglin. King Turgon and Maeglin perish.

Tuor leads Idril, Eärendil, and the other survivors safely through perils to the Mouths of Sirion.

c. 545 Tuor, feeling old, sails with Idril into the West, never to return; nor is their fate known.

c. 555 Eärendil becomes ruler of the remnants of Doriath and Gondolin gathered at Sirion's Mouths; marries Elwing. Elros and Elrond are the sons of this marriage.

Eärendil ventures far into the Western Sea in his ship Vingilot, hoping to reach Valinor with a plea for help against Morgoth; is baffled without the Silmaril, which remains with Elwing.

560 The four remaining sons of Fëanor, seeking the Silmaril, swoop down upon the fugitives near Sirion; kill many. Two sons, Amrod and Amros, perish. Elwing escapes with the Silmaril by throwing herself into the Sea.

Ulmo gives Elwing the wings of a seabird, and she flies to Vingilot. Lighted by the Silmaril, Eärendil is able to reach Valinor. Before the assembled Valar he is granted the pardon, pity, and help for Elves and Men he pleads for.

Manwë decrees that all the Half-elven shall be given the choice of becoming either wholly Elves or wholly Men.

Elwing choosing to be wholly Elven; Eärendil for her sake chooses the same.

Vingilot is hallowed and lifted up into the sky, steered forever by Eärendil wearing the Silmaril on his brow: the Morning and Evening Star (Venus).

The War of Wrath

Eärendil throws down the new race of flying Dragons sent against him by Morgoth in the War of Wrath launched at last by the Valar and the Elves faithful to them. Morgoth is seized, bound, and thrust out into the Void in permanent exile. The whole of Beleriand, right up to the Ered Luin mountains, is overrun by the Sea.

Many Elves take ship for the Undying Lands; others prefer to cross the mountains and dwell on the wide continent of Middle-earth lying behind it.

The two remaining Silmarils taken from Morgoth and entrusted to Manwë's herald, Eonwë, are seized by Maedhros and

Maglor. The Silmarils so burn the brothers that they realize their forfeiture, by their crimes, of any right to possess the Jewels.

Maedhros despairingly throws himself and his Silmaril into a fiery crevice in the Earth.

Maglor pitches his Silmaril far out into the Great Sea. Ever after, the Minstrel wanders alone on the shore singing songs of sad remorse. He never returns to Valinor.

Notes

I. A MYTHOLOGY FOR ENGLAND

1. Humphrey Carpenter, *Tolkien*, p. 59.
2. See any anthology of Anglo-Saxon poetry, like that edited by Charles W. Kennedy in modern translation.
3. *Tolkien*, pp. 71, 92, 96.
4. *Tolkien*, pp. 89–90.
5. *Tolkien*, p. 49. See *Kalevala*, trans. W. F. Kirby, I, 1–2. This Everyman edition was used by Tolkien himself.
6. *Tolkien*, p. 49.
7. *Tolkien*, pp. 64–65.
8. *Tolkien*, p. 105.
9. *Tolkien*, pp. 119–120.
10. See *The Silmarillion*, Appendix (p. 360), where *ilúvë* is said by Tolkien to mean "the whole, the all," and *atar* (p. 356) to mean "father." In their combination Ilúvatar, therefore, signifies "the father of all" or "All-Father," a title often used to describe Odin in Norse mythology. Thus the very name of God in *The Silmarillion* harks back to the Norse, although Ilúvatar, of course, is quite unlike Odin and resembles instead the Almighty Father of Christianity.
11. For a discussion of free will in Tolkien's work see Kocher, *Master of Middle-earth*, chap. III and passim.
12. *The Elder Edda*, trans. Paul Taylor and W. H. Auden.
13. *The Elder Edda*, especially "The Song of the Sybil" and "The Lay of Vafthrudnir," for Ymir and his function in the creation of Midgard. In *The Prose Edda* (trans. Jean I. Young), "The Deluding of Gylfi" (pp. 34–37) gives an account of the creation of the first man and woman, and also a myth of the making of stars, moon, and sun by Odin.
14. Arden Library, 1978.
15. In *The Silmarillion* (p. 48) Varda (Elbereth) makes more stars to brighten the sky for the Elves who are about to be born at Lake

Cuiviénen. Among the constellations she puts together is Menelmacar (Orion) "with his shining belt that forebodes the Last Battle that shall be at the end of days." Similarly (p. 44) the Dwarves expect to help Aulë in "the remaking of Arda after the Last Battle." An echo of Ragnarök?

16. "On Fairy-stories," *The Tolkien Reader*, pp. 3–84.
17. *The Elder Edda*, Introduction, p. 30.
18. *The Prose Edda*, "The Deluding of Gylfi," p. 46.
19. *The Elder Edda*, "Loki's Flyting," pp. 133 ff.
20. *The Elder Edda*, "Skirnir's Ride," stanza 7, p. 119.
21. *The Elder Edda*, "Skirnir's Ride," stanzas 17–18, p. 120.
22. *The Elder Edda*, "The Words of the All-Wise," stanzas 10–35, pp. 79–83.
23. Supportive evidence appears also in William Morris' translation of *Volsunga Saga*, which Tolkien almost certainly read (see Carpenter, pp. 46, 169). For example, when Sigurd questions the dying dragon Fafnir about the races to which the nine Norns belong he is told that "some are of the kin of Aesir, and some are of Elfin kin, and some . . . are daughters of Dvalin [Dwarves]" (p. 143). Again, when Brynhild tells Sigurd about the lore of "runes" she says that of these runes "Some abide with the Elves, Some abide with the Aesir . . . some with the sons of mankind" (p. 153). This is distinguished company for the Elves to be keeping, and it vouches for their high station.
24. *The Prose Edda*, "The Deluding of Gylfi," p. 41.
25. *The Elder Edda*, pp. 80–83.
26. *Tolkien*, pp. 89–90.

II. The Providence of Ilúvatar

This chapter concerns *Ainulindalë; Valaquenta; Quenta Simarillion*, chapters 1–3, 9, 11, 24.

1. Carpenter quotes Tolkien (p. 91) as saying emphatically, "Middle-earth is *our* world," not some other planet. And he added, "I have (of course) placed the action in a purely imaginary (though not wholly impossible) period of antiquity, in which the shape of the continental masses was different." If the world had not been our Earth no "mythology for England" could properly have been written for it.
2. In this passage the capitalization of the word "Being" is mine, not Tolkien's.
3. For a further discussion of Dwarves see Kocher, *Master of Middle-earth*, chap. V.
4. *The Elder Edda*, "Song of the Sybil," stanzas 18 and 19, p. 147, has a description of trees being given life by the Aesir gods. Three of the gods, led by Odin, find on Midgard Ash and Elm,

> Faint, feeble, with no fate assigned them.
> Breath they had not, nor blood, nor senses,
> Nor language possessed, nor life-hue:

> Odin gave them breath, Haenir senses,
> Blood and life-hue Lodur gave.

Tolkien's special love of trees is well known. This passage sounds like a forecast of the Ents, especially of their ability to speak, to move, to hear, and to feel emotions.

5. In *Grettir's Saga*, p. 79, Glam, an evil revenant from the grave, attacks Grettir. First he afflicts Grettir with such weakness that he cannot even draw his sword. Then he curses Grettir roundly: "Up until now your deeds have brought you fame, but from now on outlawry and slaughter will come your way, and most of your acts will bring you ill luck and misfortune. You will be made an outlaw and forced to live by yourself. I also lay this curse upon you: you will always see these eyes of mine, and they will make your solitude unbearable, and this shall drag you to your death." As soon as the curse has been uttered, Grettir's faintness leaves him, and he is able to cut off Glam's head. But the curse works in many subsequent episodes until Grettir is treacherously killed on solitary Drang Island.

This malediction is only an analogue, not a source for Tolkien, probably, but it serves to illustrate Icelandic saga lore.

III. THE VALAR AND THE ELVES

This chapter concerns *Quenta Simarillion*, chapters 3–5.

1. In *The Prose Edda*'s "Deluding of Gylfi" (p. 46), likewise, when Odin looked out over Midgard from his high seat in Asgard he could see all over the world. There two ravens brought to him all the news that they saw or heard (p. 63).

2. For a complete enumeration of the whole hierarchy of angels, see *The Maryknoll Catholic Dictionary*, ed. Rev. Albert J. Nevins (New York: Grosset and Dunlap, 1965), p. 268.

IV. FËANOR

This chapter concerns *Quenta Silmarillion*, chapters 5–9, 11, 13.

1. In *Volsunga Saga*, chap. 2, Volsung grows in his mother's womb for six years until she has him cut out alive. Upon emerging, he was so large and strong that he kissed her before she died from the birth. Later he became "the greatest of warriors."

2. *The Lord of the Rings* III, 395–97, Appendix E.

3. *The Silmarillion*, pp. 276, 291–92. Also *The Lord of the Rings* II, 203–04; III, 365.

4. *The Lord of the Rings* III, 53.

5. *The Lord of the Rings* II, 204.

6. For a discussion of the evil of "possessiveness" see Kocher, *Master of Middle-earth*, chaps. III, IV, V, and VII.

7. *The Lord of the Rings* II, 332–39.

8. According to Norse-Icelandic belief, Fëanor, Fingolfin, and

Finarfin all had a strict duty to avenge the killing of their father by Morgoth. In *Volsunga Saga*, chaps. 15–17, for example, Sigurd postpones all else until he has avenged the deaths of his father, King Sigmund, and other kinsmen upon their slayers, King Hunding and his sons.

V. THE FIRST TWO BATTLES OF BELERIAND

This chapter concerns *Quenta Silmarillion*, chapters 4, 10, 13.

1. Tolkien assigns the guidance of the Moon to a male Maia, Tilion, and the guidance of the Sun to a female one, Arien, much stronger than he. This arrangement is out of keeping with the Graeco-Roman myth that the god who rules the chariot of the Sun is Apollo, a male, and that Selene, a female, rules the Moon. In Norse mythology, however, as in *The Silmarillion*, the Sun is female, the Moon male. (See *The Elder Edda*, "The Lay of Grimnir," stanza 39, and "Song of the Sybil," stanza 9.) But in the Norse, both Sun and Moon are pulled by horses, which Tolkien replaces with appropriate Maiar.

2. Morgoth's pouring much of his innate strength into his creatures of evil is like Sauron's pouring much of his power into the One Ring.

VI. THE REALMS OF THE NOLDOR

This chapter concerns *Quenta Silmarillion*, chapters 14–16.

1. In *The Elder Edda*, "The Lay of Thrym," stanza 10 (p. 85), and also the Glossary of Names (p. 164) tell of the Brising Necklace, fabricated by Dwarves and owned by the goddess Freya. It apparently consisted of some precious metal worked into a twining pattern.

2. *The Elder Edda*, Introduction (p. 30): There is a region outside Midgard where Elves live (Alfheim) and another which is the home of Dark Elves (Svartalfheim). In *The Prose Edda*, "The Deluding of Gylfi" (p. 46) describes a similar division between "light elves" and "dark elves." The light elves are "fairer than the sun to look upon, but the dark elves blacker than pitch." The latter are said to live underground. Tolkien's Eöl, described as "the Dark Elf," has some of these characteristics but not all. He dwells by preference in a dark, thick forest and is friendly with Dwarves who live in caves. But he himself lives above ground. Of the Dark Elves Tolkien says in another place (*The Silmarillion*, p. 104) that they befriended Men after they were born at Hildórien and taught them many truths, as well as much rumor, about Middle-earth and Valinor.

VII. OF THE COMING OF MEN

This chapter concerns *Quenta Silmarillion*, chapters 17, 18; also 1, 12.

1. See the genealogies in *The Silmarillion*, pp. 307 and 308.

2. In *The Prose Edda*, "The Deluding of Gylfi" (pp. 70–72), Thor makes a journey to Utgard and strikes three blows with his huge hammer Mjöllnir at the head of the sleeping giant Skrýmir but is unable to make even the smallest dent. He learns later that he has been the victim of an

illusion. His blows have made deep valleys in the earth, even though a hill was placed invisibly under his hammer at each blow.

VIII. Beren and Lúthien

This chapter concerns *Quenta Silmarillion*, chapters 18–20.

1. In *Kalevala*, Runo III, a presumptuous youth, Joukahainen, challenges the wise and ancient Väinämöinen to a contest of magical songs. But the youth's songs are fended off by his adversary as shallow and commonplace. Then Väinämöinen sings songs of such power that they sink the youngster deeper and deeper into a swamp until his face is going under and he is desperately begging the ancient one to "reverse thy songs of magic,/ Loose me from this place of terror." Väinämöinen agrees to do so at last when Joukahainen promises to give him "his lovely sister, Aino." And in Runo XVI Väinämöinen, "the great primeval sorcerer," builds a boat with magic songs but lacks a spell of "three words" to fix the sides together securely. He seeks for the magical words everywhere, even going to Tuonela, the land of the dead, to procure them. Finally, in Runo XVII, he gets them from the wise giant Vipunen.

2. *Volsunga Saga*, pp. 98–99: Volsung's ten sons are captured and set in the stocks by King Siggeir, who on each night sends a huge wolf to devour one of them. When only Sigmund, the tenth, remains alive his sister Signy saves him by smearing his face and mouth with honey. As the wolf comes to kill him it first licks off the honey. This enables Sigmund to bite off its tongue, kill it, smash the stocks, and escape.

3. An interesting analogue, if not a direct source, appears in *Volsunga Saga*, "Part of the Second Lay of Helgi Hundingsbane" (p. 242), in which the Minstrel who has sung the Lay comments on the love between Helgi and his wife Sigrun. So great is it that when Helgi is killed in battle and buried in his grave mound, she goes there to lie beside his corpse and sleep with it. Soon she dies of sorrow. The Minstrel ends his Lay with the assertion that in olden times people believed that dead lovers could be born again, but that now this belief is considered an old wife's doting tale. So men say "Helgi and Sigrun were born again, and at that tide was he called Helgi the Scathe of Hadding and she Kara the daughter of Halfdan; and she was a Valkyria, even as is said in the Lay of Kara." This Second Lay is among those translated by William Morris as "Certain Songs from the Elder Edda, Which Deal with the Story of the Volsungs" and affixed by him to his translation of *Volsunga Saga* (pp. 235–42).

IX. The Battle of Unnumbered Tears

This section concerns *Quenta Silmarillion*, chapter 20.

1. It is to this disastrous Fifth Battle (Nirnaeth Arnoediad), yet to come, that Mandos refers, although the Noldor whom he curses are unaware of his meaning at the time (*The Silmarillion*, pp. 190–95).

2. For Norse anger against oath-breakers consult *The Elder Edda*, "Song of the Sybil," stanza 34 (p. 149) listing them alongside murderers and

adulterers. See also, in the same, "The Treachery of Asmund" (pp. 97–100). Likewise, in *The Prose Edda* "The Deluding of Gylfi" describes the poisonous streams through which murderers and oath-breakers must wade after Ragnarök.

3. *The Lord of the Rings* III, 365, Appendix B, relates the formation of this Last Alliance.

4. Inasmuch as Morgoth's curse falls out exactly as he intended, though invoked with malice upon a good and heroic man, the question arises why a curse pronounced by an evil being upon a person who does not deserve it should be efficacious. Theologically speaking, of course, a curse works only if Ilúvatar permits it to work as part of his Providence. I am under the strong impression, however, that in the Norse-Icelandic *Eddas* and sagas a curse almost always works, no matter what the character of the person who pronounces it or of him on whom it is pronounced. This can only be the result of a literary convention which Tolkien elects to follow in Húrin's case. Thus in *Grettir's Saga* (pp. 76–79, 86) the curse called down on Grettir by the evil spirit, Glam, pursues Grettir ever afterward. And William Morris, in his derivative *House of the Wolfings*, follows the same tradition when an evil dwarf successfully curses a suit of armor he has made so that its wearer will be unable to fight in battle. Elsewhere in *The Silmarillion* Eöl's curse against his son Maeglin also works out as planned.

X. TÚRIN TURAMBAR

This chapter concerns *Quenta Silmarillion*, Chapter 21.

1. See Kocher, *Master of Middle-earth*, chap. VII; also an essay, "Appendix on Verse-Forms," by Tolkien printed with his modernization of *Sir Gawain and the Green Knight, Pearl, and Sir Orfeo*.

2. *Volsunga Saga* (p. 148) tells how Sigurd took from Fafnir's treasure "the Helm of Awe." Although its shape was not described, it performed the same function as does Túrin's "Dragon-Helm," protecting its wearer and frightening his foes. When Túrin calls himself "Gorthol, the Dread Helm" (*The Silmarillion*, p. 205) the name closely approximates Fafnir's "Helm of Awe."

3. Unless a man who had killed another possessed wealth enough to pay *wergeld* and had strong backers behind him, he could easily find himself outlawed for a term of years by the Speaker of the Thing, Iceland's parliament. Once an outlaw, he was legally subject to ambush or open attack by his foes, and if he killed one or more of them in defending himself, that was yet another score against him by his victim's kinsmen. So he might sink deeper and deeper into outlawry, unable ever to recover. Such is the case of Grettir in *Grettir's Saga*. (See also *Njal's Saga*.) This dilemma helps to explain Túrin's fear of a possible sentence of outlawry against him by Thingol.

4. For *lembas* see *The Lord of the Rings* I, 385, 404; II, 29, 57ff.

5. Just how Morgoth bred and reared Glaurung, Father of Dragons,

Tolkien never tells. We know that Morgoth lacked the power to create life, which belonged only to Ilúvatar, and that he could only change into new forms those lives he already controlled, as he did in breeding Orcs from Elves. Balrogs, being creatures of fire, are the most probable source of Dragons, which are also creatures of fire. But Morgoth also managed to endow Glaurung with hypnotic powers, which Balrogs apparently never possessed.

6. In *Volsunga Saga* (pp. 141-43) the dragon Fafnir is killed by Sigurd in much the same manner. Knowing the path by which Fafnir usually crawls to the river to drink, Sigurd digs a pit there, in which he hides. When the Worm passes over it, Sigurd rips open with his sword the soft underbelly above him.

7. As Túrin is honored by the title "Glaurung's Bane," so Sigurd is called "Fafnir's Bane" (*Volsunga Saga*, pp. 187-90).

XI. The Ruin of Doriath

This chapter concerns *Quenta Silmarillion*, chapter 22.

1. See *The Lord of the Rings* I, 141-42 and 151-54, where the Hobbits are captured and almost killed by the half-alive spirits of the dead in the barrows on the South Downs.

XII. Tuor and the Fall of Gondolin

This chapter concerns *Quenta Silmarillion*, chapter 23.

1. The man they saw was Túrin, deceived by Glaurung's lies, hurrying northward to Dor-lómin to rescue Morwen and Nienor from the Easterlings, but they were not there (pp. 214-15).

2. Idril, being Maeglin's first cousin, a marriage between them was forbidden by Elvish custom. But little cared Maeglin for custom, or law either.

3. Glorfindel is also the name of a powerful Elf attached to Elrond's court at Rivendell in *The Lord of the Rings* I, 222-26. But he cannot be the same as the heroic Elf of that name slain in the escape from Gondolin. The latter's grave is described here (*The Silmarillion*, p. 243). The Rivendell Elf may possibly be a descendant of his, or perhaps one of his kindred named after him.

4. *The Lord of the Rings* III, 365, Appendix B.

XIII. Eärendil and the War of Wrath

This chapter concerns *Quenta Silmarillion*, chapter 24.

1. Humphrey Carpenter, *Tolkien*, p. 64.

2. *Tolkien*, p. 71.

XIV. *Akallabêth*

1. This summary is to be found in *The Lord of the Rings* III, 363-65, Appendix B, covering the entire 3441 years of the Second Age.

2. *The Lord of the Rings* III, 363.
3. *The Lord of the Rings* III, 343, Appendix A.
4. *The Lord of the Rings* II, 286.
5. *The Lord of the Rings* III, 364, Appendix B.
6. In the Appendix to *The Silmarillion* (p. 364) "tar" is described as a Quenya (Eldarin) term meaning "high." But "ar," as in Ar-Pharazôn, is an Adunaic prefix (p. 356). The replacement of "Tar" by "Ar" in the year 2899 by King Adûnakhor signifies his abandonment of dependence on the Elves and the Valar. In 3175 Tar-Palantir tried to reverse this change but in vain, for Ar-Pharazôn the usurper in 3255 cut off himself and his people completely from obedience to those who lived on the Undying Lands. And in his old age he invaded those lands, thereby precipitating the Downfall of his Island.
7. *The Lord of the Rings* II, 202.
8. *The Lord of the Rings* III, 365, Appendix B.
9. *The Lord of the Rings* III, 365, Appendix B.

XV. OF THE RINGS OF POWER AND THE THIRD AGE

1. *The Lord of the Rings* I, 289, 293ff.
2. *The Lord of the Rings* III, 364, Appendix B. For example, this city is not mentioned in *The Lord of the Rings*.
3. *The Lord of the Rings* I, 255.
4. *The Lord of the Rings* III, 365, Appendix B.
5. In Norse custom a money payment for manslaying, given by the slayer to the next of kin. See *Grettir's Saga* (pp. 31, 52) and *The Poetic Edda*, trans. Ursula Dronke, "Atlamál in Groenlenzko" (p. 91).
6. *The Lord of the Rings* III, 366, Appendix B.
7. *The Lord of the Rings* III, 373, Appendix B.
8. *The Lord of the Rings* III, 308.

Bibliography

The William Morris items listed are of special importance to us because they were of special importance to Tolkien. When he won the Skeat Prize of £5 at Exeter College, Oxford, in 1914 he spent the money on buying these books. Likewise *Grettir's Saga* is mentioned by Carpenter as one of the major Icelandic works discussed by Tolkien in the Kolbitar Club, which he organized at Oxford later on.

Remarkable for a different reason is a book titled *The Elder Edda: A Selection*, translated by Paul B. Taylor and the distinguished poet W. H. Auden. Auden had attended Tolkien's lectures on *Beowulf* when he was an undergraduate at Oxford, and later was Professor of Poetry there from 1956 to 1961. The book which he and Taylor translated together is dedicated "For J. R. R. Tolkien" and deals, of course, with materials of highest interest to the colleague he admired. Altogether, then, Auden had abundant opportunity to absorb Tolkien's ideas about Icelandic literature, and his translation of *The Elder Edda* should be read in that light.

Carpenter, Humphrey, *Tolkien: A Biography*. Boston: Houghton Mifflin Company, 1977.
—— *The Inklings*. Boston: Houghton Mifflin Company, 1979.
Eddas
   1. The Poetic (or Elder) Edda:
     The Elder Edda: A Selection, trans. Paul B. Taylor and W. H. Auden. London: Faber & Faber, 1969. All my references are to this translation.
     The Poetic Edda Vol. I: *Heroic Poems*, ed. and trans. Ursula Dronke. Oxford: Clarendon Press, 1969.
   2. The Prose Edda:
     The Prose Edda, trans. Arthur G. Brodeur. New York: American-Scandinavian Foundation, 1967.

The Prose Edda, trans. Jean I. Young. Berkeley: University of California Press, 1954. All my references are to this translation.

Faraday, Winifred, *The Edda* I: *Divine Mythology of the North.* London: David Nutt, 1902.

Foster, Robert, *A Guide to Middle-Earth.* Baltimore: Mirage Books, 1971.

——— *The Complete Guide to Middle-Earth.* New York: Ballantine Books, 1978.

Grettir's Saga, trans. Denton Fox and Hermann Pálsson. Toronto: University of Toronto Press, 1974.

Kalevala, The Land of Heroes, 2 vols., trans. W. F. Kirby. Everyman's Library, 1974.

Kennedy, Charles W. ed. and trans., *An Anthology of Old English Poetry.* New York: Oxford University Press, 1960.

Kocher, Paul H., *Master of Middle-earth.* Boston: Houghton Mifflin Company, 1972; New York: Ballantine Books, 1977.

Mabinogion, trans. Lady Charlotte Guest. Everyman's Library, 1906. The Introduction and the tale of "Taliessin" describe the knowledge and skill expected of a good minstrel.

McCulloch, John A., ed., *The Mythology of All Races*, vol. II: *Eddic.* New York: Cooper Square Publishing Company, 1964.

Morris, William, *The House of the Wolfings.* Boston: Roberts Brothers, 1892.

Morris, William, trans. *Volsunga Saga: The Story of the Volsungs and Niblungs.* New York: Collier Books, 1962.

Nibelungenlied, trans. A. T. Hatto. Baltimore: Penguin Classics, 1965.

Njal's Saga, trans. Magnus Magnusson and Hermann Pálsson. Baltimore: Penguin Classics, 1960.

Sturluson, Snorri, *Heimskringla*, trans. S. Laing. Everyman's Library, 1975.

Tolkien, J. R. R., *Beowulf: The Monsters and the Critics*, Sir Israel Gollancz Memorial Lecture, 25 November 1936. The Arden Library, 1978.

——— *The Hobbit.* Boston: Houghton Mifflin Company, 1966.

——— "The Lay of Aotrou and Itroun," *Welsh Review* IV, December, 1945.

——— *The Lord of the Rings.* 3 vols. 2nd ed. Boston: Houghton Mifflin Company, 1967. All my references are to this edition.

——— *The Silmarillion.* Boston: Houghton Mifflin Company, 1978.

——— *Sir Gawain and the Green Knight, Pearl, and Sir Orfeo* in modern translation. Boston: Houghton Mifflin Company, 1975.

——— *Smith of Wootton Major.* New York: Ballantine Books, 1967.

——— *The Tolkien Reader.* New York: Ballantine Books, 1966. Contents:
  "On Fairy-stories"
  "The Homecoming of Beorhtnoth"
  "Leaf by Niggle"

"Farmer Giles of Ham"

"Adventures of Tom Bombadil"

—— with Donald Swann, *The Road Goes Ever On: A Song Cycle.* Boston: Houghton Mifflin Company, 1967.

West, Richard C., *Tolkien Criticism: An Annotated Checklist.* Kent, Ohio: Kent State University Press, 1970.

Index

Adunaic, 278
Adûnakhor, 213, 278
Aegnor, 55, 65, 94, 116
Ainur, 5, 11–12, 18, 31, 204; Music of
the, 15–17, 253
Alqualondë, 25, 49, 63, 67–68, 85–87,
101, 119, 131
Aman, 81, 220. *See also* Valinor
Amandil, 216, 219, 221
Amlach, 110–11
Amon Ereb, 117
Amon Rûdh, 138–60
Amon Sûl, 233, 235
Amras and Amrod, youngest sons
of Fëanor, 97, 117, 191
Anarion, 222–24, 233–34, 238
Andunië, 207
Anfauglith (dust), 123, 137. *See also*
Ard-Galen
Angainor (chain), 43
Angband, 41, 61–62, 72, 77, 92–93, 177,
187; besieged by Noldor, 91–93,
122, 146; challenged by Fingolfin,
117–18; depths and heights, 81, 83–
84, 89; launches Third Battle,
90–91; Fourth Battle, 115, 122;
Fifth Battle, 148, 150–52, 161;
wins one Silmaril, 128, 132, 137,
139–40
Anglachel (sword), 158; called Gurthang, 163, 168, 170–75

Anglo-Saxon, 131, 192, 272; verse
forms, 276
Angrist (knife), 136, 139
Angrod, 55, 65, 87, 94, 100–101,
116
Anúminas, 227, 233–34, 239
"Ar," 278
Ar-Adûnakor, 213
Aragorn, 63, 124, 126, 206–207, 211,
228, 236, 246, 249
Araman, 70, 84
Ard-Galen (Anfauglith), 93, 116
Aredhel the White, 55, 100–105
Ar-Gimilzôr, 214
Arien (Sun), 79–80
Armenelos, 207–208, 215–16, 218
Arnor, 239
Ar-Pharazôn, 203, 215–21, 225–26, 233,
278
Aros, River, 96, 104
Arwen, 126, 228, 246–47, 249
Atani. *See* Edain; Mankind
Aulë, 20–22, 37, 45, 50–51; creation of
sun and moon, 79; of Two
Lamps, 254; teaching Noldor, 86
Avallonë, 208–209, 222
Avathar, 58

Balar: Bay of, 47, 96; Isle of, 47–48,
94, 122
Baldr, 6–7

Balrogs (Valaraukar), 95, 115, 150, 196, 249; at Khazad-dûm, 240; capture Maedhros, 83, 259; creatures of Morgoth, 28, 277; death of, 196; kill Fëanor, 72, 78, 187–88; rescue Morgoth, 62. *See also* Gothmog

Ban of the Valar, 207, 211, 225

Barad-dûr, 189, 212, 223, 240, 245

Barahir, 116, 118, 125, 127, 129, 133

Baran, 109

Battles of Beleriand, 145–46

Bay of Balar, 47, 96

Bay of Eldamar, 48, 193

Being, 18, 22, 253, 272

Belegost, 76, 103, 148, 151

Beleg Strongbow, 121, 141, 148, 156–62, 173–74

Beleriand, 75, 85–86, 92, 129, 135, 182, 196

Bent World, 247

Bëor the Old, 82, 107, 109–10, 113–16

Beren, 12, 47, 113, 177, 180–81, 192; guerilla fighter, 118, 123; love for Lúthien, 126–44; personal meaning for Tolkien, 124–25; saved by Huan, 136

Bilbo. *See* Hobbits

Black Enemy. *See* Morgoth

Black Speech, 250

Bor (Easterling), 120, 149, 150

Boromir, 248

Brandir, 168, 170, 172–73

Brethil, Forest of, 96, 170–71, 173, 177; Beren and Lúthien in, 135–36; Emeldir in, 116, 118; Glaurung in, 165–67; Haleth in, 112–13, Men of, 165, 167–68; Túrin at, 110–11

Brithiach, Ford of, 102, 121

Brithombar, 94, 152

Brynhild, 272

Calacirya, 48, 81

Caranthir, 88–89, 97, 109, 112, 117, 120

Carcharoth, 138–40, 141–42, 263

Carpenter, Humphrey, *Tolkien*, 124–25, 193–94, 205, 271–72

Catholicism, 4, 14, 108, 124

Caves: of Menegroth, 179, 180–82; of Nargothrond, 159, 174

Celeborn, 90, 99, 200, 208, 229

Celebrimbor, 135, 200, 205–206, 213, 230–32

Celegorm, 54, 79, 97, 102, 104, 129, 148; his lust of Lúthien, 132–33, 135–36

Celestial Hierarchy, The 35

Celtic, 3

Children of Ilúvatar, 17, 23–24, 31–32; Elves, 12, 22, 38–39, 42–44, 52, 220; Men, 64, 79, 107–114, 220–21

Christianity, 4, 193, 201–202, 271

Círdan, 100, 152–53, 200–41, 244; at feast of Reuniting, 89; builds last ship, 247; leads Elves of Falas, 78, 94

Cirith, Ninniach (Rainbow Cleft), 93

Councils: of Elrond, 230, 243–44, 248; of the Wise (White), 227, 243–45

Crissaegrim, 24, 95, 121

Crist, 1, 193

Cuiviénen, 42–43, 64

Curse: as a literary convention, 276; of Eöl, 138, 243; of Mandos, 69, 84, 91, 257; of Morgoth, 154, 276

Curufin, 97, 104, 129, 132, 135–36, 139–40, 148

Cynewulf, 1, 193

Daeron (minstrel), 89, 127, 132, 140

Dagor Aglareb (Glorious Battle), 91

Dagor Bragollach (Battle of Sudden Flame), 115, 122

Dagorlad (Dead Marshes), 223–24, 237

Dagor-nuin-Giliath (Battle-under-Stars), 75–79

Dark Lord. *See* Morgoth

Darkness: of Morgoth, 107–108; of Sauron, 216–17; Everlasting, 198

Déagol. *See* Gollum; Hobbits

Death. *See* Ilúvatar

Denethor (leader of Green-elves), 77

Denethor (Steward of Gondor), 248

Dimbar, 121–22, 135

Dionysius the Areopagite, 35

Dior Aranel, 144, 180–82, 191

Dol Guldur, 233, 240–45

Doriath, 85, 87, 155–57, 181–82; attacked by Sons of Fëanor, 29; Beren in, 129–69; founded by Thingol, 48; Húrin's revenge on, 176–79; Thingol's murder there, 179–80

Dor-lómin, 93, 116, 118, 122–23, 156, 166, 177

Dorthonion, highland of, 87, 93, 148; Men in, 109; Sauron over, 134; under siege, 91, 115–16, 118, 125–26

Dragon-helm, 156, 160

Dragons, 115, 150, 188, 196, 249; flying, 267; source of, 277. *See also* Fafnir; Glaurung; Smaug

Draugluin (father of werewolves), 134, 137

Drengist, 93

Dúnedain, 206, 239, 246

Dwarves (Naugrim), 9–11, 20–23, 88, 229, 273; aid to Maedhros, 148, 151; in Beleriand, 76–78; Fathers of,

21, 254; seven Rings for, 231, 242–43, 245

Eä, 12, 18, 22, 32, 117, 134, 143, 255–56

Eagles, 24–25, 84, 220, 255. *See also* Thorondor

Eärendil, 47, 144, 180, 183, 186, 189, 191–97, 210; and Vingilot, 29–30, 207; messenger to Valinor, 82, 219. *See also* Vingilot

Eärendur, 239

Eärnur, 240

Eärwen, 85

Easterlings, 167; allies of Sauron, 237; an external threat, 206, 249; henchmen of Morgoth, 120, 183–84, 196; treachery of, 146–47, 150, 156. *See also* Bor; Uldor

Ecthelion, 185, 187–88

Edain (Elf-friends), 82, 109, 114, 206–26. *See also* Bëor; Hador; Haleth; Mankind

Eddas, 1–3, 5–6, 8, 9–11, 13; *Elder Edda* (poetic), 3, 5–6, 13, 64, 271–72, 274, 278; *Prose Edda*, 3, 271–75

Edrahil, 130

Eglarest, 94, 153

Eilinel, 125

Eithel Sirion, 93, 116, 123

Elbereth. *See* Varda

Eldamar, Bay of, 48, 193

Elendil, 153, 207, 217, 219, 221–24, 233–37, 239

Elendili, 210–11, 213–15. *See also* Faithful, the

Elrond, 192, 195, 225, 229–30, 239, 247–48, 277; Council of, 241–45

Elros Tar-Minyatur, 192, 195, 209, 211, 217, 225, 229, 249

Elves, 106; born at Ciuviénen, 42; immortality of, 82–83; importance of, 9, 12; Light and Dark Elves, 8, 97, 274; Norse elves, 272;

Elves *(cont.)*
size of, 7–8; some turned into
Orcs, 43; three tribes of, 44–45.
See also Noldor; Sindar; Teleri;
Vanyar
Elves, Silvan. *See* Teleri
Elwë. *See* Thingol
Elwing, 180–82, 189, 191–92, 196
Emeldir, 116, 118
Emyn Beraid (Tower Hills), 233
Ents, 24, 45, 181, 202, 246, 255, 267
Eöl, 103–05, 188, 249, 274, 276
Eonwë, 25, 29, 66, 193–99, 228
Eorl the Young, 240
Ered Gorgoroth (Mountains of
Terror), 94, 126
Ered Luin, 76, 91, 116
Ered Wethrin, 93, 115–16, 123
Eregion, 213, 227, 229–30, 232
Eressëa, 200, 205–206, 214, 220, 222,
228, 231, 236
Eriador, 232–33
Erú, 211–12, 216, 221. *See also* Ilúvatar;
Meneltarma
Esgalduin, River, 96, 141
Estolad, 109
Evil, 16–17, 19, 43, 56, 73, 217–25, 229,
249; creatures, 232, 242, 249, 256,
273; origin of, 276–77. *See also* Bal-
rogs; Dragons; Morgoth; Orcs;
Ringwraiths; Sauron; Spiders;
Werewolves; Wolves

Fafnir, 272, 276–77
Faithful, the, 213–23, 233–36. *See also*
Amandil; Elendil
Falas, 94, 123, 148
Fame, 70, 73
Faramir, 212, 248
Fëanor, 50–73, 220, 229–30, 236, 240;
death of, 72, 78; leader of Noldor,
25–27, 44; life summary, 255–58;
Oath of, 29, 63–64, 73, 83, 128, 147,

189–90, 192, 197–99; sons of, 88,
96–97, 99–100, 102–103, 116–17, 128–
30, 249; Tengwar of, 86
Felagund. *See* Finrod
Fellowship of the Ring, 240
Fen of Serech, 116, 151
Fey (berserk), 70–71, 173
Finarfin, 27, 54, 57, 65, 70, 85, 88,
155–56
Finduilas, 162–66, 169
Fingolfin, 27, 54, 80, 88, 260, 262;
against Fëanor's Oath, 65–66;
against Morgoth, 91–93, 114–18;
challenge to Morgoth, 62, 83–84;
death of, 28, 118; duped by Morgoth, 56–57, 91–93; reconciled
with Fëanor, 59
Fingon, 12, 27–28, 55, 65, 118, 228, 236,
262; against Glaurung, 92–93;
against Orcs, 116, 123, 148–51; res-
cues Maedhros, 84–85
Finrod Felagund, 27–28, 55, 65, 100,
126; and Green-elves, 98, 109; and
Nargothrond, 89–90, 101, 121, 129;
death of, 133; encounters with
Bëor's people, 107, 116; feared by
Morgoth, 122; realm of, 94–95
Finwë, 45, 57, 59, 61–62, 85, 99, 133
Ford of Brithiach, 102, 121
Foreknowledge, 173–74; of Fëanor,
73; of Finrod, 129; of Melian, 126.
See also Erú; Ilúvatar; Ulmo
Forest of Brethil. *See* Brethil, For-
est of
Forest of Neldoreth, 96, 126, 132,
136, 140
Forest of Region, 96
Formenos, 57–58, 61
Fornost, 239
Fourth Age (Men), 241–42; 246,
248–49
Free Will, 4, 11, 14–17, 21, 26, 31, 65–
66, 174, 249–50. *See also* Ilúvatar

Galadriel, 27, 70, 99–100, 231, 240–41, 248; and Celeborn, 90, 99, 205, 229; sides with Fëanor, 65

Galathilion, 208. *See also* Telperion; White Tree

Galdor, 122

galvorn (metal), 103

Gandalf (Mithrandir), 200, 220, 231, 240–43, 246–48

Gelmir, brother of Gwindor, 149

Gems, 51–52

Gil-galad, 153, 228–29, 232–33, 241; King of the Noldor, 200, 205, 212, 214, 241; in league against Sauron, 223–24; in the Last Alliance, 237

Girdle of Melian. *See* Melian

Gladden Fields, 224, 239, 244–45

Glaurung, 117, 165–75, 178, 249, 277; bred by Morgoth, 92, 166, 169; father of dragons, 115, 187; hypnotic powers of, 166, 169, 174–75, 265, 276; slain by Túrin, 171

Glorfindel, 188–89, 277

Gollum (Sméagol), 224, 245–46, 248

Gondolin (Ondolindë), 24, 104–105, 118; 121–22, 148; feared by Morgoth, 151; name of, 98; Tuor in, 183–90

Gondor, 227, 234, 239–40, 246

Good, 224, 249. *See also* Evil

Gorlim, 125

Gothmog, Lord of Balrogs, 72, 151, 186–87

Green-elves (Nandor), 77, 89, 98, 109, 117

Grettir's Saga, 273, 276, 278

Grond, 118

Guarded Plain. *See* Nargothrond

Gulf of Lhûn, 228

Gurthang (sword). *See* Anglachel

Gwindor, 148, 161–65

Hador, 82, 109–13, 116, 121–22, 184; in Nirnaeth Arnoediad, 148, 151–52

Haladin, 118, 120–21, 148; rallied by Haldad, 111; to Thargelion, 82, 109

Haldad and Haldar, 112

Haleth, 112

Harad (Haradrim), 237

Havens, 192, 241

Helcaraxë, 27, 61, 70–71, 80

Helevorn, Lake, 97, 117

Helm's Deep, 234

Hildor (Mankind), 79, 82, 274

Himring, Hill of, 88, 91, 97, 117, 135

Hírilorn, 132

Hithlum, 87, 92, 95, 115–16, 122–23, 184; Easterlings in, 152

Hobbits (Periannath), 11, 228, 234, 243, 245, 277; Bilbo, 124, 246–48; Déagol, 245; Frodo, 200, 224, 232, 244, 246–48; Sam, 200, 224, 248

Huan, 132, 135–37, 140–42

Huor, 121, 123, 151, 184, 186

Húrin, 1, 121–23, 151, 155–56, 162–63, 186; cursed by Morgoth; freed, 176–77

Idril Celebrindal, 99, 103, 105–106, 183–91, 194, 277

Ilúvatar, 4–5; creation by, 64; death a gift from, 31, 142–43, 203, 218, 224; exclusive power to create life, 194, 207, 277; laws of, 30, 41; mercy of, 21–24; name of, 271; Providence of, 11, 14–30, 47, 174, 184, 250; wrath of, 15, 25–26, 221–22

Imladris, 241. *See also* Rivendell

Immortality and Mortality, Elves, 82–83, 108; Men, 114, 209, 224–25; choice: Beren and Lúthien, 263; Half-elven, 268

Imperishable Flame, 15, 18, 21, 42, 56

Incest, 172–73, 175, 178

Indis, second wife of Finwë, 54
Ingwë, 45
Inziladûn, 214
Inzilbêth, 214
Irmo, Vala of Lórien, 33
Iron Crown, 62, 117, 139
Iron Mountains (Ered Engrin),
90–92, 115, 123
Irony, 168, 172–73, 176
Isildur, 207, 218–220, 222–24, 233–34,
239, 243–44
Isle of Balar, 47–48, 94, 122
Istari (wizards), 241–43, 245
Ivrin, 89, 130

Judgment (Last), 195, 221; of Men
after death, 108, 142
Justice. *See* Manwë; Mandos

Kalevala, 1, 3, 13, 131, 156, 272, 275; Il-
marinen, 131; Joukahainen, 275;
Kullervo, 1, 155; Lemminkainen,
131; Väinämöinen, 131, 156, 275
kelvar (fauna), 79
Khazad-dûm, 28, 240
Kingdoms, North, 222–23, 227, 246;
South, 223, 246
Kingship, 54, 57, 65–66, 85, 87–89,
95, 117–18, 130
King's Men, 211, 215
Kinslaying, 257, 267; at Al-
qualondë, 25, 63, 68, 87, 99, 101,
106, 119, 131, 199; at Menegroth,
182; at Mouths of Sirion, 192
Kocher, Paul H., *Master of Middle-
earth*, 271–73, 276
Kolbitar Club, 3

Lake Helevorn, 97, 117
Lake Mithrim, 72, 83, 116
Last Alliance, 200, 223–24, 231, 232,
237–38, 276
Last Battle, 23, 41, 221, 249

Laurelin, 38–40, 79, 254–55, 259
Legolas, 228
lembas, 158–59, 161–62, 276
Lhûn, Gulf of, 228
Light, 107–108, 110, 216. *See also*
Ilúvatar
Lindon, 228, 241
Loki, 7
Lórien, 52, 75–76, 79, 132, 240, 247
Lothlórien, 27, 200, 205, 229, 233, 240.
See also Lórien
Lúthien Tinuviel, 12, 47, 125–27, 192;
cloak of invisibility, 132–33, 185;
daughter of Melian, 75–76; love
of Beren, 127, 140–44, 190; mercy
of, 134, 136; mother of Dior, 180–81

Mablung, 89, 141, 148, 157, 169, 173,
175, 180
Maedhros, 29, 64; alliance with
Easterlings, 120, 146, 150–51; at-
tack on Havens, 191–92; friend of
Fingon, 70, 84–85, 148–51; on
Himring, 88, 97, 111, 117, 119–20;
March of, 88, 90, 96–97, 152; in
Nirnaeth Arnoediad, 148–52; in
sacking of Menegroth, 182; sui-
cide of, 199
Maeglin, 103, 105–106, 121, 185–87,
249, 277
Maglor, 182, 192, 196–99; against
Orcs, 90–91, 97, 117, 119; minstrel,
29, 69; self-exile, 254
Mandos, 57, 59, 200, 202; curse
(doom) of, 41, 44, 69, 71, 84, 101,
114, 128, 132, 135, 152, 185–86; Halls
of, 142–43; justice of, 15, 20, 25–28,
57
Mankind. *See* Children of Ilúvatar;
Easterlings; Edain; Hildor;
Southrons
Manwë, 189, 193–97, 202; finds the
Ents in the Music, 15, 19, 23–24;

judgment, 118, 143, 228; justice of, 43–44, 189, 193, 196, 209, 220; making of sun and moon, 79; mercy of, 55, 58, 71, 73

Mardil, First Steward of Gondor, 240

Melian, 46–47, 75, 90, 99–100, 125, 128, 132, 144; Girdle of, 78, 95–96, 116, 126, 129, 147, 180, 255, 266; warning to Eöl, 158

Melkor (Morgoth), 76–77, 81; called Morgoth, 256; imprisoned, 44; lord of Sauron, 217–18, 228; malice of, 7, 15–19; separated from Valar, 34–35

Menegroth, 11, 76, 79–82, 89–90, 116, 140, 156–58

Menelmacar (Orion), 41, 272

Meneltarma, 207, 212, 217–18, 220, 225

Mercy. See Ilúvatar; Lúthien; Manwë; Ulmo

Meres of Twilight (marsh), 89, 96

Midgard (Middle-earth), 5, 9–11, 18, 271–72, 274

Mîm, 158–61, 178, 249

Minas Anor, 223, 235, 239

Minas Ithil, 223, 235, 237, 240

Minas Morgul, 223, 240

Minas Tirith: in Gondor, 223; on Tol Sirion, 119

Miriel Serindë, 51–52

Mirkwood, 233, 242

Misty Mountains, 237, 245

Mithlond, 204, 247

mithril, 205, 247

Mithrim, Lake, 72, 83, 116

Mjöllnir, 274

Moon (Tilion), 78–80, 258, 274

Mordor, 222–23, 237

Morgoth (Melkor), 160–61, 182–84, 186–87, 192, 196–99, 227–30, 234–36, 254–62; capture of, 201; curse of, 163, 176; evil of, 11–12, 57, 229; lies of, 55–56, 60, 100, 178

Moria, 205, 240

Morris, William, 64, 272, 275–76

Morwen, 156, 164–68, 174, 177–78, 277

Mount Dolmed, 151

Mount Doom (Orodruin), 230, 232–33, 238, 242, 244, 246

Mount Rerir, 97

Muspell, 5–7

Nandor. See Green-elves

Nan Dungortheb (Valley of Dreadful Death), 95–96, 102, 104, 126, 135

Nan-tathren, 152

Nargothrond, 135; caves of, 89–90, 159; Finrod at, 89–90; Guarded Plain of, 112, 129, 132, 158; refuge at, 115–16; Reuniting at, 89, 101; Túrin at, 162–74

Narog, River, 165

Narsil (sword), 237–39, 241

Nauglamir, 90, 176–82; 266–67, 274

Nazgul. See Rings of Power, for Men

Neldoreth, Forest of, 96, 126, 132, 136, 140

Nenniel (Lake Evendim), 233

Nenning, River, 94

Nerdanel the Wise, 54

Nevrast, 90, 93–94, 98

Nienor, 156, 164–67, 169–76, 277

Nimloth, 208, 214, 218, 220. See also Telperion

Niniel. See Nienor

Nirnaeth Arnoediad (Fifth Battle, of Unnumbered Tears), 149–53

Nogrod, 76, 103–104, 179, 148

Noldor, 25, 59, 82; birthrate, 91; decline of, 12, 183–87; forgiven, 199; lied to by Morgoth, 55–56; qualities of, 45, 50–51, 86–87; speech

Noldor *(cont.)*
  forbidden, 101; warned by
  Manwë, 56
Norns, 4–5, 11, 272
Norse, 12, 271–77, 279; creation
  myth, 4–5; oath, 275–76; Pan-
  theon, 4–5; Ragnarök, 5
Númenor, 194, 203–26, 239, 248

Oath: of Beren, 128; of Finrod, 89,
  116; of Húrin and Huor, 121–22; of
  Reuniting, 260; of Thingol, 127;
  Norse, 275–76. *See also* Fëanor
Odin, 4–6, 14, 271
olvar (flora), 79
Olwë, 46–47, 67–68, 70, 85
Orcs, 156–69; against Thingol, 77–
  78; attacked, 91, 130, 188, 196; 223;
  slaves to Morgoth (Melkor), 42–
  43, 62, 122, 187, 232
Orodreth, 55, 65, 94, 119, 130, 135, 148
Oromë, 40, 42–43, 47, 54, 59, 79, 132
Orthanc, 235, 242, 245
Osgiliath, 223, 234–35
Ossë, 36, 48, 206
Ossiriand province, 96, 116, 144
Ost-in-Edhil (city of Elves in Ere-
  gion), 232

Palantíri, 52–53, 202, 213, 220, 223, 234–
  36, 240, 248
Pass of Sirion, 94, 97
Pelóri Mountains, 39, 80–81
Petty-dwarves, 158, 175, 178
Pity, 143, 196
Possessiveness, 56, 60, 64, 72, 147,
  176, 179
Powers (angels), 19, 209, 254, 273. *See
  also* Ainur; Maiar; Valar
Pride, 56, 148, 228. *See also* Túrin
Providence. *See* Ilúvatar

Quenya (Eldarin), 278

Radagast (wizard), 245
Ragnarök, 5–7, 507, 272
Region, Forest of, 96
Rerir, Mount, 97
Reuniting, at Nargothrond, 101; at
  pools of Ivrin, 89
Ringbearers, 204, 246–47
Ringil (sword), 117–18
Ring of Barahir, 126, 128
Ring of Doom, 57, 67
Rings of Power, 200, 203, 213, 227,
  230–31, 243; for Dwarves, 231, 242,
  245; for Elves (Narya, Nenya,
  Vilya), 231, 241, 247; for Men
  (Ringwraiths, Nazgul) 223, 231,
  237, 239–42, 245–46, 248; Sauron's
  One Ring, 200–201, 213, 222, 224,
  230–32, 237–39, 241–45, 247–48
Ringwraiths. *See* Rings of Power,
  for Men; Nazgul
Rivendell (Imladris), 200, 232, 241–
  42, 277
River Aros, 96, 104
River Esgalduin, 96, 141
River Narog, 165
River Nenning, 94
Rivil's Well, 126
Rochallor, 117
Rohan, 240, 249
Rohirrim, 240
Romenna, 214
Rumil's Tengwar, 45, 52, 86

Sacrifice, human, 218
Saeros, 157
Saruman (Curunír), 227, 242–44,
  246, 248
Sauron Gorthaur: First Age, Lieutenant of Morgoth, 37, 119, 125–26,
  132, 134, 137; Second Age, Rings of
  Power, 200, 215, 227, 230; on Númenor, 216–21; reincarnated, 222–
  26; Third Age, 195, 227–46

Sea, Bent, 222; Encircling, 38, 142, 208

Second Age, 194, 204

Serech, Fen of, 116, 151

Shelob, 62

Sigurd, 272, 274, 276–77

silima (basic substance of the Silmarils), 55

Silmarils: made by Fëanor, 55, 57, 60, 64–65, 69, 72; stolen by Morgoth, 61–62, 83, 99, 117; recovered: by Beren and Lúthien, 139–40, 142, 179–82; by Eärendil, 191–96; by Fëanor's sons, 197–99

Sindar (Grey-elves), 75, 89, 115–16, 200; and men, 82; decline of, 183; language of, 86–87, 92; Morgoth's lies to, 100, 119

Sirion, 90, 95, 189; Pass of, 94, 97, 104, 117, 119, 137, 152; Tol Sirion, 94, 119

Skrymir, 274

Smaug, 166

Song Contest, Finrod against Sauron, 130–31, 134

Song of Parting, Beren's farewell to Earth, 137

Southrons, 237, 249

Spiders, 232. See also Shelob; Ungoliant

Stewards of Gondor, 245–46

Straight Road, 222, 247

Sun (Arien), 78–79, 274

Sybil, 6

Taniquetil (Oilossë), 39, 58, 86, 93, 222

"Tar," 278

Tar-Ancalimon, 211

Tar-Atanamir, 209–11, 219

Tar-Minastir, 213, 232

Tar-Minyatur. See Elros

Tarn Aeluin, 125

Tarondor, 239–40

Tar-Palantir, 215, 278

Taur-Im-Duinath (forest), 97

Teiglin Crossing, 112

Teleri, 46; and Fëanor, 55, 67–68; and Kinslaying, 25–28; betrayed by Noldor, 99–101, 132; language of, 86–87; Silvan Elves, 228

Telperion, 39–40, 79, 254–55

Tengwar. See Fëanor; Rúmil

Thangorodrim, 62, 72, 83–84, 137, 154, 176, 197

Thargelion province, 96, 102, 109, 117

Thingol (Elwë), 46–48, 75–77, 116, 147, 156–58, 166–68, 174, 177–79; aid from, 120–21; claims to kingship, 85, 87; father of Lúthien, 127–28, 132, 141; forbids entry to Men, 110; healed by Lúthien, 144

Third Age, 83, 204, 227

Thor, 4, 18, 274

Thorondor, 84–85, 118, 121–22, 140, 188, 196

Thráin (Dwarf), 243

Thuringwethil (vampire), 137

Tilion. See Moon

Tirion, 27, 45, 57, 59, 62, 90, 98, 193, 220

Tol Galen island, 144

Tolkien. See Carpenter, Humphrey

Tolkien, Christopher, 204–205

Tolkien, Edith Bratt, 124–25, 184

Tolkien, J. R. R., "Children of Húrin," 1; "The Fall of Gondolin," 1, 184; "Gest of Beren and Luthien," 124; The Hobbit 25, 166, 243; "The Homecoming of Beorhtnoth," 155; "The Lay of Aotrou and Itroun," 201–202; "The Lay of Eärendil," 191–94; The Lay of Leithien," 124, 130,

Tolkien *(cont.)*
137; *The Lord of the Rings*, 18, 25, 28, 94, 220, 227–28, 230–32, 234–36, 240–49, 277; "On Fairy-stories," 272; "Sir Gawain and the Green Knight," 276; "Smith of Wootton Major," 8
Tol Sirion (Isle of Werewolves), 119, 132–35, 137
Tragedy, 177, 248
Treason, 69, 120, 135, 146
Trolls, 223
Tumladen, 90, 98
Túna, (hill), 86, 90, 220. *See also* Tirion
Tuor, 12, 113, 116, 183–90
Turgon, 55, 65, 102, 105, 118, 177, 194; aids Fingon, 148; death of, 28; orders ships, 122; warned by Ulmo, 89–90, 98–99, 121
Túrin, 12, 113, 155–75, 176, 177, 183–84, 249, 276, 277; assumed names of: Agarwaen, 162; Gorthol, 160; Mormagil, 163–64, 168; Neithan, 157, 160; Turambar, 160, 169–75
Two Trees, 39–40, 55, 59, 64, 79, 189, 218, 254. *See also* Laurelin; Telperion

Uldor (Easterling), 149–50
Ulfang, 120, 149
Ulmo, 32–33, 44, 47–48, 65, 183–87; counsel of, 89, 165; mercy of, 189; music, 40; present in water, 82, 94, 98, 121; trusted by Teleri, 67–68, 165
Undying Lands, 241, 246. *See* Eressëa; Valinor
Ungoliant (Unlight), 58–59, 61–62; 95, 102, 207, 257
Utgard, 8, 274
Utumno, 38, 41, 43, 92

Valacirca (Great Bear), 41, 134
Valandil, 239
Valaquenta, 25–32. *See also* Valar
Valar, 12, 15, 82, 182, 189, 193–98, 216–17, 222, 228, 236, 246. *See* Ban; Powers
Valaraukar. *See* Balrogs
Valier, 32–34, 79
Valinor, 12, 185, 189, 193, 218–19, 222, 228–29, 247–48; defending, 38–39; return to, 180, 200, 205. *See also* Aman
Valmar (Valimar), 39, 57, 143
Vanyar, 45, 54–55, 59, 86, 199
Varda, 56, 59, 202; kindler of stars, 32, 41, 134, 207, 255, 271–72; of sun and moon, 79–80, 258
Vengeance, 63, 266, 273–74
Viking Club, 3
Vingilot, 29, 193, 207, 268
Vinyamar, 90, 93, 98, 185
Void, 4–5, 15–16, 28, 135
Volsunga Saga, 64, 275–77
Voronwë, 153, 185

Walls of the World, 38, 201
War of Wrath, 191, 213, 227–28
Werewolves, 132–34, 139, 249, 263. *See also* Carcharoth; Draugluin
wergeld, 159, 238, 276
White Tree, 208, 214, 217–18, 223, 234, 237, 239, 246. *See also* Galathelion; Nimloth; Telperion
Witch-king of Angmar (Ringwraith), 239–40
Wizards. *See* Gandalf; Radagast; Saruman
Wolves, 132, 150, 161, 262–66
Wormtongue, 248

Yavanna, 23–24, 37–39, 41, 59, 60, 82
Yggdrasil (World Ash), 39
Ymir, 4–5, 9, 271